Blue Vaudeville

Blue Vaudeville

*Sex, Morals and the
Mass Marketing of
Amusement, 1895–1915*

ANDREW L. ERDMAN

McFarland & Company, Inc., Publishers
Jefferson, North Carolina, and London

> *The present work is a reprint of the illustrated case bound edition of* Blue Vaudeville: Sex, Morals and the Mass Marketing of Amusement, 1895–1915, *first published in 2004 by McFarland.*

LIBRARY OF CONGRESS CATALOGUING-IN-PUBLICATION DATA

Erdman, Andrew L., 1965–
    Blue vaudeville : sex, morals and the mass marketing of amusement, 1895–1915 / Andrew L. Erdman.
    p.   cm.
    Includes bibliographical references and index.

    ISBN-13: 978-0-7864-3115-1
    (softcover : 50# alkaline paper) ∞

    1. Vaudeville—United States—History—20th century.
2. Vaudeville—United States—History—19th century. 3. Sex in the performing arts. I. Title.
PN1968.U5E73   2007
792.7'0973'09041—dc22   2004004057

British Library cataloguing data are available

©2004 Andrew L. Erdman. All rights reserved

No part of this book may be reproduced or transmitted in any form or by any means, electronic or mechanical, including photocopying or recording, or by any information storage and retrieval system, without permission in writing from the publisher.

On the cover: Lilliam Herlein (Billy Rose Theatre Collection, The New York Public Library for the Performing Arts, Astor, Lenox, and Tilden Foundations)

Manufactured in the United States of America

McFarland & Company, Inc., Publishers
  Box 611, Jefferson, North Carolina 28640
  www.mcfarlandpub.com

To Mom, Dad, and Harley

Acknowledgments

As with many undertakings, the writing of a book is rendered more difficult without the support, guidance, advice, help, and counsel of others. For all these things and more, I am deeply indebted to a number of individuals without whom this book would not have come to pass.

I would like to thank Profs. Daniel Gerould and David Nasaw of the City University of New York Graduate Center, for their wisdom and guidance when this book was in its early stages. I would also like to thank Prof. Jill Dolan of the University of Texas at Austin for her input, as well as the late Prof. George Custen of the College of Staten Island.

In addition, I have been lucky to have been surrounded by family and friends who encouraged me and helped me never lose sight of my goals. Chief among these individuals is Harley Erdman, my brother, and a respected theatre historian and dramatist. I would also like to thank my father Joseph Erdman, for his faith in me and for helping me gain a love of the stage at an early age. And like my father, my mother, the late Audrey Erdman, helped me to understand the marvels that the theatre can hold. I have been blessed with a loving family.

Others who merit the deepest thanks include Caroline France, who helped prepare this manuscript for publication, and Austen Hayes, for her guidance and kindness. Finally, this book would never have come to be in its present form without Maura and Emer Crisham, who offered their hospitality and affection, and gave me a place to finish the manuscript.

Table of Contents

Acknowledgments vii
Introduction 1

One—"Dressed in the Form of Art"
　　The Censorship and Curtailment of Popular Entertainments 21

Two—"Clean, Great, and National"
　　The Mass Marketing of Amusement 43

Three—"Of Pleasing Face and Form"
　　The Sexual and the Sensual on Stage 83

Four—"Wild Woman"
　　Eva Tanguay as Temptress and Sexual Rebel 127

Five—"The Signal of Distress"
　　Film and the Fall of Vaudeville 163

Chapter Notes 169
Selected Bibliography 187
Index 193

Introduction

In 1910, an article called "The Decay of Vaudeville" appeared in a widely read periodical called the *American Magazine*. The article's author chose to remain anonymous. But her attitude toward what had become a vastly popular form of entertainment—the vaudeville theater—was unmistakable. She argued that this variety-format entertainment, whose popularity had grown in large measure thanks to its alleged suitability for all audiences, had become decidedly unsuitable for all audiences. Indeed, vaudeville, in her judgment, had done "more to corrupt, vitiate and degrade public taste in matters relating to the stage than all other influences put together." To put the finishing touch on her moral reproach she suggested that the bill of fare at a typical "first class" theater which did not contain material so offensive as to "make a decent woman deeply ashamed of her presence in that theatre," was "about as rare as snow in Panama." This writer went so far as to suggest that censorship be explored as a remedy.[1]

If this nervous theatergoer and commentator were the only one to complain about the racy, immoral content of the hugely popular vaudeville theater, which boasted national theater chains and houses in nearly every major (and many not-so-major) cities in the United States, that would have been one thing. Or if her rancor had represented the opprobrium of only one segment of society—say, reform-minded Christian women—it might be of slightly less significance in understanding social attitudes toward vaudeville. But such was not the case. Rather, her moral queasiness, her feeling that the vaudeville stage was sullied with acts of naughtiness and license, was shared by others, even men, even foreigners, even those somewhat outside the Anglo-Christian caste that dominated American society.

In an article in *Cosmopolitan* in 1905, British playwright and social activist Israel Zangwill wrote that he had at one point held high hopes for vaudeville and saw the potential for it to be a "purified" and "intellectual" form of entertainment. "Alas, the few glimpses of vaudeville performances I have had did not quite bear out this roseate vision." Zangwill, whose voice joined the growing chorus of vaudevillebaiters, saw the popular variety-format shows as rife with vulgarity. What was worse, in Zangwill's view, was that the offending infection could not be pinned down to any one kind of joke or song or monologue, where it might easily be excised like a tumor nipped in its incipiency. No, for Zangwill, the filth and vulgarity were woven inextricably into the "whole texture of a song or a scene." Accordingly, whereas others may have called for censorship, Zangwill thought the patient was too far gone: "[N]o censorship on earth will refine the [vaudeville] stage."[2]

Even those voices in society which might have been expected to show unwavering support for vaudeville theater began to join in the fray. The *New York Dramatic Mirror*, one of the leading theatrical newspapers of the day, on whose reviews and articles vaudeville had in part come to national prominence, wagged its finger as well, accusing it of "dropping into the evil habits of some of the older and more hardened sins of so-called variety." In New York City, observed the *Mirror*, there had been produced in a vaudeville theater an act that was "reeking offense to the morals of even that hardened community." The anxious author did not actually describe what is was that made the act reek, as it were, but the point is clear: If it could offend even New Yorkers, then it certainly had no place on the public stage.[3]

Why are these anxious, righteous, finger-pointing critiques of vaudeville of interest? Certainly, on one level, they are indicative of a larger public concern at the time over the effects of popular entertainment, which was sweeping through American cities, in its various forms — nickelodeon movie houses and amusement parks, to name a few — like a tidal wave. It was a time when big businesses were forming to entertain people, many of whom were in America's growing cities, and less apt to be influenced by such traditional cultural institutions as family and church.

But in the case of vaudeville, what is especially surprising is that here was a form of popular entertainment (what might be called a forerunner of our present mass "pop culture") which had succeeded largely by having distinguished itself as a "clean," "wholesome" entertainment, fit for the entire family. In a sense, vaudeville anticipated the Disneys of today by promising inoffensive fare for the whole family as a major selling point.

Benjamin Franklin Keith and Edward Franklin Albee ran the largest, most successful, and most powerful chain of vaudeville theaters, known as the Keith circuit.[4] Albee, who was the chief marketing genius of the Keith-Albee operation, the "power behind the scenes,"[5] once proclaimed, "The old variety houses used to be filthy places, but we changed all that. We believed in soap and water, and in a strict censorship of the stage." Keith too, though never quite the showman that his partner was, made his share of pronouncements for the public ear (and, no doubt, to instill the fear of God to those who both were, and might one day be, on his payroll): "I made it a rule at the beginning ... that I must know exactly what every performer on my stage would say or do. If there was one coarse, vulgar, or suggestive line or piece of stage business in the act, I cut it out."[6] In fact, the following placard was famously posted backstage at Keith theaters, a sort of Ten Commandments for playing his houses:

> Notice To Performers: Don't say "slob" or "son of [a] gun" or "Holy Gee" on the stage unless you want to be cancelled peremptorily. Do not address anyone in the audience in any manner. If you have not the ability to entertain Mr. Keith's audi-

ences without risk of offending them, do the best you can. Lack of talent will be less open to censure than would be an insult to a patron. If you are in doubt as to the character of your act, consult the local manager before you go on the stage, for if you are guilty of uttering anything sacrilegious or even suggestive, you will immediately be closed and will never again be allowed in a theater where Mr. Keith is in authority.[7]

In similar fashion, the ad copy on a poster advertising the Chase circuit of vaudeville theaters declared, "It is the constant aim of the management to prevent the use of a single word, expression, or situation that will offend the intelligent, refined and cultured classes."[8]

Eventually, the Keith central office developed a list of some seventy-three specific pieces of content that would supposedly result in censorship or debarment from the stage. Bare legs too were stricken from the stage of Keith's biggest and most famous theater, the Palace. In a Keith theater, you allegedly couldn't even show pictures of "fires, train wrecks, and similar disasters" which might somehow cause disquiet to pregnant women.[9] It was attitudes and practices such as these that led to the unofficial branding of the Keith chain as "the Sunday School Circuit," a nickname which Albee and Keith both embraced.[10] As those who were beginning to launch the Hollywood movie studios, and their associated cinema chains, would discover, those churning out the popular fare had to keep one step ahead of the moral reformers. Theater closings and other legal antidotes never loomed very far away. Therefore, "the 'Sunday School Circuit' reputation could soothe the anxieties of moral reformers and attract family audiences. Self-censorship meant bigger audiences and bigger profits," writes Robert Snyder in *The Voice of the City: Vaudeville and Popular Culture in New York*.[11] It was all very canny; it kept the crowds coming in and the stump-speech reformers at bay.

It also, quite frankly, permitted the vaudeville chains greater leeway in what they could actually get on stage. After all, moral posturing and public promises of purity were appealing to just so many kinds of theatergoers. Others, many others, clearly wanted a taste of the variety and burlesque theater upon which they, as consumers of popular entertainment, had been weaned. To that economic end, the Keiths and Albees of the world shrewdly wove into their bills many an act whose main appeal was sexual titillation. Consider, for example, this description of the popular performer Charmion, "the Parisian Sensation," at Koster & Bial's vaudeville theater in 1897:

> She ... attempted one or two [trapeze] tricks, but seemed to find her clothes a bother, so she began to unhook her waist... Finally, the waist came off. Then she hung by her feet and the skirts, etc., naturally fell down over her head, leaving a view of lace unmentionables, black stockings, purple garters, and a large amount of pink silk fleshings between the garters and her hips.... [So] she loosened and removed "skirts," "unmentionables," chemise, shoes, garters, stockings, and hat until clad in the conventional costume of the female acrobat.[12]

Though she would not reveal nude body parts (that would be accomplished by numerous "art," "posing," and "living picture" acts in vaudeville), Charmion based a large part of her appeal on provocative disrobing. A month after her initial appearance, Charmion had worked into her routine the flinging of garters into the audience. She was "the talk of the town," according to the *New York Dramatic Mirror*.[13] Charmion's New York engagement lasted six months—remarkable in an era when vaudeville acts typically played a week or two at most.[14]

There would seem to have been, then, conflicting efforts at work in the American vaudeville theater, a contrast between what the promotional mechanism claimed and what the production apparatus actually delivered to hungry audiences. On the one hand, the managers and owners who controlled the form publicly declaimed its moral purity and freedom from sexual, suggestive, or smutty material. Yet on the other hand, vaudeville provided enough off-color, suggestive material to draw the ire of certain reformers and critics. It claimed to be free from sexual suggestion and fit for the entire family, unlike the burlesque hall and concert saloon; yet women who disrobed or wore tight, revealing, or form-fitting outfits were some of vaudeville's biggest and most successful draws. Though the refined entertainment presented in vaudeville was supposedly intended to lure in middle-class women and their children, men made up the majority of theatergoers, and it is clear the vaudeville producers made every effort to cater to patrons used to the "rough and tumble background" of vaudeville's antecedent forms.[15] Vaudeville impresario E.F. Albee claimed that at least one of his patrons had written to thank him for presenting an entertainment so pure that she felt "she could attend on the Sabbath and still feel that she was in direct communion with her God," yet Albee admitted himself that the only way to be successful in vaudeville was to traffic in female "backsides"[16] (as we will see). In fact, it is remarkable that the big vaudeville chains retained a reputation for moral purity, when in actual practice they provided so many scantily clad bodies (usually female), comics whose stock-in-trade was the double entendre, singers whose songs were loaded with suggestive lyrics, and "cooch" dancers who might as well have been appearing on the burlesque stage.

At least once Albee openly acknowledged this two-way pull. When Annette Kellerman, famous for both her prodigious swimming skills and her propensity to appear in a tight, revealing bathing suit, failed to adequately please audiences, Albee ordered an alteration to the stage setting for Kellerman's aquatic act: he had mirrors put up all over the place, especially those which would afford spectators a view of Kellerman's shapely rear in a revealing swimsuit. "Don't you know," Albee lectured one of his production underlings, "that what we are selling here is backsides, and that a hundred backsides are better than one?"[17] If it took a hundred backsides to make his paying spectators happy, so be it.

Thus, if the bottom line were in part based on keeping up appearances of purity, it was also based, quite literally, on bottoms. As one recent historian of the vaudeville stage has ably noted, the "entrepreneurs" who built vaudeville into a "mass culture machine" and a "vast bureaucracy that manufactured culture" could do so only by effectively addressing the "deep fissures in late-nineteenth-century American culture," with those favoring the so-called "feminine" (refined, highbrow) legitimate theater on one side and those used to the decidedly male-oriented concert saloons and wine houses "associated with vice" on the other.[18]

But E.F. Albee was too good a businessman to break so sharply with offerings that had proven so popular and profitable. One historian of the vaudeville stage argues that Albee (and, it may be inferred, others like him) "had no objections to the raucous pre–Tony Pastor type of entertainment that had kept the old variety shows from catering to the family trade,"[19] alluding to theater producer Tony Pastor, who is often cited as among the first to attempt to improve the variety theater's moral climate, thus helping instigate the vaudeville era. Another vaudeville chronicler, himself a retired performer, noted "the customer got to longing for a peep at the undraped figure…."[20] As vaudeville gained in popularity, the customer got much more than "a peep at the undraped figure"; rather, he got it reliably, in spades. Indeed, the big vaudeville enterprises played a crucial role in fostering such longings and desires.

Navigating the boundary between naughty and respectable was not easy. Vaudeville managers and producers had to put sass in their acts, but avoid getting sassed by authorities with the power to close or hamper their enterprises. A keen-eyed and witty journalist, who went by the pen name "Rush," took note of this delicate balancing act in a column he wrote for a then relatively new publication called *Variety*. In 1909 an act called Kid Gabriel and Co. appeared at Keith's Fifth Avenue Theatre. Kid Gabriel was a "plastic posing" act, which meant that it reproduced well-known works of art in tableaux form. Like many other such acts which populated the vaudeville stage, the performers were either nude, partially so, or covered in a thin film of silk or white dust so as to approximate "classical" statuary. Though presented as a high-brow form of cultural enrichment, the act was appealing to many theater patrons because it presented living female bodies on the stage that were unclad or appeared so. In Keith's Fifth Avenue theater, mocked Rush, "an effort has been made to educate the clientele of 'refined vaudeville.'" But the real aim of these "art" acts was not refinement. Rather, it was to offer up "the bare flesh of the living nude." According to Rush, vaudeville producers always favored bare flesh, "the barer the better." But make no mistake, the *Variety* reporter noted, those same producers will at the same time hang up a sign near the stage reading: "The use of the word 'dam' [sic] not permitted in this theater."[21] Rush is arguing, in a sense, that all such efforts at making vaudeville seem clean or free of sexual suggestiveness were simply rhetorical or discursive tactics in the service of a larger economic strategy. Others, looking back at vaudeville, seem to concur that although supposed constraints on content were often circumvented, "the image of vaudeville as being 'clean' remained intact."[22] Not a bad marketing strategy—nor is it one totally unfamiliar to modern day consumers of mass-market entertainment, especially television.

Therefore, the attempt to portray vaudeville in a favorable moral light was really part of a far-reaching marketing, publicity, and advertising effort, one that had as its goal the advancement of a public discourse of moral purity. To some extent, as we have seen, this effort aimed at separating vaudeville from its seamier antecedent forms, such as variety and burlesque, not to mention a shrewd attempt to put some distance between vaudeville and the theater more generally, which has been subject to moral outrage since at least the time of Shakespeare.

But this may not explain the entire aim of this project of moral assuagement. There seems to be something in it directed at larger, deeper, more pervasive anxieties in the minds of many in the consuming public. Specifically, it can be argued that in going out of their way to proclaim and publicize vaudeville as "clean," "wholesome," "respectable," and free from sexual suggestiveness, the powers behind vaude-

As if to acknowledge the suggestive nature of many vaudeville acts, the *New York Dramatic Mirror* changed the art accompanying its weekly vaudeville column in 1900 from a circle of playful clowns, dancers, and musicians to a she-devilish temptress. (Billy Rose Theatre Collection, The New York Public Library for the Performing Arts, Astor, Lenox, and Tilden Foundations.)

ville were in some measure addressing anxieties over the consumption of a mass-market product. For vaudeville was among the first forms of staged amusement in the United States to emerge as, quite simply, a mass-scale product. Unlike earlier entertainments, which involved small groups not acting in concert with one another, vaudeville developed as a hierarchically arranged, centrally controlled, large-scale commercial entity. The *New York Dramatic Mirror* posited that B.F. Keith, founder of vaudeville's biggest chain, "saw the writing on the wall" as he created the first modern mass amusement back in the 1890s. From that time on, there were "syndicates" of theaters run by a vast network of hierarchically arranged professionals.[23]

It is crucial to understand that in the world of vaudeville, acts were booked centrally, content was controlled and overseen by a small group of powerful individuals, routes were planned that spanned not one or two cities but entire swaths of the country, and successful artists became national, and even international, personalities. It was the beginning of standardized entertainment on a mass scale, scarcely seen before. Vaudeville, it has been written, left its biggest mark in American life by managing to "erode the local orientation of nineteenth century audiences, and knit them, despite their diversity, into a modern audience of national proportions."[24] Vaudeville, in the words of one recent scholar, "came far closer to constructing an undifferentiated mass audience than legitimate" theaters ever did.[25] The emergence of vaudeville, therefore, truly marked the beginnings of the emergence of a nationwide entertainment market. This market continued to grow in the twentieth century. In this light, we may view "vaudeville" as entertainment's first national, branded product. Essential to crafting this brand, then, was the implicit promise of cleanliness. By repeatedly advertising a "clean" product, the vaudeville owners were preparing the first national market for an entertainment product; their repeated efforts to paint vaudeville in the pure white hues of cleanliness may be viewed as in fact efforts to allay or mitigate anxieties in the minds of prospective theatergoers over the massness that was a chief characteristic of the form. This may not have been the only reason they did so, but it was a critically important one.[26]

For now there had been born a new creature on the American landscape—not merely the spectator or the ticket-buyer or the audience member, but rather the *consumer*. The Keiths and Albees of the world had to appeal to the consumer—in particular the white, middle-class consumer—a species they and other mass-marketers had in part helped to create. These "consumers" took a new view of the act of commercial transaction. They understood themselves to be part of something larger, to be "participants in a national market composed of masses of people associating with big, centrally organized, national-level companies."[27] One historian of American culture even holds that being a "citizen" increasingly meant in fact being a "consumer" within the "democracy of goods."[28] Put another way, you were what you bought.

In their continuing efforts to advertise and publicize vaudeville as clean, morally pure, and safe, those who controlled the vaudeville industry were helping to transform the entertainment "customer" of the nineteenth century into the entertainment "consumer" of the twentieth. This was a crucial transformation, and one whose effects are still with us today. It not only prepared Americans for a mass market in entertainment, it helped further develop the commercialization of leisure time. That is, rather than making available more free time, there became simply more and more things to spend money on. One never stopped being a consumer even in one's "free" time. An "unacknowledged social decision" saw to it that industry produced "unlimited quantities of goods rather than leisure."[29] Thus, vaudeville in particular, and the nascent mass entertainment media more generally, became such "quantities of goods," provided for working, urban Americans to consume in place of enjoying purely free time.

The vaudeville chiefs—Keith, Albee, Proctor, Martin Beck, and others—were not alone in trying to find a national mass market for a product. For the years that marked vaudeville's coalescence and rise to widespread popularity were also, to be sure, the same years that saw the emergence of the first national brands and the creation of a demand for mass-market goods and services. Vaudeville, it has been written, "grew alongside many other mass culture industries, such as professional sports and department stores, and incorporated these kindred developments into its own success."[30] Some of the early entrants into the mass-marketing game, such as Coca-Cola, Sears, and National Biscuit (Nabisco), are still around, while many others are not. But at all events, one can see that the efforts used by these firms were similar to the promise of cleanliness, purity, even sterility in a sense, that often resided at the heart of vaudeville's mass-marketing and advertising strategies. In 1911, for instance, Philip Morris Cigarettes advertised, above all else, that they contained "Pure Turkish tobacco—nothing else,"[31] while the makers of Cracker Jack candies told the potential customer that their product came "In Sealed 'Triple Proof' Packages"[32] to ensure the sterility of the contents. Plexo, a popular brand of face powder, based its entire marketing effort around anxieties over contamination and dirt. "Why use an unsanitary Powder Puff at home and carry the still more unsanitary Powder Rag while shopping, traveling, etc." read an advertisement from 1909, "when PLEXO Powder, the kind in a box *with the puff attached* entirely *eliminates* all this danger, bother and expense?"[33] Schlitz beer heavily promoted the fact that its bottles were steam-cleaned—when, in fact, rival companies did the very same thing to their bottles.[34] As early as the 1880s, the Quaker Oats company was stressing the "purity" of its packaging to would-be consumers.[35]

These initial examples are few and their parallels in language may seem superficial. But it can be argued that they aimed at achieving roughly the same goal as did the vaudeville magnates, using similar rhetorical and discursive strategies. What can be gained by such comparisons, then, is a more in-depth and accurate view of the first national mass-marketing campaign for entertainment in the United States within its proper historical context.

Looked at another way, the influential individuals who controlled the vaudeville industry not only created a new kind of product, they also affected the way huge numbers of people *thought* about that product. In so doing, they were acting not merely as captains of industry but as "captains of consciousness" to borrow a term from historian Stuart Ewen. "Captains of consciousness" wanted more than simply to sell a wide array of standardized goods and services to large numbers of consumers. Rather, they "looked to move beyond their nineteenth-century characterization as captains of industry toward a position in which they could control the entire social realm. They aspired to become captains of consciousness."[36] The "captains of consciousness" in the entertainment industry in this sense may be said to have originated in vaudeville and created a mold that has continued to influence the creation and marketing of mass-scale amusement fare to the present day.[37]

By publicizing and marketing vaudeville as free from the taint of sexuality, and yet at the same time offering a plethora of unclad bodies and lewd dance acts, the captains of the vaudeville industry were also urging along another transformation in American culture. They were paving the way for the liberalization of mores and attitudes toward the female body. The more they built up a public face of cleanliness, the more easily they could offer patrons glimpses of disrobing women like Mlle. Charmion or posing ladies such as those of the Kid Gabriel troupe. Thus, as vaudeville developed, many American entertainment-seekers not only grew used to the idea of mass-scale amusement, they also grew used to—one might argue that they grew hungry for—acts whose popularity was based on the sexualized female form. It was a winning formula: assuage anxieties with a rhetoric of purity, then present acts that increasingly departed from an older, Victorian prudishness.

This accompanied and fit in well with the far-reaching efforts of would-be mass-marketers in other industries, who were influencing many Americans to let go of an older Victorian outlook and embrace a new culture based more on pleasure, spending, permissiveness and some measure of political apathy. The older culture that was falling away was one of small entrepreneurs and locally-oriented producers of goods and services, whereas "the new culture epitomized a consumption-oriented society dominated by bureaucratic corporations."[38]

The changes wrought by vaudeville are a perfect example: a mass market for entertainment was built on the shoulders of a few large, bureaucratic corporations; at the same time, these large corporations learned to traffic in the sexualized female form based on a morality of permissiveness. In a sense, anxieties over mass-market consumption were outweighed by a rhetoric of purity and a (presumably heterosexual male) desire to see the female body on stage in increasing states of undress.

Take for example performers like Mlle. Charmion who disrobed or changed costumes in full view of the audience. It is significant that Charmion was not alone in her stage antics. Rather she was part of a wave of such performers, nearly all female, who remained popular throughout the duration of vaudeville's tenure as the leading form of entertainment in the United States. In May 1898, for example, the Olympia theater presented the following bill: "Marguerite Sylvia made her vaudeville debut here last week. There was nothing very novel or startling about her turn, but she managed to score quite a success. She sang a couple of songs in a long dress and then changed into tights, in which her figure showed to very great advantage. The sensational part of the programme was furnished by Adgie, who combines the talents of the lion tamer and disrober. There is no telling where this boudoir business is going to stop," wrote the *New York Dramatic Mirror*.[39]

This "boudoir business" was often presented in some form of clever disguise or coding. On the face of it was a promise never to offend. But the body often betrayed "more than a hint of innuendo and more than a trace of provocative movement" for "the viewer who wanted to find it."[40] Looked at from this perspective, theater owners and managers agreed to look the other way while performers relied increasingly on sexual titillation in order to sell their acts.

Others have advanced the less likely argument that the performers began push-

Mlle. Charmion in a characteristically seductive pose. The trapeze was her vehicle for an elaborate disrobing number—one which smacked of burlesque. (Billy Rose Theatre Collection, The New York Public Library for the Performing Arts, Astor, Lenox, and Tilden Foundations.)

ing the envelope unbeknownst to most of the executives and producers who controlled vaudeville, who were themselves "more worried about the stock-market quotations than what was going on on their stages." Thus there emerged a sort of grassroots rebellion from the ranks of theatergoers who placed upward pressure, with the help of journalists and other professional nay-sayers, on the vaudeville producers and executives who, in turn, started enacting rules designed to get their performers to behave.[41] But it seems difficult to fully believe that the men who had meticulously begun to plot the first form of truly mass-scale nationwide entertainment should have lacked the perspicacity to keep tabs on their very own bill of fare.

It may be more useful to see such titillating acts, laden with morally questionable material, as having simply survived and been rerouted and repackaged, from the pre-Tony Pastor days into the age of mass-market amusement, rather than as some kind of infection which sprang up all of a sudden. For vaudeville's antecedent forms were the concert saloon, the burlesque house, the variety hall. The clientele was largely male and alcohol and tobacco were present in abundance.[42]

Then, according to the common wisdom of the day, the producer Tony Pastor came along and changed the rules. He opened a theater in Tammany Hall on Fourteenth Street in New York City, then the burgeoning center of theatrical life in the Big Apple, on October 24, 1881. Pastor was said to have been the first to play to a "double audience" (meaning women as well as men). "It was the first 'clean' vaudeville show in America and to its bill, as [actor] Fred Stone used to say, a child could take its parents."[43] Thus, out of a rough-edged and densely sexual form which catered to men in smoky rooms where the whisky flowed freely, there emerged, thanks to Pastor, a wholesome new entertainment at which the entire family could pass its leisure hours. Later, much later, after vaudeville had become little more than the subject of nostalgia, Tony Pastor was recorded as the American theater's first Puritan. Given the mass-scale vaudeville that followed, it may have been something of a misnomer. But every movement needs its figureheads.

Pastor has been credited with maintaining a theater in which audience members were not only safe from smutty material on the stage, but were equally safe from their fellow theatergoers—no small feat in an era when sitting next to a stranger in a house of nocturnal urban amusement promised no small measure of anxiety. In fact, when "stripped of their offensive setting" (in the concert saloons and beer halls of the Bowery), many acts all of a sudden seemed less offensive to urban crowds who might never have considered going to such a place as the variety theater.[44]

Pastor banned smoking and drinking (his way of discouraging certain types of roguish men), and also instituted a policy whereby "mashers who attempted to approach women in the audience would be promptly ejected"[45] (his way of getting rid of certain other types of roguish men). Whether Pastor's policies were fully successful or not in actual practice is hard to say, but word of his intentions got out, and that meant an unarguable success, economically speaking. Others, therefore, have seen Pastor's strategy as nothing more than shrewd business, "a definitive and canny bid to double the audience by attracting respectable women—wives, daughters, sweethearts."[46] As sellers of mass entertainment have realized up to the present day, sometimes the best way to find an audience is to appeal to those left out of one's competitors' purview, rather than trying to lasso the ones those rivals are struggling to retain. In any case, Pastor's commercially motivated rhetoric worked. The famous performer Lillian Russell declared that "Pastor's Theatre set a standard that was unique and drew as many women as men. Every act was scrupulously clean and free from any suggestiveness."[47] Keith, Albee, and others, no doubt, took note of this "unique" reputation and worked it into a marketing and production scheme of national proportions. For them, like Pastor, bowdlerization, or the appearance thereof, was the marketing lubricant needed for success—but on a much bigger scale. "Money was probably more important to Keith and Albee than morality," writes one well-known chronicler of the vaudeville stage. To get that money, as Pastor had figured out, one had to get the wives and daughters in the door as well. Thus Keith's "cloak of morality." But as with Pastor, censoring or threatening to censor what the crowd did was just as important an element in the overall scheme of things as was keeping the performers on some kind of supposed leash. Via cards printed in Keith theaters, audiences were warned sternly, if politely: "Gentlemen will kindly avoid the stamping of the feet and pounding of canes on the floor, and greatly oblige the Management. All applause is best shown by the clapping of hands. Please don't talk during the acts, as it annoys those about you, and prevents a perfect hearing of the entertainment."[48] Albee also demanded that patrons remove their hats, and refrain from smoking, spitting, whistling, and crunching peanuts.[49]

The behavior of both performers and patrons in the emergent vaudeville theater, as distinguished from what had come before, may not only have made it a little pleasanter for refined wives and daughters to enjoy the show, but might also have allayed their anxieties in another crucial way. These changes gave vaudeville the imprimatur of a bourgeois or middle-class form of amusement. It was safe, not rough; trustworthy and purified, rather than suggestive of society's dark underside, its "connections with working-class culture and with working-class sexuality" severed. Thus, it paved the way for what might be seen as a middle-class sexuality, a tolerable, if not openly advertisable, way to get the titillating goods from the burlesque hall and the variety theater onto the refined, stamped-safe-for-the-middle-class vaudeville stage. Indeed, even the change from the term variety to vaudeville,[50] with its French roots and hint of European sophistication, symbolized "not so much a change in performance structure as changes in the form's institutional structure, social orientation, and audience." Thus, it was not so much immorality, per se, that Keith was trying to dodge, as it was the "taint" of the working class.[51] In a sense, then, the presence of women (other than prostitutes) in the house helped signify that the vaudeville theater was a trustworthy form of entertainment consumption for the middle class, rather than for those lower on the social ladder. Masculinity had somehow become intertwined with the unruly wage-earning classes.[52] The working classes sought after a French word called "burlesque," while their middle-class counterparts were to prefer the francophonic "vaudeville."

Of course, as the present argument suggests, it is not clear that vaudeville and burlesque were polar opposites. In fact, the closer one looks at vaudeville theater, the more it seems that the form—whether at Pastor's, Keith's, Koster & Bial's, or elsewhere—kept a foot, if not more, planted firmly in the burlesque tradition. We have already seen, for example, that certain female performers in vaudeville made disrobing onstage a key part of their act.

Or consider Alice Eis and Bert French, two of vaudeville's perpetual favorites. During the last week in July 1909 the two put on an act called "the Vampire Dance" at the Keith-controlled Fifth Avenue theater. Of Eis and French, *Variety*'s Rush had this to say: "The pair at the Fifth Avenue this week go into a disagreeable number with a degree of vivid detail that is almost medical…." The act featured Eis as "a Parisian woman of the streets" striking "a particularly snakey posture." At the performance's climax, Eis removed a "thin red veil" and "reveal[ed] … a tight-fitting dress" with "a skirt slashed almost to the waist line and the only underdressing is a covering of fleshings." *Variety*'s competitor, the *New York Dramatic Mirror*, said that the Eis/French number was simply the "latest of dips into the world of suggestion and vulgarity, and it is or ought to be to the shame and discredit of those in charge of the [Keith-controlled] United Booking Offices or the Fifth Avenue theater that this act was given a public showing…. To call it a dance is a libel against the name of art." Nonetheless, the two played to a capacity house the following week and became a solid "drawing card."[53] In fact, Eis and French gained such a following for presenting sexually suggestive material in vaudeville that when they appeared at Keith's famed Palace theater some six years later in another dance number, called "The Lure of the North," *Variety*'s "Sime" joked, "[I]t's funny to see the French-Eis people all dressed upon the stage."[54]

The way Rush writes about vaudeville here, he might as well have been writing about burlesque, for all its emphasis on the sexually provocative female form—and the *Variety* journalist seems to have known it. In January 1910, singer Lillian Herlein played at Keith's Fifth Avenue. Rush wrote in his review that Herlein was "bound to make talk. The talk will come from her appearance in full tights during her final song called 'Swim, Swim, Swim.'" According to Rush, Herlein was a "statuesque brunet with a twenty-two-inch waist, and other proportions which are striking to say the least." Her act had one main purpose, in his view—display of her "figger"—and this, as its sponsors knew, was its "principal aim" and "drawing card."[55] For as Rush's colleague Sime noted, "figger goes a long way toward getting salary from the box office."[56]

Rush's words are significant because they could have been written about dozens of other acts that were seen on the vaudeville stage during the form's rise to massive popularity in the closing years of the nineteenth century and the opening years of the twentieth. Indeed, it is hard to find a review of a female performer in which the (always male) reviewer makes no mention of her "beauty of face and form," "statuesqueness," or fails to point out that she "looks fine in tights." It seems, then, that the sexually provocative female body was part of the vaudeville theater's stock-in-trade—that it indeed placed the "emphasis on anatomy" that at least one writer on vaudeville has ascribed to burlesque and burlesque alone.[57]

In fact, by 1915, burlesque may have been in some ways *cleaner* than vaudeville. That was the year that the American Circuit of burlesque halls undertook to create "clean burlesque," marking the culmination of "several years of determined efforts by circuit officials." Among the show elements barred were "cooch and Oriental dancers," "bare legs," "smutty dialogue," and "vulgar jokes and actions."[58] Noted *Variety* a few years earlier, "The Burlesque Wheels [or circuits], one at least, can now claim as clean a show as vaudeville. Not perhaps in their entirety, but in spots."[59] The clear line between burlesque and vaudeville may not have always been all that clear after all.

Perennial vaudeville favorites Alice Eis and Bert French performed erotic dance duets which usually resulted in Eis boasting various states of undress—such as is seen here. (Billy Rose Theatre Collection, The New York Public Library for the Performing Arts, Astor, Lenox, and Tilden Foundations.)

If vaudeville retained certain key similarities to burlesque, then it begs the question, just how important were women in vaudeville audiences? It is a common assumption, as we have begun to see, that the presence of women in the audience was one of the key factors that differentiated the form from burlesque and the earlier concert saloon and variety hall amusements. Many observers have concluded that vaudeville theaters were always filled with all members of the family, one even quoting actor Edwin Royle, who supposedly said of the vaudeville houses that they were "the only theaters in New York where I should feel absolutely safe in taking a young girl without making preliminary inquiries."[60] The vaudeville producers got women and girls in the door and in so doing, disassociated themselves from the unseemly, male-dominated burlesque world so approved-of by the working classes. Even "variety" had come to mean little more than a "stag show," while female patrons showed all concerned a marked departure from "masculine saloon culture," in favor of a venue for "women, children and more wealthy patrons."[61] So the story goes.[62]

But there is evidence to suggest that, perhaps beyond an initial burst of popularity, women in fact scarcely attended vaudeville in such great numbers, and that, indeed, vaudeville was, like burlesque or the concert saloon, a form of entertainment that relied much more heavily on male ticket-buyers for its success than on female ones. Anna Marble, in her "Women in Variety" column in *Variety*, observed in December 1906 that vaudeville seemed to appeal more strongly to men than to women. According to her informal survey, some two-thirds of the average audience was "made up of the sterner sex" (even at matinees!), including many whose "appearance proclaimed them merchants, bookkeepers, and other workers."[63]

The only statistical survey of New York vaudeville audiences, conducted in 1911, seems to confirm her findings. It revealed the modal audience to be sixty-four percent male, thirty-six percent female. It further determined the crowd makeup to be sixty percent "working" class, thirty-six percent "clerical" class, and four percent "vagrant, gamin, or leisured."[64]

And even though vaudeville producers often placed their theaters near busy shopping and retail districts in order to attract a female clientele, women made up only a third of the audience in New York in 1910 and less than half the audience in cities like San Francisco and Milwaukee.[65] Tony Pastor himself even had to eventually resort to gimmicks and premiums to keep women coming to see his shows, consisting of "gifts of hats, dress patterns, and other feminine gewgaws," not to mention dolls, flowers, candies, and even a special "Ladies' Night"—though to little avail. Similarly, as late as 1902, vaudeville magnate Frederick F. Proctor had to offer "dainty souvenirs" to lure women into his matinee shows in New York City and Newark.[66] (Of course, even when women were present as vaudeville patrons, they were not necessarily deterred by unwholesome material. In fact, some clearly enjoyed it.)[67]

On occasion, though, the vaudeville stage did succeed in differentiating itself markedly from the burlesque. But this was due to the presence of an undraped *male* body, typically belonging to an athlete or weight-lifter. In March 1902 the *New York Dramatic Mirror*, reporting on the show at Keith's Union Square, joked "[Strongman Eugene] Sandow's attire, or rather the scarcity of it, suggests that he might do well to give out, besides his dissertations on how to develop the physique, a few friendly tips on how not to develop pneumonia." The following week, the *Mirror* observed that the strongman Sandow "is applauded for an exhibition that if attempted by any woman would be promptly suppressed."[68] As we have seen, scantily clad women were common in vaudeville and were rarely dismissed. Men in tights may have been brought in by vaudeville producers to appeal to the "sexual interest" of women in the house as well, though neither the producers nor these female ticket-buyers could really openly admit as much.[69] Still, Sandow and other such specimens of male musculature were hardly a regular component of American vaudeville. Whereas the scantily clad woman on the vaudeville stage evoked pleasure or, alternatively, moral outrage from male trade paper reporters, scantily clad men like Sandow elicited humor or gentle scorn.[70] Ironically, the more they may have appealed to women in the audience by strutting their near-nude, well-muscled, athletic bodies, the more men like Sandow may have been regarded by many a dismissive male onlooker as oddly effeminate.[71]

Even Tony Pastor himself seems to have recognized at a certain point that he could not entirely excise the vestiges of burlesque in his vaudeville offerings. In 1897, well after Pastor's alleged conversion to "clean variety," the Washburn Sisters played his Tammany Hall theater. The theatrical and sporting trade paper the *New York Clipper* noted, "The Washburn Sisters appeared in very pretty, though brief, frocks ...

the new member of the firm is an excellent substitute for her predecessor, being of pleasing face and form, but her stock of 'ginger' far exceeds the demands of refined variety audiences." To theater journalists at the turn of the century, "ginger" denoted the sexually suggestive, off-color, or ribald, and it was often said that a performer who pushed the limits of respectability was rather "gingery." But ginger was not the only spice which symbolized unwholesomeness or sexual titillation. Nor was it the only spice at Pastor's. Maud Nugent, who enjoyed a "long and successful run" at Pastor's, specialized in the performance of "spicy" and "peppery" songs. "She is not likely to be soon forgotten," remarked the *Clipper*.[72]

Though not as spicy as Maud Nugent or the Washburn Sisters, impressionist C. W. Littlefield pushed the limits of purity at Pastor's as well by doing an imitation of "the boy smoking his first cigar." The *Dramatic Mirror* called Littlefield's act "not a thing for a house frequented by refined people." Still, Littlefield was allowed to appear again several months later, the smoking routine completely intact.[73]

As we have seen, such impurities were allowed to pass on the stage, where audiences clearly enjoyed them, thanks in part to a promotional rhetoric which gave the entertainment consumer what he wanted while simultaneously easing his anxieties about mass consumption, entertainment or otherwise. In so doing, the vaudeville magnates, like their peers in many other industries, were appealing to a "preoccupation with purity and unity" among individual consumers who had now to turn to faceless national firms for their goods and services. Historians have suggested that many Americans at the time associated purity and unity with the small-scale communities to which they had been accustomed.[74]

As we will see, the national, mass-market firms that came increasingly to control both the consumption habits and livelihoods of a great many Americans, like the vaudeville chains, responded in part by making purity, and even the salutary, a central promise in their promotional discourse. Sears, for example, in order to craft a national market for its catalogue goods (its retail stores came later), had to change the minds of individuals used to turning to their local small-scale retailer, perhaps a general store, which "constituted the nexus between the wants of farmers and villages and the 'manufactories,'" according to *Catalogues and Counters: A History of Sears, Roebuck and Company*. To that end, Richard Sears, in addition to providing constant reassurances that his watches, bicycles, and cream separators were of the highest quality and could be returned no-questions-asked, had also to craft an image of the Sears, Roebuck company as being comprised of people who were as "honest, dependable, and financially reliable" as a local merchant or store owner. He succeeded. In 1897, Sears, Roebuck and Company sold $2.8 million worth of mail order goods; ten years later, that figure had leapt to $40.8 million.[75]

Similarly, Keith, Albee, Martin Beck (father of the Orpheum vaudeville chain) and others oversaw and controlled what has been termed "[t]he growth of a centralized vaudeville empire" in which those selling its wares "chose a mass audience over a local audience."[76] In the field of public entertainment, they were pioneers, and their efforts marked the creation of a national market that is still with us today. At the same time, though, as we will see, the vaudeville powers were very much products of their era. They were businessmen who took advantage of advancements in transportation, communication, and technology to enrich themselves mightily by selling to a burgeoning mass market. "What iron and steel are to the industrial market," wrote *Variety* in 1912, "so vaudeville is to the amusement seeking public of the united forty-nine states."[77] The writer of those words was Joseph M. Schenk, General Booking Manager of the Loew vaudeville circuit; Schenk would later go on to distinguish himself as a producer at United Artists in Hollywood in the 1920s.[78] Schenk captures both the mass scope of vaudeville's economic project while also suggesting that a new community—a national community defined by regularized, widespread consumption patterns—had replaced the old, local, irregular communities of the past. The vaudeville magnates had made of entertainment a professionally run and highly schematized industry, as others were doing in their respective fields of commercial endeavor. Tellingly, it has been written that Keith and Albee were to vaudeville "what Frick and Carnegie were to steel."[79] Keith and his peers deserve credit (or blame, depending on how one looks at it) for their mass-market thinking. But like the powers behind Standard Oil, Coca-Cola, and Sears, Roebuck, they were historically located individuals—empire builders in an age of rampant empire building; mass-marketers in an age when mass-marketing began to make sense. And it is with an understanding of this historical context that one may more fully and properly understand the issues of sexuality, wholesomeness, and, where applicable, corporate self-censorship in American vaudeville. Some have even suggested that vaudeville's approach to these nettlesome questions formed a kind of reusable template, a "core and example," for future hawkers of mass entertainment, particularly movies, radio, and television.[80]

In the mighty entertainment factory that was vaudeville, for the first time, a policy, an official and public *stance*, on sexuality and censorship on the stage had been developed and, at times, implemented across merely local communities. This was aided by the far-reaching bureaucracy of the Keith and other circuits.[81] Furthermore, since vaudeville not only created an effective working paradigm for mass national amusement but also evolved into a key part of the motion picture industry,[82] it is reasonable to conclude that vaudeville's various practices, policies, and conflicts both foreshadowed and directly influenced those of American popular entertainment forms later on in the century.

Certainly, not all attitudes and policies were handed down directly from the central offices, most of which were in New York City. Local managers had some discretion in asking a performer to cut this or that bit of a monologue or a song—or, similarly, request that particular routines be expanded. After all, what played in Philadelphia or New York did not always play quite as well in Topeka, Kansas or Springfield, Illinois—at least not without some regional tweaking. Even without taking into account regional differences in taste, the manager of one Keith theater, say, might simply have had a different standard for vulgarity and entertainment value than that of his peer at another Keith outlet. Accordingly, vaudeville performers had to construct their acts in such a way that any bit or routine could be jettisoned at the last minute or, contrarily, built upon if need be. The acts were thus modular in nature, rather than based on some kind of sacred and unalterable text.[83]

But the modularity and sometime regional variation in stage fare need not contradict the fundamental truth that vaudeville was largely a mass-scale, largely standardized entity. It does not mean that there were *no* regional or local variations of material, nor that people in one particular sub-pocket of American culture felt and responded precisely as their peers in another city or village—peers of perhaps a slightly different ethnic, economic, or sociopolitical makeup—would have. For part of what permitted vaudeville to acquire its national scope and scale was an understanding that some concessions to locale and region had to be accommodated—and then incorporated into the overall business model.

So, even if there were variations in what entertainment consumers around the country saw and felt, there is little doubt that the businessmen in charge of distributing entertainment (and, for that matter, every other emergent mass-market ware at the turn of the century) were trying quite clearly to impose a national economic paradigm on the American market. That is, even if it constitutes a kind of fiction to suppose that there exists or existed an "American market," it is precisely this fiction that motivated and mobilized the likes of B.F. Keith, Richard Sears, and others, enfolding and incorporating regional tastes within a nationwide scheme. In short, while it may not be possible to construct culture from the top down, it seems to have been possible to craft and seek after markets in precisely this way.[84]

Big-time vaudeville was a business that relied on a product that fell more or less within certain parameters (even while it could be varied locally) and which could be scheduled to play at a large chain of venues, owned by one or a few interests, around the United States. This was simply how it worked. Certainly, local managers could insist an act conform to different standards than that act faced in the previous city, but it is also true that such negotiations occurred under the aegis of a mass-scale marketing discourse which allegedly promised purity, content control, and, in the rare instances when it became necessary, censorship. For while values and tastes may have evolved in so many ways at so many regional locales, mass-marketing began to occur at the national level for the first time in the history of the American economy. It was at this moment, as the Keiths and Searses of the world were beginning to make their mark, that Americans, particularly in cities, were indelicately coaxed from local consumption patterns into a universe of "mass-produced goods," participants in a nation-size market made up of millions of people "associating with big, centrally organized, national-level companies."[85] This kind of participation, as has been suggested, brought with it understandable anxieties; and it was such anxieties that powerful business interests sought to address with promises of cleanliness, purity, control, and moral or hygienic authority. As we will see, so much of the popular discourse of the day—advertising copy, newspaper columns, magazine articles, letters to editors, popular songs, even legislation—betrays, reveals, and illustrates both these anxieties and what some folks at the time thought ought to be done about it. Texts like these, then, are not only reflective of the tempest that was American culture at the time, but must also be seen as a tool that shaped and transformed public opinion, tearing down an older era and constructing a byway to the new.

On the subject of eras, new and old, it may be important to include a short note about the timeframe of this study. Though vaudeville theater in the United States in some sense may be said to have begun in the 1880s with the work of producer Tony Pastor and others like him, we will be more immediately concerned with the period from 1895 to 1915. It is this period that bookends vaudeville's rise to peak popularity, development as an industrially organized amusement, and evolution into a national preoccupation. It was in 1895 that the *New York Dramatic Mirror* inaugurated its weekly "Vaudeville Stage" column. Wrote the *Mirror*, "The vaudeville branch of the profession is an important one, and if present indications count for anything, it will soon demand as much attention as the dramatic profession." This important change in the *Mirror*'s editorial practices reflected key changes underway in the realm of public entertainment.[86]

By 1915, however, big-time vaudeville was in the first stage of what would eventually prove its inexorable decline. B.F. Keith was dead, and his demise was of symbolic, as well as material, importance. Motion pictures, long in the ascendancy, had unquestionably replaced vaudeville—initial host of the movies' own emergence—as a distinct and more popular form of entertainment.[87] Also, the period of World War I marked significant changes in both gender relations—a central concern of this work—and patterns of middle-class amusement-going, having largely to do with socio-economic upheaval and Prohibition.[88] Finally, following the War, but especially after about 1920, we begin to observe the real, imagined, and discursive decline of the American city, for by this time, "no one could deny that the cities were poor and that the suburbs, relatively speaking, were rich." The racial makeup, and polarity, of the American city in this era changed dramatically. [89]

Such sweeping changes in city life spelled the end of vaudeville, for the vaudeville theater had been perhaps the exemplary public, urban entertainment of the age. And when the middle classes so desperately sought after (if not always recruited) by Keith and Albee began withdrawing to the suburbs, their (the vaudeville magnates') project fell in many ways in an uncontrolled descent.

Although the move away from cities, and the subsequent demise of urban recreations (coupled with the rise of "clean, safe" places of amusement such as the multiplex movie theater[90] and the sports complex marketed toward those who could *drive* to the games—not to mention the ultimate "safety" of home-based amusements such as radio, during the 1920s, and television in the later 1940s) did not happen fully until after World War II, its beginnings may be clearly seen after 1918.[91]

Finally, though it may seem self-evident, it may yet be helpful before plunging in further to define "vaudeville" as distinct from the earlier variety theater, concert saloon, contemporaneous burlesque hall, and cabaret venue. While both vaudeville and the variety theater presented a concatenation of different acts with no narrative through-line, there are key differences. The variety theater was a decidedly small-time operation. Local owner-managers booked whatever talent happened to be in town, opened their doors, and hoped for the best. Vaudeville, by contrast, grew up as a centrally-managed operation in which the owners managed formidable circuits of theaters and often planned an entire season's fare at once. Thus, what might be seen at Keith's Boston theater was largely the same, particularly in overall conceit, as that which could be seen at a Keith theater in another city hundreds of miles away. Increasingly, through the work of powerful booking agencies (owned or controlled by the vaudeville chains), the theatrical product became standardized and served up on a mass scale.

Vaudeville differed from the nineteenth-century concert saloon in that vaudeville theaters were not simply bars with a pianist, dancer, or comic on stage, vying for attention while the crowd immersed itself in chatter, tobacco, and liquor. Rather, the vaudeville theaters that emerged in the 1890s were carefully controlled, corporate-run entertainment environments. Men like Keith and Albee took great pains to mediate every element of the theater-going experience, from sightlines to furnishings to the mix of acts on stage. These were places in which one's attention was directed toward the stage, and where decorous applause or laughter was the only form of noise encouraged by the management. These were not places to unwind for several hours, whiskey or cigar in hand, while talking up one's fellow attendees. Rather, they were places where one paid a modest admission for a carefully-packaged show and then departed after the last act went off stage.

The differences—and striking similarities—between vaudeville and the burlesque hall have already been covered.[92] For the purposes of the present work, all that need be pointed out is that the burlesque "wheels" (as they were known) never propagated a public discourse of purity and cleanliness as did vaudeville. Rather, they largely and unabashedly appealed to male patrons seeking disrobing acts and lewd humor. And while similar types of acts could be seen on the vaudeville stage, it was burlesque that earned the reputation for being overtly racy and licentious despite some reform efforts in the mid-1910s. Vaudeville's reputation remained functionally intact—despite the complaints of vocal moral crusaders—even when its stage offerings bore a striking resemblance to those of the burlesque hall.

Finally, vaudeville may be distinguished from the cabaret theater by the latter's loftier artistic and political aims and greater popularity in Europe than in the United States. Though vaudeville theaters in the United States had become, by the last decade of the nineteenth century, "grandiose, elaborate palaces of stereotyped amusement," they were rarely home to overtly political (with a few exceptions, such as the occasional suffragist act) or "artistic" content—at least according to the dictates of high culture. In inventing mass entertainment, the business magnates who controlled vaudeville chose clearly to exclude what they felt might alienate the greatest number of paying customers, and include that which would result in the greatest gross receipts. In contrast, the cabaret world appropriated from vaudeville and other mass forms (the circus, for example) a certain "vitality, immediacy, and vivacity"—but then put these crowd-pleasing elements to work "in order to convey a rarefied artistic style or a liberal political message or a skewed vision of the world."[93] Thus vaudeville spawned a kind of entertainment that was electric in its appeal, easily spread, and the perfect fare for amusement-hungry new urbanites in the final decades of the nineteenth century, and opening decades of the twentieth. Some might put the tools of vaudeville to other uses—political, artistic, etc.—but not Keith, Albee, and their brethren. As far as they were concerned, there was simply too much money to be made.

one

"Dressed in the Form of Art"
The Censorship and Curtailment of Popular Entertainments

If the vaudeville chiefs were concerned about promulgating the notion that theirs was a form of popular entertainment free from moral taint and vulgarity, they had another good reason to do so, beyond that of allaying anxieties in the minds of their patrons: censorship and theater closure. In an era when municipal governments, urged on by indignant urban reform groups, threatened to block content and in which, on at least one occasion, New York City's mayor ordered a closing of popular entertainment venues,[1] avoiding the appearance of impropriety may have been even more important than keeping it off the stage.

In this regard—never falling seriously afoul of governmental bodies and/or many of the "progressive" groups lobbying them—vaudeville established a highly successful track record, with one or two exceptions. And when compared to the motion picture, whose popularity grew in large part because vaudeville theaters began showing short movies within their programs,[2] vaudeville's avoidance of serious governmental interference seems all the more remarkable. It is, in a sense, an indication of certain crucial, underlying differences between the world of big-time vaudeville and that of early motion pictures—not to mention the brilliantly effective rhetoric of purity that those marketing vaudeville entertainment put to such constant use.

One reason why calls for government censorship never dogged vaudeville as they later did the motion picture industry may have been that while the emergent motion picture companies were largely controlled by European-born Jewish immigrants, who were perceived as unkempt outsiders by the dominant Catholic and Protestant elite,[3] vaudeville was largely controlled by individuals with whom that elite could more easily identify. B.F. Keith's wife, for example, was well known for her devout Catholicism and it is argued that she helped her husband devise the Keith chain's putative self-censorship code.[4] Noted Boston's Cardinal O'Connell, "The business in which Mr. Keith was engaged was one surrounded by all sorts of temptations and dangers, a business which could be turned to the loss of souls, but Mrs. Keith constantly kept watch over that...."[5] Purveyors of popular fare in the early decades of the twentieth century were lucky if clerics weren't busy damning them in sermons; here was an out-and-out endorsement.

E.F. Albee, Keith's partner, was not himself a religious man. Nonetheless, he coaxed investment backing from the Catholic church, both because it had some of the deepest pockets in New England and for the air of purity its sustenance would lend the budding vaudeville chain. He also actively solicited and won the input of Protestant leaders by having them serve as community liaisons and occasional censorship consultants. Again, the public relations value was immeasurable. Joked one former vaudevillian, "Had Boston boasted a larger Jewish population, it is certain that Albee would have worked a rabbi into the scheme of things."[6] Indeed, other early mass-marketers at the turn of the century enlisted the endorsement of religious authorities to help legitimate their mass-produced wares. The company that manufactured the shortening Crisco, for example, recruited rabbis to declare that the product was kosher.[7]

Vaudeville did eventually, if briefly, fall afoul of certain religious authorities when its lucrative Sunday shows conflicted with traditional worship time. Nonetheless, it never suffered the degree of censure that plagued Hollywood almost from the beginning and which, in some ways, continues up to the present.

It should be noted too that vaudeville, while extremely popular, was never as vastly popular, and therefore as thoroughly threatening to the social fabric, as the mass-market films produced by Hollywood. If vaudeville was a rogue wave, movies were nothing short of a prolonged hurricane, ripping into the urban order, threatening to overturn or damage a number of Victorian-age cultural values and practices. More than staged entertainments and dime novels, "the movies threatened to gain control over the representation of crime and punishment, of class and ethnicity, and, especially, of familial and sexual relations."[8] If vaudeville was perceived by some as "Sunday school," the movies were tantamount to getting the facts of life from one's teen peers on a street corner.

A well-publicized policy, if not actual practice, of self-censorship, though, helped the vaudeville chains keep calls for government censorship at bay during a time when the possibility of censorship, restraint, and control trailed close behind nearly all the emergent modes of mass communication. Its "emphasis on purity and refinement for family audiences" rendered it largely "immune" from the civic sanitizing that scorched the movies.[9]

Still, those who controlled the form did well to be careful. As early as 1848, the illusion of nudity offered by "living pictures" at Palmo's Opera House in New York drew "vigorous protests" and was eventually banned by the city.[10] Living pictures and tableaux, which sometimes won moral approval and other times suffered moral censure, were consistently the subject of police raids, bench warrants, and crusading efforts. Jack McCullough, in *Living Pictures on the New York Stage*, points out that the form saw repeated attacks not only in the years leading up to the Civil War but especially in the period from 1875 to 1893.[11]

But living pictures were not the only target of moral outrage. In 1866, *The Black Crook* at Niblos's Garden was repeatedly objected to because it featured female performers in flesh-colored tights during its two-year, 474-performance run. In 1900, Clyde Fitch's *Sapho* [sic] was shut down altogether for its sexual content.[12] It was not merely the (potentially) sexually titillating content that aroused the ire of authorities, but also the fact that the arousal came at such a cheap price. Ever since what has been termed the "commercialization of leisure" in the eighteenth and nineteenth centuries, so-called "cheap amusements" have been suspect, according to at least one historian, "precisely because they arouse strong desires and strong antipathies in an untrustworthy public."[13] One even comes across the occasional police action taken against a vaudeville act, though typically adjudication and punishment was meted out toward the performer or performers in question rather than the producers or chain owners — another decided difference between what vaudeville suffered and what the movies, in which systemic remedy was demanded, suffered.

In 1909, the popular performer Mlle. De Leon was arrested for presenting a dance considered "indecent."[14] De Leon had made a name for herself as a "coochee-coochee" dancer who appealed to audiences through "the gradual discarding of sundry articles of raiment," according to the *New York Dramatic Mirror*.[15] In 1910, famed performer Sophie Tucker was enjoined from singing the song "Angle Worm Wiggle" by police and eventually lost her case in court.[16] By 1904, the Committee of Fourteen, a conservative group of professionals and social reformers, began turning a wary eye on vaudeville and the other leisure activities so closely associated with the rise of the American city. Though primarily concerned with getting rid of prostitution, the Committee "also attacked the problems presented by the new amusements,"[17] including, at times, vaudeville.

If the cloud of out-and-out censorship only occasionally darkened the landscape of the growing vaudeville industry, it was ever hovering above that of vaudeville's close cousin — with whom it shared performers, producers, and dramatic material — the legitimate stage. Some social elites, religious leaders, and moral reformers of the era feared the stage as a kind of mass medium which the public at large was neither educated nor ethically sound enough to handle. As early as 1907, an editorial favoring theater censorship appeared in the *New York Times*. It read, "The theory of theatrical censorship is admirable. It aims to protect public morality by guarding the mind of the multitude, as far as possible, against contaminating influences. It tries to check irreverence toward religion and to avoid needless public offense to the sensibilities of friendly foreigners." And while the *Times* found that the actual practice of censorship has often "dismally failed," it argued nonetheless that "[a] well-directed censorship of plays and novels, too, might be beneficial."[18]

Two years later, the Catholic Men's Society passed resolutions condemning "the immorality of the stage now so frequently exhibited in grand opera and in theaters, as well as in the humbler moving-picture shows." The Society declared, "We ask the Catholic and the secular press to aid in this work of protecting the children by denouncing the infamous business now carried on by unscrupulous men seeking to enrich themselves by providing the indecencies which are put upon the stage and in the picture shows, whose sure effect is to corrupt the minds of those who witness them."[19] Evident in the discourse of the Men's Society is a paternalistic attitude toward consumers of public amusements, rather like that of a parent toward a child craving sweets: They don't know what is good for them, so it is up to us to "protect" them. Twice that year, the New York City aldermen proposed bills on play censorship.[20] Though they never became law, a play censor *was* appointed in the nearby town of Plainfield, New Jersey. In that municipality, which had bristled following a local production of Clyde Fitch's *The Blue Mouse*, the mayor wrote, "There seems to be a growing tendency on the part of theatrical managers, of moving picture shows, and of vaudeville houses to produce plays and show pictures that are not only not elevating, but are absolutely indecent and demoralizing."[21] And at least one New York legitimate theater manager said that, in his opinion, "there should be a stage censorship."[22]

Three years later, in 1912, prominent New York Catholics again banded together, inaugurating the National Catholic Theatre Movement. The Movement aimed to introduce "a systematic scheme whereby all plays regarded as immoral would be put on the 'black list' in every city of the United States." Said New York's Cardinal Farley, a key member of the Movement, "I hope the time will come when no play can be presented in New York before it has passed a National committee." An Irish-American Cardinal wrote a statement for the cause in which he argued, "The stage at the present day is a powerful engine for the swaying of men's minds for good or evil. Unfortunately, it is seldom used for good, and generally for evil, with fatal effects."[23] In its anti-theatrical discourse, the clergy implicitly acknowledged that a new era had arisen in which commercial entertainment, controlled by industrially organized, financially motivated businessmen had replaced the church, family, and local community as the primary influence on individual morality.

There is too the persistent comparison of such entertainment to disease, contamination, and infestation. Another member of the National Catholic Theatre Movement lamented that in his confessional, he could only deal with "victims already infected." As far as he was concerned, his project, like that of a Pasteur, to be effective had to attack the "source of the plague"—that is, the playhouses; if they, "like breeding pest houses, are allowed to spread their infection, the health of the whole community is threatened."[24] No wonder that vaudeville producers advertised their amusement as "clean" and "pure," even if it wasn't always so, and no wonder that purveyors of other mass-market goods and services stressed the sterility and purity of their products. Changes in consumption patterns had indirectly provoked a moral crusade.

The real problem, as the clergy saw it, then, was the free market as it applied to public amusement. A new structure of morality, in which the permissible equaled the commercially viable, threatened to replace an older paradigm in which culturally authorized elites, or at very least parents, decided what should and should not be disseminated to the masses. Theatre Movement member Monsignor McGean cannily pointed out that in fact, the "theater managers give a supply for a demand," hence their success at getting people to see plays. Accordingly, rather than attack the supply side, "We therefore must educate the demand and that will automatically shut off the supply." He urged parents to declare, "I will not attend any play or let any members of my family attend any play which I have heard is dangerous, which is stained with the vices of the day." McGean's tack was different from that taken by others toward the movies, which was decidedly supply-side (and much more effective). "We must cause a demand for something better," McGean hoped in vain.[25]

Still, the idea of a self-determining market, without input from cultural authority figures, was a concern that ran deep amongst anti-theatrical sorts. Protestant leaders, up in arms about the proliferation of plays such as *Kismet* and *The Garden of Allah*, which featured "Mohammaden prayers constantly being said," also joined the fray, arguing for a modification of *laissez-faire* practices in the realm of staged entertainment. Said the Rev. Francis Rolt Wheeler, "Critics? Oh, no, no, no! Indeed, no, nor censors either. We are just experts who will view the various plays to determine which ones are wholesome; that's what ethics are for, you know—specialists...."[26] Men like Wheeler hoped to intercede in the process of mass cultural production, positioning themselves near the top, like the guardians of Plato's *Republic*. The very idea that a consuming public might determine the output of such a system threatened them on so many levels that its existence had to be likened to a pestilence or a plague.

Those who sought to censor—or at least "clean up"—the theater, both legitimate and vaudeville, while agreeing on the problems of the free-market model, sometimes took divergent views on who was to blame. Some, like the Catholic clergy mentioned above, pinned the onus on producers and managers, whom they saw as unscrupulously feeding the unenlightened masses a diet of filth. An anonymous contributor to *Variety* in 1913 attacked the United Booking Office and William Morris, for having "countenance[d] the attractions that will draw the money to the box office quickly, regardless of whether the said attraction contains suggestive lines, almost nude women or anything else." The United Booking Office was the centralized organization which (for a commission) scheduled vaudeville acts across the country and which was controlled by Keith interests; William Morris, whose name is still with us, was one of vaudeville's key talent agents. More importantly, the anonymous author picked up on vaudeville's clever marketing strategy—the means by which it had fashioned itself as a mass-market brand, suitable for consumption in cities and municipalities around the country: through the commercial rhetoric of purity. Acts relying on "suggestive material," argued the *Variety* author, were featured "where the trade mark of any successful vaudeville theater is most prominently displayed, throughout the city or town, 'Clean and inoffensive entertainment.'"[27]

Other elements in society tended to blame audiences for the moral backsliding. This group counted in its numbers reform-minded intellectuals, journalists and writers—individuals more favorably disposed to a free market model of cultural production, but doubtful about the masses' ability to handle it. In discussing the question of stage censorship in *Cosmopolitan*, Alan Dale tried to defend plays and performances with sexually suggestive material on the grounds that "vulgar and contemptibly stupid though they be, they are not so vulgar and so contemptibly stupid as their audiences." Dale, having attended a play recently, could not hide his disgust at the people who would "flock" to see plays with vulgar appeal. "I saw a collection of paunch-faced, obese men, each with a huge cigar in the corner of his mouth, and labeled with the tout and wine agent label. I saw a collection of frowsy, overdressed, and tittering women, very loud, very unattractive, and very unmistakable." The journalist, like an anthropologist revolted by the subject of his daring fieldwork, concluded: "Who present was to be contaminated? Could the play, however bad it might be, be worse than its audience? Could anything make that audience worse than it was?"[28] For Dale, unlike his Catholic contemporaries who targeted the rapacious, unprincipled theater owner or manager, the problem of mass-market entertainment was the masses. It was they, ultimately, who dragged down the moral quotient of the theater, not the playwrights and producers. Perhaps whereas his counterparts in the National Catholic Theatre Movement might have wished for a theocratic oversight board for the stage, Dale might have longed for an aristocracy of theater critics.

Several years later, an editorial in the *New York Clipper* pinned the blame for a wave of "suggestive songs" on the audience, pinning on the crowd a "morbid desire" for "anything that has a *double entendre*—for anything that is off-color." In such a scenario, how could one rightly blame those on stage (or behind it, for that matter), who were in a sense, marionettes that moved, danced, and sang in a manner "as broadly suggestive as possible" to gain applause from those who helped determine their trade value?[29]

If vaudeville faced only indirect threats of public censorship for the content it purveyed, it faced a more palpable attack from individuals who sought to control and circumscribe its spatial and temporal flexibility. Critics, like those who attacked the nickelodeon movie, saw the vaudeville house as a potentially dangerous geographical space, one perhaps where promiscuous men and women could interact away from the prying eyes of family and clergy. In 1909, the *New York Dramatic Mirror* inveighed against some of the potential perils of this new public urban space. Specifically, it warned of the "the 'continuous' masher," which is to say, the "men who have nothing better to do" than go to a vaudeville house in the middle of the day "and allow their mashing proclivities full play." Since many of the New York vaudeville houses featured a continuous cycle of entertainment, men in search of women could wander in at any time and try to find an interested party. According to the *Mirror*, such a man would "ogle, wink at, nudge or engage in conversation any woman who may be unfortunate enough to sit beside them."[30]

One almost wonders if the *Mirror* had conscripted a masher to write this piece, for he seems intimately familiar with the methodology of mashing. Having found a pleasing target, according to this report, the masher "begins a system of turning, leering, and nudging, which puts the girl, if she is at all sensitive, into a state bordering on nervous prostration." Of course, the piece noted, some women went into continuous theaters looking for this very thing, arguing that "there are hundreds of women who visit the vaudeville houses for the purpose of doing a little mashing of their own account, and they are more than pleased at the attention they attract." To certain concerned parties, the vaudeville house, like the emergent cinema and, later, the dance hall, represented a new urban space physically, culturally, and symbolically distinct from the world of late nineteenth-century socio-sexual norms. Its very existence frightened some, while it drew heated calls for regulation from others. The *Mirror* determined that "eternal vigilance" was needed to deal with the mashing nuisance.[31]

If vaudeville houses and other sites of public amusement represented a spatially and geographically threatening locale—an arena of free mashing—they also posed a temporal one in the minds of certain critics and reformers. The turn of the century saw a series of sustained attacks on so-called "Sunday shows," or the production of certain performances on Sunday. In early 1900, politicians, city officials, and police met to discuss the enforcement of existing laws which prohibited or circumscribed performances on Sunday.[32] Arrests were made on at least one occasion later that year, but the issue died down until about 1905 when two theater managers, Mark Leuscher and Louis Werba, were summoned before a New York City magistrate for having violated the Sunday law. The judge, however, ended up letting the two go, "as he believed a theater to be a better place for a man to spend Sunday evening than the back room of a saloon," according to one trade paper.[33]

Not everyone agreed. The "Sabbatarian League" formed shortly thereafter and began putting pressure on the police to enforce the Sunday laws. The League, which also lobbied New York's Mayor George B. McClellan, saw the vaudeville house as a direct competitor to the house of worship. One Protestant minister who visited a Sunday vaudeville show claimed he saw "more of his congregation there than had been in church."[34] The new sites of amusement offered in the burgeoning city symbolized and directly contributed to the breakdown of an existing social structure with a clearly defined spatial/temporal regimen and rules of control.

For their part, the vaudeville producers tried, predictably, to seem compliant via an effort to enforce the "Sunday clause" of the New York City charter, not only for fear of losing their licenses but because they wished to seem in favor of producing "clean, amusing entertainment." *Variety* noted that complying with the law would cost the major vaudeville producers in New York roughly a million dollars per season in lost ticket revenues.[35] In any case, the New York Supreme Court had upheld the statute.

The peace was a fragile one, however, and the following year moral crusaders renewed their assaults on Sunday shows, probably because vaudeville managers, hungry for increased ticket sales, reinstated the presentations. Understandably, it was clergymen who led the effort. When New York City assemblyman Gluck suggested the introduction of a bill explicitly permitting Sunday shows, he was shouted down by both Catholic and Protestant leaders. Archbishop Farley argued heatedly that "no proposed legislation has ever threatened to such an extent to operate against every person in this city as this bill does," while Presbyterian minister Canon William Sheaf Chase took a slightly less hyperbolic course, suggesting that Shakespeare might be fitting fare for a Sunday show, "Julius Caesar rather than Salome," the latter referring to iterations of a provocative disrobing act wildly popular in vaudeville at the time. The trouble was, according to Canon Chase, the "people who go to Sunday shows want a low-type of play, filled with more or less obscene jokes and allusions,"[36] and there could be only one solution to that: darken the houses.

Though clerics Farley and Chase had differing reasons for opposing Sunday shows, their admonitions betray a common anxiety. It derived from the notion that houses of worship, long a (literally) sacrosanct cultural locale, would soon be subject to the whims of free market competition. That is, to lure people into houses of worship, perhaps they too would have somehow to compete with the amusement fare offered by entertainment industry businessmen, and against professional showmen like B.F. Keith and Willie Hammerstein, they would surely lose.

In the fall of 1907, Chase called on his peers to unite in an effort to quell Sunday vaudeville. His resolve was remarkable considering his life had already been threatened on at least one occasion for his anti-theatrical preaching. "Do you know that you are making a lot of people unhappy and losing money? I warn you[,] you are marked to die," read an anonymous letter Chase received in March, 1907.[37] In September of that year, Chase called for the arrest of local theater managers who violated the Sunday laws; several weeks later, police closed down Sunday shows at Keith & Proctor's Jersey City venue, and made arrests at vaudeville theaters in Brooklyn. By the end of October, one judge, in considering the evidence against Willie Hammerstein, declared that singing acts did not violate the Sunday law, but circus acts did.[38]

Methodist ministers in Manhattan and Brooklyn, not content with the ruling, came on board as well. The Methodist Reverend Dr. John Wesley Hill harshly criticized the city, arguing that lax enforcement had made the existing laws "look like shams," causing him to pontificate with near-apocalyptic zeal: "It is high time that we of the Church should do some telling work against an evil that is undermining the foundations of the Sabbath from one end of the city to the other."[39] The religious groups undertook to make that Sunday in December 1908 a day to test the enforcement policies of the municipal government. By calling public attention to, and trying to stir outrage over, the Sunday statutes during a time of pronounced paranoia over the new urban amusements—New York's nickelodeon movie theaters were to be ordered temporarily shut down several weeks later—the clerics were forcing civic leaders to *do* something or risk their political lives. Those in favor of Sunday legislation could point to the passage of similar statutes in nearby states, such as Massachusetts, which had passed its own law eight months earlier.[40]

By the end of the month, those opposing Sunday shows had prevailed, causing police and city leaders to take action, even if they did not fully understand the arcane Sunday code already in existence in New York, and leaving vaudeville managers scrambling over how to handle the problem. Police Commissioner Theodore Bingham called the city's vaudeville producers down to his office to inform them of the change in policy, where the following exchange, itself reminiscent of a vaudeville comedy sketch or a Marx Brothers movie, actually took place.

> BINGHAM: Gentleman, I've brought you down here to tell you about the law.
> MANAGERS: What is the law anyway?
> BINGHAM: I don't know. Go down to the Corporation Counsel's office and find out. But if you violate it I'll arrest you anyway.[41]

Upon reaching the Office of the Corporation Counsel—the attorneys for the city—the vaudeville managers, including Willie Hammerstein and Percy Williams, were read the provisions of Sections 265 and 277 of the Penal Code which pertained to Sunday presentations. A passage of the Code's text is worth reproducing here, for the arcane and highly specific nature of its wording renders it too somehow comical. Forbidden were:

> The performance of any tragedy, comedy, opera, ballet, or farce or any part thereof. Negro minstrelsy. Any dancing.... Wrestling, boxing, with or without gloves, sparring contests, trials of strength or any part thereof. Circuses or equestrian perfor-

mances. Dramatic performances or exercises. Any performance or exercise of jugglers. Acrobatic or club performances. Rope dancers. Any theatrical play or sketch or a part thereof, with or without theatrical costume. Any vaudeville show. Any impersonation of any character with or without theatrical costume. Any moving pictures giving a play or part of a play.

What could be presented were "orchestral or other instrumental music or vocal music played or sung but not in connection with any theatrical exhibition, nor in costume; lectures and recitations, forming no part of any theatrical piece; moving pictures of an instructive or educational character."[42] Thus, that which bore the imprint, however vague, of highbrow art or educational refinement would pass muster. But entertain—by blackface minstrelsy, boxing, juggling, or any other amusement so many urban crowds loved—and you were asking to get shut down.

Both theatrical managers and city officials may have been confused about the provisions of the Sunday laws, but the latter nonetheless made every effort to enforce the statute as they understood it. All around the city, performers were arrested and shows were threatened with closure by vigilant police, many of whom disguised themselves in plain clothes and sat in the audience. Performer Cliff Gordon, who delivered "political" speeches in costume, omitted the costume during the first Sunday of enforcement. But because he employed a German dialect in his routine, Captain Maher of the West 37th Street station ordered Gordon's arrest "on the ground that he was impersonating a German." Anything that smacked of the mimetic brought instant censure or arrest. When the musical Faust brothers finished their act at the Fourteenth Street Theatre, one singer with an injured leg limped off stage. The limp drew unintentional laughs from the audience. "The police said 'vaudeville' and arrested them, with the manager of the house." During another musical performance, one tenor smacked another tenor with a rolled-up newspaper between numbers. "Cut that out," called a policeman from the house, "that's vaudeville if it isn't acting." One clever performer, who gave lectures while films were being shown, was careful not to adorn his words with anything that might be construed as entertaining rather than "instructive or educational" as per the statute. During the film "Travels in Northern Europe," he would fall silent for long stretches then simply point to the screen and state, "Railroad track. More railroad track. Reindeer." Despite what might be considered the act's sarcastic humor, he was not bothered by the police.[43]

Crusading religious leaders were pleased for the time being. The Reverend Dr. John Wesley Hill, who had spearheaded the effort, proclaimed a spiritual victory over those who would permit things such as Sunday performances. Hill, masterful at marshalling the most explosive rhetoric of the day, said that laxity of enforcement was "a step toward anarchy" and that things like Sunday shows threatened "a spread of moral malaria throughout the community."[44] Theatrical owners and producers opposed to the Sunday laws tried to fire back with their own rhetoric that played on fears of totalitarianism and economic loss, which they hoped would readily recruit public sentiment in their favor. "This sort of treatment," said an attorney who represented some of the city's motion picture theater owners, "can go in Russia, but it can't go in this country. There are 12,000 men employed in the 550 [motion picture theaters]." But it was to no avail. Early 1909 saw another wave of arrests.[45] Sunday ordinances continued to dog vaudeville and motion picture houses for much of the

This humorous cartoon from *Variety* (31 July 1909) literally illustrates the number of sexually suggestive acts in vaudeville—acts which, it was feared, would fall afoul of the incoming New York City police commissioner. Note Eva Tanguay singing "I Don't Care" inside a concealing box. (Billy Rose Theatre Collection, The New York Public Library for the Performing Arts, Astor, Lenox, and Tilden Foundations.)

next ten years, even receiving a shot in the arm in the form of the Stillwell Bill, which more carefully detailed the kinds of acts that were forbidden, in 1913.[46] And although a court found the Sunday laws in violation of the New York State constitution, that ruling was overturned nine months later.[47]

The specter of censorship, public outrage, and governmental control trailed other modes of leisure-time amusement in the emergent mass media, not just vaudeville and film. In addition to plays and vaudeville, newspapers, books, dime novels, schoolbooks, and other commercially-produced cultural texts were held in suspicion by elites, moral crusaders, and other guardians of culture. Between 1870 and 1890, some 20 literary censorship societies were founded in the United States. One of the best known was the New York Society for the Suppression of Vice. Its secretary, and the most famous figure of the censorhip movement, was Anthony Comstock. Comstock got himself appointed an unpaid "special agent" of the postal service, with authority to enter any post office and confiscate any material he found there which offended him. Like the Catholic clergy seeking to censor the theater, Comstock often evoked and relied on images of physical illness and infestation—cholera, cancer, syphilis—in his attacks on vice.[48] In his moral assault on George Bernard Shaw, for example, Comstock, who admitted that he was not directly familiar with Shaw's plays, assailed the Irish dramatist nonetheless for believing, as Comstock saw it, that the "proper method of curing contagious and vile diseases is to parade them in front of the public." For Comstock, this was neither an excuse nor a solution to the problem of "obscene literature."[49] The crusader also harped on themes of the dangers of city life, "and that one of its chief dangers was sexual," in the words of one Comstock biographer.[50]

Though Comstock paid more attention to literary than theatrical vice, he was indirectly indicting vaudeville and other public amusements which grew up as an essential and inseparable part of the nation's burgeoning urban scene. "Vaudeville," after all, according to at least one authoritative historian of the form, means *voix de ville* or "voice of the city."[51]

As might be guessed, moral crusaders, reformers, and cultural guardians were especially concerned about the effects of the new commercial media on children and youth (and, to a lesser extent, on women). According to Herbert George Wells, writing in *Cosmopolitan* in 1903, "the sexual consciousness of a great proportion of our young people is being awakened [by] the half-penny 'comic' papers which are bought so eagerly by boys." Though primarily concerned with mass market literature, Wells made an aside to single out the theater by pointing out that the producer of "adult" plays who failed to keep those under eighteen out of the house would "have to take his chances, and it would be a good one, of a prosecution." Similar to other critics of literature and performance of the era, Wells saw the real threat as emanating from the more popular forms of entertainment, rather than that which had received the approval of high culture: "We want to make the pantomime-writer, proprietor of the penny 'comic,' the bill-sticker and the music hall artist extremely careful, punctiliously clean, but we do not want, for example, to pester Mr. Thomas Hardy."[52] Presumably, Wells and others like him felt that certain modes of discourse, especially those likely to be mediated by culture's elite institutions such as universities and literary societies, were of little or no harm particularly to children.

Others did not quite agree. In 1905, the thirty or so free libraries of New York City removed several works by George Bernard Shaw from their shelves. Naturally, the concern over their public availability took the form of a concern for the works' potential for harming children. Arthur E. Bostwick, chief of circulation for the libraries, figured that it was "all right for people of mature years to read Shaw" but not adolescents. Society's younger members were much more likely to misinterpret Shaw's "radical" social critiques. What if Shaw's now-classic *Man and Superman* were to fall "into the hands of a little east sider?" worried the librarian? "Do you think it would do him any good to read that the criminal before the bar of justice is no more of a criminal than the magistrate trying him?" No, argued Bostwick. It would lead to higher rates of juvenile crime. Hence, off the shelves came *Man and Superman*.[53]

A *New York Times* editorial questioned Bostwick's actions using logic that might as well have come from Herbert George Wells. It was not that Shaw ought not to be censored, but that doing so might lead to the barring of works by recognized cultural icons such as Shakespeare. "Is it possible that Mr. Bostwick puts 'King Lear' on his restricted listed?" asked the *Times* editorialist. At all events, pointed out the writer, if children felt the dire urge to familiarize themselves with *Man and Superman*, all they had to do was go to a public library in Brooklyn, where Shaw's works were left on the shelves in all their social-critiquing glory.[54]

Two years later, Worcester County in Massachusetts removed the "boy books" of Horatio Alger from its library shelves in order to protect children and teenagers from works that civic authorities deemed "not truthful" and "too sensational," according to the *New York Times*—though it is hard to imagine how Alger's works, many of which illustrate the triumph of hard work and social order over idleness and vagrancy, should have caused alarm.[55] And the following year, Confederate veterans in Texas prevailed upon the state legislature to remove "objectionable material" from school history books and replace it with a "number of matters relating to Texas history."[56] No steps were too extreme, according to certain pro-censorship advocates, when it came to the effects on the hearts and minds of youth.

But books, periodicals, and popular literature were not only a threat to youngsters. As moral reformers, especially the clergy, saw it, the proliferation of free-market-driven mass entertainment and media threatened codes of decency among all age groups and at all levels of society. In 1908, some of the same elements who would later form the National Catholic Theatre Movement created a committee to purify the press and to "induce newspapers to eliminate from their columns such details of testimony and criminality as would tend merely to gratify prurient curiosity," wrote the *New York Times*. Again, not only was an organ of the media—in this case, the press—attacked but so too implicitly was the free market model on which it operated. The reformers penned an open letter to the *New York Times* which sounded more like a Jeffersonian declaration than the furious sound emanating from a church pulpit, putting forth the authors' "aim of securing newspapers for our homes which shall at all times be free from lewd or suggestive articles detrimental to morals, offensive to decency, and damaging to self-respect." Why not, then, just go out and buy newspapers which omitted all such offending material? Alas, such a thing, perhaps possible in an earlier, gentler age, was now out of reach: "[U]nfortunately, there comes periods when overwhelming public interest and unworthy public curiosity provoke the editors of some of the best of our journals to ... lay before us ... libidinous details of criminality which are revolting even to men charged with the punishment of those who prey upon society." These pro-censorship advocates not only linked sexuality to criminality, but argued that it is not in society's best interest to let a buying public determine what gets published and what does not. "The community—all communities," they went on to write, "were shocked by the long continued revelations of the Thaw case,"[57] referring to the murder trial of Harry Thaw, convicted of killing famed architect Stanford White who was alleged to have once had an affair with Thaw's wife, Evelyn Nesbit, but before she was married to Thaw. If readers wouldn't demand an end to lurid details in their newspapers, they would be assaulted and potentially damaged by them. Though probably aware of this moral opprobrium, the powers behind the vaudeville industry capitalized on the sensational appeal of the Thaw affair. Evelyn Nesbit appeared at Hammerstein's in New York, run by Willie Hammerstein but booked through the Keith-controlled United Booking Office, clearing some $80,000 in box office revenues. Her popularity at Hammerstein's was initially spurred by Harry Thaw's escape from prison, though she went on to tour around the country to great success, for many seasons, largely thanks to Keith bookings.[58]

Newspapers too, then, had become fair game for censors and crusaders who believed the buying public unfit to regulate its own media intake. The same year that reformers wrote their open letter to the *Times* arguing for a cleaned-up press, steps were taken in nearby Paterson, New Jersey, "to suppress the publication" of *La Questione Sociale*, purportedly an "Anarchist paper."[59] The seeds of censorship and content control were laid effectively enough that by the time of America's entry into World War I, the Committee on Public Information could engage with impunity in the "suppression of speech or publication inimical to the doctrines for which America was fighting," according to two historians of American propaganda during the First World War.[60]

Yet for all the outcry in favor of censorship and content control, there were other voices in American society that saw things differently. These voices were in favor of a significantly more open free-market model of public discourse. They urged Americans to let the public decide what was fit for presentation and publication rather than leaving it in the hands of an elite few. The *Nation* attacked just such "suppression" and prior restraint in 1899, suggesting that such tendencies did not befit the current moment in world history, at least in America, where a free society and democracy were beginning to flourish and take root. The *Nation* impugned "the assumption that the ruler who imposes these restrictions is a better judge of what a man ought to read than the man himself." Such an assumption, argued the political journal, "was perfectly comprehensible in the Old World." But in modern America, it had no place, for here was a government "based on the hypothesis that each man is as good a judge as any other man of what our legislation and administration should be." Censorship, endemic to "certain despotic countries like Russia and Turkey," had no place in the free market of ideas (and, implicitly, the growing free market of entertainment and information) found in America.[61]

Likewise, many theater producers seized upon a rhetoric of free-market determination in place of censorship or prior restraint. Legendary legitimate stage producer Lee Shubert said he and his associates had "always believed in the censorship of the public," trusting that the ticket-buying public could be "trusted to select their own stage diet so as to avoid any serious moral dyspepsia." These worked better, in Shubert's view, than "schoolmaster methods" which might, one may infer, impede business proceedings. Shubert's fellow producer Henry Harris likewise averred that a play with a "distasteful" or "repugnant" theme "needs no censor to stop it," while Henry Savage stated that "enlightened public opinion" comprised "the most just and competent censor" imaginable."[62] Winthrop Ames, a theater director, like so many with a decided professional and economic interest in combating government censorship and curtailment of theatricals, echoed themes of freedom and democracy overcoming tyranny: "[T]he question of what shall or shall not be said and done on the stage is not to be settled by any one man, and most certainly not by one man merely because he holds a municipal office…."[63] Those associated with the legitimate stage chose the rhetorical strategy of propagating the politically high-minded ideals of free expression and an enlightened populace which could choose for itself. For their part, the vaudeville producers felt they had to promise at least the trappings of self-censorship—even banning the occasional act in the face of public outcry in order to make it an example—while closely following the dictates of free market determinism. Such was their stratagem (similar to the tactics of many other entertainment and mass-media industries to follow). They were, after all, in the process of crafting the beginnings of mass entertainment and needed a ready public to consume their wares.

Observers other than self-interested theater producers also began to put forth the idea that a free market of ideas was ultimately more salutary to society than some form of institutionalized content control. Should the paying, theatergoing public, in his view, find a work to be "subversive of morality," its producers, no matter how powerful, were left with "no alternative but to defer to the views of its patrons and masters, that is to say, the people." So wrote "A Veteran Diplomat" in the *New York Times* in 1909. As he saw it, the powerful syndicates who controlled the legitimate stage would not hesitate to "blacklist, on the score of impropriety, certain objectionable plays"—but only if a paying public deemed them to be so.[64] An editorial, also in the *Times*, stated simply that while there existed "many stage exhibitions lately of a low, vulgar character," the suppression of widely-regarded "art, literature, [and] the drama" could not be justified on the grounds of its supposed uplifting effects.[65]

The *Times* argued that accusations of immorality and calls for suppression were, more often than not, disingenuous, typically coming from "those purveyors of public entertainment who do not happen to have profitable indecent shows in their theaters."[66] Charles Burnham, President of the Association of Theatre Managers, and Marc Klaw, impresario of both the legitimate and vaudeville stages, even suggested that producers were helpless in the face of abundant public demand for salacious productions. "A manager to be successful must cater to the audience," said Burnham, as if such utter simplicity betrayed a folksy truth no one would be silly enough to argue with. The *New York Times* went so far as to portray Burnham and Klaw as merely giving ticket-buyers what they wanted and, in so doing, finding "the public were more responsible for the plays presented than the managers"—a curious image for two of the most powerful and Machiavellian theatrical producers of their day.[67]

Others who opposed censorship and content control did so because they felt the best way to address social problems, no matter how unpalatable, was to air them out before the public eye. Following the thinking of Zola, Ibsen, and Shaw, they saw no need for censorship if what was presented on stage could be defended as truthful. When his play *The Easiest Way* was attacked by clergy on charges of indecency, playwright Eugene Walter argued that all he had done, in writing *The Easiest Way*, was to put forth for the audience a display of "the terrific influence of a certain element of newly rich or irresponsible rich sons who find pleasure in playing with weak and unfortunate women as others do with their dogs and horses." The game-winning trump card in such arguments was often (and still is, largely) an appeal to documentary-style veracity: "It is the truth, and what harm can there be in the truth?" pondered the dramatist. As if that weren't enough, Walter added a reformist appeal to keep the reformists themselves at bay: "And if one woman's soul is saved from the human wolves of the 'Tenderloin' then the play has done something. *The Easiest Way* is true to life." Finally, in addition to supposed claims to truth and social remedy, Walters, like other artists of his day, fearful of prosecution, suggested that to oppose censorship and champion a free market of ideas was peculiarly and proudly American.

Whereas a French author would "subordinate the wife and justify the mistress," and his English counterpart might "hide everything and pretend it didn't exist," he has instead opted for the American method going "directly to the question this way: 'There's something wrong here; let's find out what it is and then fix it.'"[68] Like others who would contrast America with Russia or Ottoman Turkey, Walters acknowledges the emergence of a marketplace of ideas coupled inseparably with the emergence of a marketplace of commercial entertainments. If the consumers who comprise the market demand a particular kind of play—and are willing to pay for it—it is wrong to refuse them. Thus, one sees the stage artists and producers developing a counter-arsenal of rhetoric to that brandished by the concerned clerics and threatened cultural elites.

Like Walters, others began arguing that vice was best treated by being brought out into the public sphere and analyzed rather than hushed up. If cool heads could prevail, the benefits would be enormous. In 1911, the *Nation* reported that a "remarkable change has of late years come over the public on this very question of vice." In former days, the literature had been "scanty and often untrustworthy." But a sort of light had come on as society recognized the value of open debate and discussion of distasteful topics, "under proper conditions," that would lead man to "correct his judgment by the experience of knowledge of another." It was best to "treat the evil without hysteria or sensationalism." Still, cautioned the *Nation*, such a stance did not imply controversial subjects were to be "bandied about at all times and places or to become a matter of after-dinner discourse."[69] There were still some limits. Perhaps the pages of a magazine were the proper locale. Writers and thinkers of this ilk espoused the view that mass public audiences were perfectly capable of seeing vice and license depicted before them, and judging such things with cool reason.

This attitude suited theater and vaudeville producers just fine, for it permitted them to start putting on acts and plays depicting prostitution, drug use, and the seamy side of life for which the public clamored, all under the guise of truthfulness. For example, in 1912, Hammerstein's produced a sixteen-minute play entitled *A Woman of the Streets*, which depicted Antoinette, "a French woman of the underworld who has become world-wise, cunning and craftily suspicious of those who uphold laws...." Wrote "Mark," a *Variety* reporter who reviewed the piece, "[T]he Hammerstein crowd accepted it in silence until the end when it applauded quite heartily."[70] Perhaps the stage, then, could provide some of the "proper conditions" for cool heads to prevail.

Still, when it appeared that vaudeville producers were merely trying to pander with depictions of vice, onlookers were quick to criticize. In 1910, a short play called *The Derelict* was produced at a New York vaudeville theater. The work, which featured "three men and three women of loose morals... enjoying a hilarious time at a supper where the bubble water flows freely," came under fire from the *New York Clipper*, which assailed the work as one that "could not fail to leave a bad taste in one's mouth." The *Clipper* wondered why "women of the *demi monde* make such appealing subjects for the dramatists," which, in its view, "cannot be pleasing to the better class of theatergoers," but should find favor only with a few perverts in the crowd, the "lovers of the salacious." But the hearty applause at the curtain suggests otherwise.[71]

Even the *Nation* was quick to point out that when a stage work, under "the guise of contributions toward the study of the social evil" but in fact still "abominable in [its] theme and still more abominable in [its] intention"[72] got on the boards, it was still just "filth," plain and simple. It is as if each group of players within the social matrix quickly learned to seize upon the argument that would best forward its own agenda in the name of higher-minded ideals.

Some producers riposted by suggesting that they would not permit such productions in their theaters. Abraham Erlanger of the powerful legitimate and vaudeville producing firm of Klaw & Erlanger issued a public statement declaring, "We are not going to let our theaters deteriorate to the condition from which they were rescued." Nonetheless, the firm booked the play *The Queen of the Moulin Rouge* even though it had come under "severe criticism" for being "indecent" and "immoral." Charles Frohman, another influential and successful theater producer, tried to redeem his and his peers' position by stating, "A play that is primarily fine drama and incidentally represents an unfortunate side of life justifies its production on the score of fine drama."[73] Thus, by introducing notions of taste, quality, and distinction, Frohman, like others, tried to elide accusations of moral impropriety.

Though the threat of censorship was to take its fullest form in relation to the motion picture industry, it nonetheless informed the development of vaudeville and tells us much about American culture during vaudeville's rise to prominence. For struggles over what is unacceptable and what is not, and within what format or venue, reveal differing views of the cultural landscape from a number of vantage points. "Whatever their outcome," writes one historian, "those contests reveal what is at stake whenever people at a given time in a given social setting negotiate the boundaries of what may be said and heard, or shown and seen."[74] People mobilize, form groups, and decry this or that form of expression, in favor of this or that other substitute, all the while proposing methods and apparatuses of mediation to determine what may prevail. By promising, and occasionally practicing, self-censorship, while trying to feed the often less-than-wholesome tastes of a mass audience, the powers behind vaudeville effected a balancing act, poised between risks and rewards, appropriate to the moral climate at the turn of the century.

The greatest danger, and many of the greatest rewards, would come from the presentation of sexually suggestive material—unclad bodies, lewd jokes, "blue" songs—on the vaudeville stage. Many acts which provided those elements were some of the form's biggest hits, and went a long way towards liberalizing attitudes and limits of acceptability with regard to the female body in popular entertainment. Yet sexuality was an especially tempestuous issue around the turn of the last century. With gender roles, consumption habits, and modes of mass communication all in upheaval, human sexuality became a flashpoint for the discussion of culture at large—much as censorship was.

Sexuality, if provoked and catered to by popular culture, could unleash forces threatening to the fabric and structure of society. In 1899, the *American Journal of Sociology* lamented that "[e]very day we hear of assaults and murders provoked by the sexual excitement and the passions which accompany it." One can almost hear the author wringing his hands, as he recounted how recently, "an excellent young man, amiable, laborious, and helpful to the family, became, after he had been enticed into relations with a woman of evil life, lazy, thievish, and violent, going so far as to beat his own mother." Not only could untrammeled sexuality lead to criminality, it could, implied the author, transform humans into veritable beasts, especially at "the period of oestrus" whereupon "animals are all more pugnacious and more ready for violent reaction." Sexuality unleashed threatened to turn our most basic hierarchies of order and control on their head: "Even the dog becomes less obedient to his master." Finally, noted the *American Journal of Sociology* author, uncontrolled Eros could catalyze uncontrolled Thanatos, recalling the numerous, though unspecified, "cases of amorous couples who drown the transports of their embraces in a violent death."[75] One wonders if the writer of this article was thinking more of fictive and literary couples—the Romeos and Juliets—than real-life unions. Perhaps the theater was to blame after all, if not for the perils of sexual embrace, then at least for one writer's anxieties.

Sexuality was therefore viewed as a potentially dangerous force, one that was not to be treated lightly. It functioned, according to certain observers of the day, like a current capable of overcoming any form of control it might encounter. "This flow of sex comes like a great river athwart the plain of our person and egoistic schemes, a great river with its rapids, with its deep and silent places, a river of uncertain droughts, a river of overwhelming floods, a river no one who would escape drowning may afford to ignore," wrote Herbert George Wells in *Cosmopolitan*, Thus, sex and the sexual, while natural, were closer to natural disasters than natural bodily and emotional functions. That which appealed to and provoked sexual urges was to be monitored very closely, like a river barely dammed, for the uncontrollable ramifications it could have.[76]

Some even implied that sex outside of procreation was a deleterious act, one that harmfully detracted from the procreator. Parents who chose to indulge in sex without the intent of creating a fetus were, according to an article in the *New Republic*, "deliberately wasting substances which should go to the increase of their own bone, muscle, blood and brain, and to the like endowment of their children."[77] Again, sexual activity, when not harnessed for what many considered its proper use (and even then, only under certain circumstances) could cause decay, decline, and, by implication, death. It has also been argued that turn-of-the-century American society was suspicious of sexual passion for the psychological and economic damage it might cause, by distracting men "from success," weakening their "resolve," and "ultimately destroy[ing] their will," in the words of a well-known social historian.[78]

There were others who took a more enlightened view, social thinkers and critics of the period who cautiously felt that discussions and representations of sexuality and the sexual in popular discourse could be perhaps helpful or were, at the very least, inevitable. But this depended on their treatment. A contributor to the *Nation* felt that if "the sex motive in fiction" could be handled "cleverly," as French writers were inclined to do, or "gracefully" as were the English, then such elements would not pose so great a problem. In any case, there was no fighting it. "Heaven knows, they give us enough of it! Sex—*sex*— SEX!," he wrote.[79]

Others called for a more open discussion of sex and sexuality in the organs of public discourse, not necessarily for prurient appeal but to educate people and thereby place sexuality under the dictates of reason. In an article in the *Arena* in 1894, Edward Chamberlain argued in support of Moses Harman, a Kansas editor who had been arrested for disseminating information on human reproduction through the mail and was subsequently convicted on federal "obscenity" charges. Without proper knowledge of human sexuality, argued Chamberlain, mankind was bound to reproduce its worst and weakest elements, rather like a horse breeder lacking "information on the reproductive organs and functions of the horse." Echoing the Darwinian ethos of his day (or perhaps presaging the rise of more sinister racial "sciences"), Chamberlain felt that man "propagates recklessly, with no regard to racial development." As a result, "humanity is cursed with all sorts of abnormalities and perversions," and society at large ends up paying a huge bill because, under such conditions, "Hospitals flourish, insane asylums are swarming, prisons are overcrowded, suicides shock us daily, prostitutes throng the streets and greed saps national integrity." With such uneducated procreation going on, Chamberlain seems to be suggesting that the apocalypse itself was looming near: "The deformed, the weak, the vicious confront us at every turn. Society is one vast conglomeration of vain-glory and misery, cant and vice, debauchery and scandal."[80] Chamberlain takes a bleak view of humanity, to be sure. But he feels that by opening up, rather than further censoring, discussions of sexuality and the sexual, perhaps humanity can be saved. In other words, his perhaps racist anxieties lead him at least to suggest that humankind would benefit from a greater formal understanding of sexuality, rather than continuing forth blindfolded by socially authorized ignorance.

If discussions of sexuality might prove salutary in the long run, then perhaps, others reasoned, there was also little or no sin in observing the unclad human figure. As we have seen, the naked or near-naked (female) figure was one of the popular elements of the vaudeville stage. On the one hand, if mores surrounding sexuality and nudity were relaxed, vaudeville producers who trafficked in naked bodies were less open to moral criticism. On the other hand, if representations of nudity became too common or unexciting, patrons might not be willing to seek them out in the theater by buying a ticket. Arthur Schukai, writing in *Harper's Weekly*, tried to debunk the "general impression that nakedness is wickedness." Predictably, though availing himself of some of modernity's deepest values, Schukai, in addition to pointing that under our clothes we are all naked, opined that the "human body is the wonder of creation and that in addition to its wonderful endurance and efficiency is [it] should also be often beautiful to look upon is only another wonder added." What disgusted him, though, was not so much those who viewed the unclothed body as "wicked," per se, but rather, those who would treat it as an object of illicit license. The mobs who "crowd the theater to see a few pitiful girls dance in scant attire" were, to Schukai, "a mockery of wickedness ... first-class idiocy."[81] Of course, as long as nakedness had at least a touch of wickedness associated with it, people were much more likely to "crowd" the theater—and this is how the vaudeville producers wanted it, though they could not expressly say so.

To avoid charges of moral impurity, vaudeville producers often presented nudity—female nudity—in the guise of "art," either as living pictures or classical statuary. In 1912, a performer named Miss Robbie Gordone executed a "series of reproductions of famous statues" in which she "show[ed] her beautiful form" at Keith's Fifth Avenue theater. Gordone's poses, which appeared at a Monday matinee, included "Persecution of a Virgin," "The Awakening of Galatea," "The Lion's Bride," and "The Death of a Dancing Girl."[82] In this package, the nude body could allegedly be offered for its pure aesthetic or artistic beauty, rather than for the sexual curiosity it might provoke. As *Scribner's Magazine* argued around the same time, artists took joy in the nude not for prurient value, but rather, out of "pure delight in the beauty of the human figure." Perhaps the unlettered masses did not understand such a thing. But as the presumably better-educated readers of *Scribner's* must know, the magazine implied, in history, the "Greeks and the Florentines" delighted in "a beauty of form, in which the human figure exceeds all other beautiful things." Therefore, somehow, the unclad human figure, if posed as an object of artistic distinction, had little to do with sexuality. Of course, the implicit assumption here was that cultural elites—scholars, curators, critics—would be the ones to make the determination about what was art and what was not, and where its proper place in society, physically and temporally, was. The *Scribner's* authors, who felt that artists had "a right to paint the nude" and that doing so did not necessarily mean a painter was "influenced by the commercial value of his product, that he purveys for those of evil mind," nonetheless added an important caveat: "[T]he exhibition outside of a school of an avowed study from the nude is a mistake."[83] To use the nude figure in a mass market entertainment was thus seen as an abuse.

In a piqued argument over the nude in motion pictures, the *New York Clipper* wrote in 1915 that although nude models were used by visual artists to create "masterpieces," it was not the same thing "by any stretch of the imagination, [to] allow these same women the freedom of the public on the motion picture screen." The difference, in this editorialist's opinion, was that when the nude appeared in the art studio, although naked, she was nonetheless "dressed in the form of art and not in the guise of amusement." Thus art, with its aim, in his view, to "educate and not to amuse" had a legitimate claim to the nude body, its product to be "gazed upon and admired by mature minds" in a pristine setting such as a fancy private art collection, rather than for a few pennies before so appetitive a beast as the "curious throng." By contrast, in a movie theater or vaudeville house, nudes "appear before the eyes of a mixed and motley audience."[84]

The implication is clear. If displayed in a locale where there was no hindrance of access, where simple mass market motives afforded a glimpse to anyone who could pay the modest price of admission, the nude body became sexualized, commercial—and therefore dangerous. The vaudeville house, which, unlike a fancy private art gallery, was indeed open to "the curious throng," the "mixed and motley audience," had to suggest its nudes were nonetheless artistic or polite—the sort of thing elites would approve of. It was a simple matter of economics.

The debate over nudity and sexuality onstage reflected, too, anxieties over the changing roles of women in marriage, in family, and in culture at large. On the one hand, reformers, feminists, and social thinkers called for greater parity between men and women. Ellen Key, described as "probably the most distinguished feminist in the world" by *Harper's Weekly*, longed for "woman's perfect equality with man in education for work, opportunity to work, wages for work and duty to work," which, in her view, would herald the "final victory over sexual morality, legal or illegal." Still, she acknowledged that this transition had to be handled carefully to avoid more of "the confusion and error which the new sex morals have brought in their train."

While women deserved economic equality and marriages bred on "inner necessity and not [on] outward pressure," the overt display of female sexuality had to be handled carefully, if not discouraged altogether. She especially assailed women who sought in sex pure "sensual gratification." As far as Key could see, the worst offenders in this regard were rich women who did not need to work, "parasites upon the father or husband, satisfying their craving for pleasure or luxury, without accomplishing anything to pay back what they received from society." For women in this "parasitic state," taking without giving, "sex has become the whole content of life." However, Key was a feminist, such as one might have defined it in the day, and thus, such parasite-women were not entirely to blame for their erotic overdevelopment; one also had to consider their behavior an understandable backlash after "centuries of their sex slavery" in which a woman's only real worth was sexual. It was a time of change, upheaval, for those, like Key, who tried to look more closely and sensitively at women's sexual lives. The new possibility of leisure time, coupled with the rise of titillating urban amusements, threatened to undo woman's delicate, yet critically important, moral nature. "Through her motherhood" and, presumably, the work that went with it, argued Key, "woman's sexual nature becomes gradually purer than man's."[85] There seemed to be many different answers to culture's thorny gender questions, some better than others.

Yet the vaudeville stage and other popular, urban, mass market amusements offered images of unfettered female sexuality in the form of entertainers like Sophie Tucker, Mae West, and Eva Tanguay. These women both shaped and reflected important changes in attitude toward sexuality and the female body; they represented a marked departure from the Victorian conception of womanly purity and morality. In a seeming paradox, they were permitted to perform as they did by male theater magnates who marketed them to a mass audience, on a scale never before seen, by deploying a discourse, a rhetoric, of moral and sexual purity. Though wildly popular, these actresses also stirred anxiety over the involvement of women in urban entertainment. For the city was a place that seemed, to many onlookers at the turn of the last century, a maelstrom of uncontrolled social forces that threatened to upset the genteel order of things as they had come to be. Women, their bodies, freedoms, and roles were in many ways at the center of that maelstrom. The anti-vice frenzy circa 1908 focused not only on Sunday vaudeville and salacious nickelodeon fare, but was linked to widespread panics over "white slavery" and a deep-rooted fear "that 'good' women coming into the city for work were being seduced into prostitution" in the words of one historian.[86]

The burgeoning sites of urban public amusement had to handle sexuality carefully, therefore, for it was supposed that their very existence furthered the scourge of sexual vices. No wonder that theater, dance hall, and cinema owners tried to emphasize a kind of "careful segregation of passion from respectable amusements" beginning around 1900. Only with the rise of the cabaret later on would sexual expressiveness find a more open climate.[87]

The age of vaudeville, then, in relation to human sexuality, was an age of contest and change. Between the restraints of Victorian moral codes, and the rise of new mores, practices, and market-driven norms lay a period of upheaval. Vaudeville was perhaps the key public entertainment during this period. Though women were beginning to enjoy new sexual freedoms and pleasures, they were still in subordinate positions. As one social historian has put it, women "were the violins; men were the players." Still, the work of thinkers like Havelock Ellis and, after him, Freud, suggested the emergence of new ideas on sexuality, "an optimistic attitude toward human beings and useful sexual lives."[88] (It is debatable whether all of Freud's view of human sexuality, over the course of his career, may be termed "optimistic." Nonetheless, his discourse served to further open it up as a field of authorized inquiry, thus helping lay the groundwork for treating sexual and emotional dysfunction.)

As both the purveyors of sexually stimulating mass market material and those who called for censorship and control each knew, the emergence of the new sexual norms were directly tied to similarly emergent notions of mass market determinism. At least one historian has pointed out that since the rise of the Industrial Revolution, "passion and desire" constituted the new order, leaving "no clear conceptual boundary between its sexual and economic manifestations." In short, nothing firmly distinguished "the marketplace in goods and services from the marketplace of sex."[89] There was perhaps no place where the link between economics and sexuality was more manifest—bringing about struggles, new modes of discourse, and numerous other dramatic transformations—than on the vaudeville stage.

two

"Clean, Great, and National"
The Mass Marketing of Amusement

As gender roles, concepts of vice and virtue, and attitudes toward sexuality—especially female sexuality—spun in flux in the last years of the nineteenth century and first years of the twentieth, a group of businessmen were taking the first steps to build the beginnings of a nationwide entertainment industry. Such a statement may make it seem as if the two developments happened in a mildly interesting, though unrelated, parallel fashion. But as we will see, this seems to have been far from the case. For, in readying an audience for a formulaic,[1] mass entertainment, the vaudeville magnates advertised the cleanliness and moral purity of their form as a way of symbolically demonstrating that there was a strong, patriarchal authority running the show, even as the product was disseminated far and wide to diverse audiences in cities hundreds, sometimes thousands, of miles apart. The content of their stages may have both shaped and reflected what was occurring in so many other cultural locales, but that content was firmly delivered in a package marked "safe" from such cultural and sexual confusions.

Of all the vaudeville patriarchs, none was more important than Benjamin Franklin Keith. The *New York Dramatic Mirror* said quite simply that "more than to any other individual," B.F. Keith could take credit for the "extreme popularity of vaudeville in this country."[2] And noted the *New York Star* at the time of his death, "Mr. Keith left his impress on the contemporaneous theater to a larger degree than any other man of his period."[3] Hyperbole is common in eulogizing, but this was a reasonable claim.

There is little in B.F. Keith's immediate background to suggest that he would one day head one of the world's great theatrical empires. One biographer has described him as "a little man, both in stature and mentality," possessed of "a curiously cold and colorless personality."[4] Keith was born in Hillsboro Bridge, New Hampshire, on January 26, 1846, one of eight children of Samuel C. and Rhoda S. (Gerould) Keith, who were of Scotch and French ancestry, respectively. Apparently, the Keiths had few resources at their disposal and young Benjamin was sent away at age seven to work on a farm in western Massachusetts, where he remained until the age of eighteen. The details of his early education are sketchy, but an article in the *Philadelphia Telegraph* stated that he attended "the little red schoolhouse and the village academy." During this time, Keith showed little inclination toward the theater, though at age seventeen, he saw a circus produced by Van Amburgh's traveling show. "For several years after that he met life in a number of its phases but was intensely attracted to the amusement business" noted the *Telegraph*.[5] Still, Keith would not set foot into a theater until the age of twenty-one.[6]

After his years working on a farm, Keith went to New York where he secured employment with Bunnell's Museum in the 1870s. Unlike the museums that were to arise in later decades and which provided a home for culture's rarified treasures, Bunnell's was a "dime museum," meaning it assessed a small fee from visitors who were then shown not paintings and sculptures but rather, a motley assortment of oddities and curiosities. One account has Bunnell's attractions including "wax figures, two-headed chickens, and bearded ladies." Oddities, yes—but not odd fare for dime museums of the day.[7]

After his stint at Bunnell's, Keith furthered his education in the realm of popular amusements by working in the circus, first for Barnum, where he ran a candy concession, and then Doris & Forepaugh. He also tried on at least three occasions to take traveling variety shows on the road but in each case, noted the *New York Clipper*, Keith returned home "with his finances completely exhausted."[8]

By 1883, believing he had enough experience to make a go of it (more or less) on his own, Keith and a partner, Colonel William Austin, rented a vacant storefront at 565 Washington Street in Boston and converted it into a rudimentary show-hall. The Washington Street location was significant, for rather than being in a neighborhood of low-class dives and saloons, it was situated near Boston's business district, near respectable hotels, restaurants, and retail establishments.[9] It was a bid to attract the respectable mainstream, rather than the margins, of society in order to fill his seats, an early attempt to find a place in the burgeoning world of the urban mass market dictated by the tastes of the growing clerical and white-collar classes.

Still, Keith's operation, initially known as the Hub Museum,[10] was far from highbrow. For ten cents, patrons could glimpse whatever freak or curio Keith managed to book. At the beginning, the offerings were slim. "My only attraction," Keith once admitted, "was Baby Alice, a midget that at the age of three months weighed but one and a half pounds."[11] Soon, Keith added a small stage and began featuring more conventional variety performers—singers, dancers, comics—in addition to the often bizarre dime museum fare. The reason for this was simple. Visitors to the museum would have become bored in short order with the same unchanging collection of questionable artifacts and not-always-so-odd oddities. As for living, breathing "freaks," they were hard to come by. The solution, then, lay in variety-format amusements. Keith could tap into the ready supply of traveling talent, in an array of crowd-pleasing specialties, to keep things fresh, giving prospective patrons a reason to visit over and over, not unlike a cinema changing its marquee each Friday.[12]

Thus, unlike Tony Pastor and others who came to vaudeville from a theatrical background, Keith came from a grounding in broad-based popular amusements, acutely aware of what would sell to a large audience, without being overly identified with the performers on stage. Groucho Marx, who cut his teeth on the vaudeville stage, once remarked that Keith, along with partner E.F. Albee, "was the owner of a large cotton plantation and the actors were his slaves."[13] Perhaps "patriarch" is a slightly more accurate term than "plantation owner." In any case, Keith was the king, even if Albee was eventually the true chief of operations.

At this crucial and formative point in his career, Keith was beginning to learn that marketing to a mass audience would mean offering a wide variety of entertainments. E.F. Albee later claimed that Keith, even at this early date, though possessed of a small operation, dreamed of a large-scale theatrical empire that would transcend local boundaries. By the early 1880s, according to Albee, his future vaudeville-building partner "began to dream of making variety of good repute and building it into something clean, great, and national."[14] These words may be laden with sentiment and nostalgia, however, it is likely that Keith looked at businessmen in other fields such as retailing, mail order, banking, and manufacturing, who were beginning to have success with a national marketing approach, and speculated that such a scheme might be brought to the field of staged entertainments as well.

Keith must also have seen that a mass entertainment needed not only to be affordable but diverse as well. Vaudeville's multitude of offerings eventually proved one of the pillars of its marketing strategy; its catchphrase, "something for everybody," was more than a hollow promise. The vaudeville stage was a kind of clearinghouse of late-nineteenth-century popular entertainment. On the vaudeville stage one could see blackface minstrel acts, balladeers, musicians, comedy sketches, one-act plays and condensed versions of larger works from the legitimate stage, conjurers, opera singers, what would be today called standup comics ("monologists" in the vaudeville era), and even sports stars, strongmen, and others there to display their physical or athletic prowess.[15]

In the early days, demand for the curios and variety acts was modest, but Keith was nonetheless encouraged to rent out a room upstairs from his storefront where he installed a more traditional theater space that featured variety performances on the hour. He now called his operation the Gaiety and Bijou—the former name presumably denoting the museum downstairs and the latter the variety theater upstairs. In all, the Keith enterprise was able to seat in excess of 400 people, though it seems clear that the house was rarely full, despite bills that included zither-playing midgets, fat ladies, puppet shows, comedians, sketches, and "the biggest frog in the world."[16]

To lure in patrons in greater numbers, Keith experimented with a format he called "continuous." Rather than bringing down the curtain and darkening the house between shows, Keith simply brought the first performer on the bill back on stage again and started all over. Apparently, Keith had learned from his circus days the truism that "nothing attracted a crowd like a crowd," in the words of one expert on the history of popular amusements.[17] The advent of continuous performance was a significant development in the history of vaudeville, not because it was an unqualified success—indeed, Keith still struggled to make ends meet—but because it showed Keith searching to find a formula that would appeal to the urban masses he hoped to attract. He had realized, even at this early stage, that some sort of innovation would be necessary to win the business of patrons who were beginning to have a number of options when it came to spending their amusement dollar. Indeed, Keith later abandoned the continuous format (after others, notably F. F. Proctor, had copied it) in 1906,[18] but he never stopped searching for the next big thing that would win him more customers. To that end he eventually built palatial, luxurious theaters, featured performers who were established successes on the legitimate stage, and mastered the relatively new practices of modern advertising, marketing, and public relations. For example, he built "B.F. Keith's Electrically Illuminated Advertising Wagon," a gaudy, horse-drawn coach with the names of his theaters and the words "popular prices" and "continuous performance" painted in bold letters on the outside.[19] Similarly, the promise of "clean" and "wholesome" entertainment was yet another, if vastly important, stratagem in the effort to locate a mass audience.

Perhaps the most important development in Keith's professional life, though, occurred in the mid-1880s, when he first came into contact with Edward Franklin Albee. Like Keith, Albee was an empire-builder, a man who sought after a mass product and grew adept at marketing it. Noted the *Billboard* in 1914, shortly after Albee took the reins of the Keith vaudeville interests following B.F. Keith's death, "[I]t is [Albee's] hands that fashioned the monster vaudeville machine, systematized and regulated it so that it became the most efficient and powerful organization known in the amusement field."[20] Systematization and regulation were indeed central to Albee's project.

Edward Franklin Albee, "of stern Puritan ancestry," was born in Machias, Maine, near the Canadian border, on October 8, 1857. Unlike Keith, Albee spent little time in rural New England as a youth. His parents took him, "when he was a child in pinafores," to Boston where he attended primary school and sold newspapers. Albee appears to have had little formal education beyond this, and as a boy took a job doing errands for a Boston department store. About this time, he was selected, along with three other children, to play a foundling in a melodrama called *No Thoroughfare* starring Charles Fechter. The run lasted three weeks and Albee was paid some fifteen dollars for his troubles.[21]

In 1873, Barnum's "Greatest Show on Earth" played in nearby Lowell, Massachusetts. After obtaining his parents' permission, the sixteen-year-old Albee went to see it. "He saw it and joined out, as the expression ran in those days, in the capacity of a 'tent boy,'" wrote the *New York Times* many years later. Though, like Keith, he never performed, he managed a variety of tasks for the circus including taking care of the hippopotami, making peanuts and popcorn, and brewing up lemonade, "pink, white, and dark red." Also like Keith, Albee was undoubtedly familiarizing himself with the possibilities for mass entertainment, noticing what appealed to diverse audiences, what succeeded in a multiplicity of venues, and what marketing techniques were necessary to repeatedly fill the seats and earn a handsome return on one's investment. He eventually traveled with nearly all the major circuses of the day, including the Great London, Van Amburgh's, Sells Brothers, and Burr Robbins. "In my opinion," Albee was later to say, "the advantages gained which fit a man for later years in business cannot be found in any other calling; the diverse experiences which one encounters in traveling with a circus—the novelty, the contact with all classes, the knowledge of the condition of the country, its finances, its industries, its farming."[22] In a sense, Albee was engaged in a kind of crude market research which would not only supplement Keith's wisdoms, but hinted at the efforts of the entertainment industries years later.

Working for some of the same organizations in the same industry, it is possible, likely even, that Albee and Keith crossed paths during the 1870s. What is certain, however, is that in 1883 Albee approached Keith at the latter's "museum" on Washington Street in Boston. According to one version, a twenty-six-year-old Albee walked into Keith's museum and, without requesting employment, simply began doing random and lowly tasks around the "pitiful little" operation. One of Keith's three other employees asked their boss who the new guy was, to which Keith responded, "I dunno." Albee was soon hired formally.[23]

Albee's first major marketing coup significantly altered Keith's career. A legitimate theater on the same street was putting on a production of Gilbert and Sullivan's *The Mikado*, charging $1.50 "and turning hundreds away." Albee figured that he and Keith could produce an abridged version—short-form derivations of full-length plays being common in the nineteenth century—and draw in some of those who could not gain admittance to the legitimate *Mikado*. They had little to go on. Pirating and pasting together a script, they took what capital they had between them—some $300—bought costumes from a local department store, hired a cast and recruited an orchestra consisting of a mere pianist. Given their limited resources, the abbreviated *Mikado* could not have been terribly spectacular. But the price was attractive. For their entertainment, Keith and Albee charged ten to twenty-five cents—a mere fraction of what their competition demanded for the full musical. They paid their actors little. Star Raymond Hitchcock received a salary of $25 per week. The two would-be impresarios opened the doors at eleven o'clock in the morning "and ran continuously until midnight or even later." It was a huge success. The crowds were so big it was necessary to enlist the help of the Boston police to keep order and, more importantly, keep the lines headed for the box office coursing smoothly along.[24] To add an exotic touch, they dressed up their venue like a Japanese garden, complete with women in geisha costumes at the door, and advertised with the following slogan: "Why pay $1.50 when you can see our show for 25¢?"[25] Already, at this early stage in their careers, Keith and Albee were showing signs of being masterful businessmen, entrepreneurs, and marketers.

Thus established, Keith and Albee began what would become a lifelong project of expansion, consolidation, reinvestment, and further expansion. In 1886 they leased a regular theater, the Bijou, which had a seating capacity of 900. Like other Keith theaters, the Bijou was located near busy shopping and retail establishments and in the same general vicinity as well-attended legitimate theaters. In 1887, they opened the Gaiety Museum in Providence, in 1889 the Bijou in Philadelphia, and in 1893 they struck into the New York market with the Union Square theater, near Tony Pastor's already established, popular, and "respectable" venue.[26]

The Keith/Albee expansion, though, consisted of more than real estate and investment capital. It was as much a brilliant and calculated advertising and publicity campaign aimed at soothing anxieties over participating in an emergent innovation: mass-marketed, centrally planned, industrially organized entertainment. Keith never let prospective patrons forget that, behind the glamour and the players, the sets and auditoriums, was a strong, patriarchal figure of purportedly the highest moral caliber. According to one well-known historian of the vaudeville stage, Keith "mastered and exploited a rhetoric of cultural refinement and moral elevation to legitimate a new kind of theater."[27] His approach worked. In 1903, looking back on Keith's remarkable career (which had yet to reach its apex), the *New York Star* wrote, "The public began to trust him a little; then much, and finally, until the day came when, with beautiful theaters in Boston, Providence, New York, Philadelphia, and other cities, the name of Keith stood for worth and value, and honest theatrical menus."[28]

The theaters *were* beautiful, too. Keith and Albee made sure of that. They were, in the words of one contemporary scholar, "theater environments that realized bourgeois dreams of European upper-class splendor."[29] An elegant, embossed, illustrated brochure they put out described every detail, every furnishing, every convenience that was available to patrons of Keith's New Theatre in Boston. Its description of the foyer was itself as ornate and overblown as the décor on which it held forth; the supposedly genteel pitch to allegedly refined theatergoers was just a bit too enthusiastic and breathless to have been acceptable to the real moneyed crowd, the kind of people who prefer their luxury couched in decidedly discreet articulations:

> [The main foyer] is unquestionably the most magnificent apartment connected with any amusement establishment in the world. The walls are treated in rich old rose, the surfaces of which are broken alternately at regular intervals by mirrors and superb panel paintings by the eminent artist Tojetti. The floor is of white marble tiling.... There are over three hundred incandescent lamps ... the fixtures of which are brass, with richly burnished gold finish, all manufactured for the theater from special designs of the Louis XV order.... Elegant vases and jardinieres, filled with beautiful and rare plants and flowers, are scattered about in lavish and graceful profusion. A magnificent hall clock of unique design marks the passage of time, beautiful antique cabinets hold superb collections of bric-a-brac and Dresden china....[30]

But the appearance of luxury and wealth was not the only allure. Keith made sure to advertise the fact that not only would the onstage offerings be pure and clean but so too, literally, was the physical plant itself. "The absolute cleanliness which pervades every nook and corner of the building is a matter of comment," read the brochure. Anxieties in the minds of would-be patrons, among the first paying customers in a systematized mass-amusement scheme, were assured that "although thousands of people cross the threshold daily the same bright, fresh and wholesome appearance, so noticeable at the opening, is still apparent." That "fresh and wholesome" environment was kept so by over a hundred physical plant employees exercising "the utmost vigilance, and the carrying out of a carefully arranged system of routine work," rendering "the accumulation of dirt" an "impossibility." Ultimately, of course, the cleaning which "never stops here but is continued uninterruptedly day and night," succeeded not because of the dozens of chambermaids and janitors scrubbing floors, but due to the scientific organization scheme drafted and overseen by the men at the top. The maintenance staff, "perhaps connected with any playhouse in the world," the promotional pamphlet surmised, was "divided into different departments, each in charge of a superintendent who is directly responsible to General Manager Albee for the condition of affairs and the conduct of those under his supervision."[31]

A similar piece in the *Dramatic Mirror*, penned by Albee, informed readers that two dozen char women attended to matters of cleanliness at one Keith venue and that "every portion of the floor space not covered with carpet ... [is] scrubbed every morning."[32] Putting things more succinctly, *Scribner's Magazine* wrote, "[T]he proprietor of 'The Sunday School Circuit' is the inventor of vaudeville as we know it. This which makes for righteousness, as is usual, makes also for great and abiding cleanliness—physical as well as moral."[33] In Keith and Albee's marketing approach, physical and moral cleanliness were inextricably bound, the former standing as a material symbol of the latter, even while the latter was rarely, in fact, observed. "Not content with a careful supervision of the songs, words and gestures used by players in his employ, he spends many thousands of dollars each year in soap, scrubbing brushes, brooms and white paint, so that every portion of each theater under his direction is always without the shadow of a blemish," wrote the *New York Dramatic Mirror*.[34] What better way to suggest that the contents of the stage were acceptably clean (even when they may not have been) than by literally ushering your patrons through lobbies and vestibules whose refined accoutrements fairly gleamed from elbow grease and disinfectant?

In addition, while Keith and Albee's words (in their brochure) convey the cleanliness and purity of the environs, they also link such efforts inherently to a rational, almost scientifically planned system of management. They let prospective customers know that though they may cross the threshold daily along with "thousands of people," a scrupulous system was in place which assured that nothing untoward or unpleasant would be included in the experience. The discourse of cleanliness and purity, whether applied to the content of staged entertainments or the physical plant itself of Keith theaters, proved the perfect means of illustrating that an amusement could be massive in scope and yet altogether in the careful, caring control of competent professionals. As his career wore on, Albee in particular took great pains to demonstrate that while his theaters reached diverse audiences in numerous urban settings, nothing was left to chance. "We go into every detail scientifically, artistically, and psychologically," Albee wrote of his theater design schemes in *Theatre Magazine*. The scientific was to be balanced with the artistic, the aesthetics "suave, cheerful and restful as well as beautiful." Acoustics and sightlines were handled in such a way as to maximize enjoyment of the show, while keeping unsightly functional elements concealed or camouflaged by ornament. The placement of the seating was intended to "avoid strain, cross rays, glaring footlights and borders and any effects that tire the vision," while the seats themselves were designed for maximal posterior comfort. Everything else, from ventilation and heating, to aisle width and slope, to the angle and height of the stairs, were planned to the letter. Albee assured the reading public that "these and a hundred other points are gone into and precisely checked and planned when a new Keith vaudeville theater is underway."[35]

Not only were the physical elements of Keith theaters carefully attended to, but, as already pointed out, audiences were kept carefully in check as well. On at least one occasion, two men were refused admittance to Keith's Union Square for failing to wear jackets, despite the fact that it was August.[36] For Albee, scientific planning, careful management, and aesthetic beauty were part and parcel of the same overarching project. His words above presage the efforts of other widely successful corporate mass marketers in twentieth-century America, such as Disney and McDonald's, who leave nothing to chance in the creation of mercantile milieus.

Even the playbills at one of Keith's theaters were the "most elaborate, artistic, tasteful and expensive" ever printed. Each page was "framed in a delicate border of lavender and gold, filled in with artistic sketching of a superior order.... The most attractive style of type and the finest quality of ink are used, and the paper is of a superior quality," gushed the *New York Dramatic Mirror*.[37] For Keith and Albee, the artifice of elegance, refinement, and cleanliness was central to the creation of a brand that would ultimately have mass appeal.

The Keith brand thus came to signal not only comfort and beauty but healthfulness and precise planning. To complement such tactics, Keith wasted no effort in publicizing his admittedly large-scale operation as morally above reproach—even if the acts on the stages he controlled were at times close relatives of burlesque hall fare. A master of public relations and what today's business experts might call "brand management," Keith wrote or had members of his press corps such as Harvey Alexander Higgins[38] write numerous articles advancing his image of clean vaudeville. In 1900, Keith wrote in the *Criterion*: "In many instances, indeed, they [variety theaters] were offensive to the essentially wholesome and clean-minded American majority. I have endeavored to reform the abuses at which I hint, by eliminating from my bills everything savoring of vulgarity or salaciousness."[39] The following year, no doubt reflecting the hard work of his press agents, the *New York Dramatic Mirror* reported that Keith "has trained the performers into giving an entertainment that pleases without offending the most fastidious." Keith and his public relations crew must have rejoiced when they read the sentence, "Cleanliness, in every sense of which that word may be used, has always been Mr. Keith's watchword."[40] Several weeks later, however, Keith's Union Square scored a big hit with "Art Studies," sixteen living picture tableaux rife with nudity or the appearance thereof, yet cloaked in the packaging of artistic refinement.[41] A few months later, a sketch called "The Bridegroom's Reverie," a kind of sexual fantasy, also at the Union Square, depicted "a succession of comely girls" in provocative attire emerging from a picture frame while a young man sat back and enjoyed "his last cigar as a bachelor."[42] At very least, sketches like this must have held little appeal to wives and other presumed proponents of the institution of marriage.[43]

But Keith's high-minded moral rhetoric stood him in good stead with reformers, critics, and anti-vice crusaders who often targeted popular amusement fare as a symbol of cultural decadence, especially the Catholic church whose leaders, we have seen, were often in the vanguard of criticism. Commenting in the 1920s on the Keith enterprises, Cardinal O'Connell of Boston applauded Keith for shunning the ubiquitous "temptations and dangers" which surrounded anyone in the entertainment field. With Mrs. Keith's help, O'Connell testified, Keith vaudeville had not resulted in an operation that had fostered "the loss of souls," but quite the opposite. Unlike the movie moguls, who never fully escaped the moral attacks of clergy and reform-minded elites, vaudeville came to symbolize the coalescence of wholesomeness and hard work. O'Connell intoned this myth by crediting the Keith family's virtuous "industry and perseverance, and one may well say ... the blessing of God" for its financial gain. And although large fortunes had too often rent families morally asunder, in the case of the Keiths, "thanks to the excellent Christian training which Mrs. Keith gave her son [Paul, who took over for his father following B.F. Keith's death in 1914]," such vicious backsliding was hardly the case here.[44]

Keith made sure that as his enterprise grew it secured the imprimatur of recognized moral authorities. For example, he hired a superintendent of a religious school in Boston to observe his shows and write down any infractions.[45] While the early movie moguls—largely Jewish and foreign-born—were to be portrayed in the discourse of the day and for many years after as vicious and unprincipled panderers, the vaudeville moguls were depicted as devout Christians and shining examples of the American work ethic. It helped, of course, that the Keith family had donated small chapels here and funds to the church there.[46] By 1904, Keith's shrewd publicity ploys were already earning him moral plaudits. "The people who have been his patrons appreciate Mr. Keith's efforts, because they know that their morals and their clothes are perfectly safe when they buy their tickets," wrote a trade paper.[47] As already noted, the moral cleanliness promised, if not always delivered, in Keith theaters was heralded by the cleanliness of the physical environs. In effect, Keith's real promise was that popular mass amusements would come in a "safe" and predictable package. Accordingly, E.F. Albee himself from time to time publicized the fact that he would personally have to approve all acts booked at his theaters, though he appears rarely to have cut or censored them—particularly if they were popular.[48]

The cloak of moral and religious conviction, dubious though it may have been, was, as has been seen, essential to the vaudeville magnates' primary project: the building of the beginnings of a massive entertainment empire, a goal they began pursuing from the 1880s onward. It was this effort that would forever alter the workings of the amusement market in the United States. It has been written that vaudeville's "most important contribution to the development of American popular culture was to erode the local orientation of nineteenth century audiences, and knit them, despite their diversity, into a modern audience of national proportions."[49] In this regard, some viewed Keith as a visionary—after the fact. In 1919, the *New York Dramatic Mirror* said that B.F. Keith "in his shrewd mind saw the writing on the wall" in the 1890s. "Hereafter there were to be syndicates of theaters instead of single ones and combinations where there had been one." And in 1906, the *Mirror* stated that the Keith company "is given most of the credit for the organization and successful carrying out of the plan to amalgamate the interests of many vaudeville houses."[50]

Keith and his retinue may not have been visionaries so much as businessmen in an era of an emergent national market. But their efforts certainly changed the way entertainment worked. Because of Keith and his industrial kin, operations for booking acts, ticket sales, production, upkeep, and everything else associated with large-scale, industrially organized entertainment took root from the 1890s onward. Performers themselves were now but one kind of specialist in an industry run by a relatively new kind of specialist—the professional business manager. [51]

E.F. Albee was perhaps the chief figure of the new managerial class that came to control American entertainment. "Big salaries, big business, and scientific control make everybody happy," wrote Albee in the *New York Clipper*.[52] He delighted in having built a large-scale corporate entity with a rationalized division of labor, as he delighted in trumpeting the "[d]iversity, speed, entertainment, and wholesomeness" of the Keith enterprises. "Originality, personality, legitimate sensation is the demand

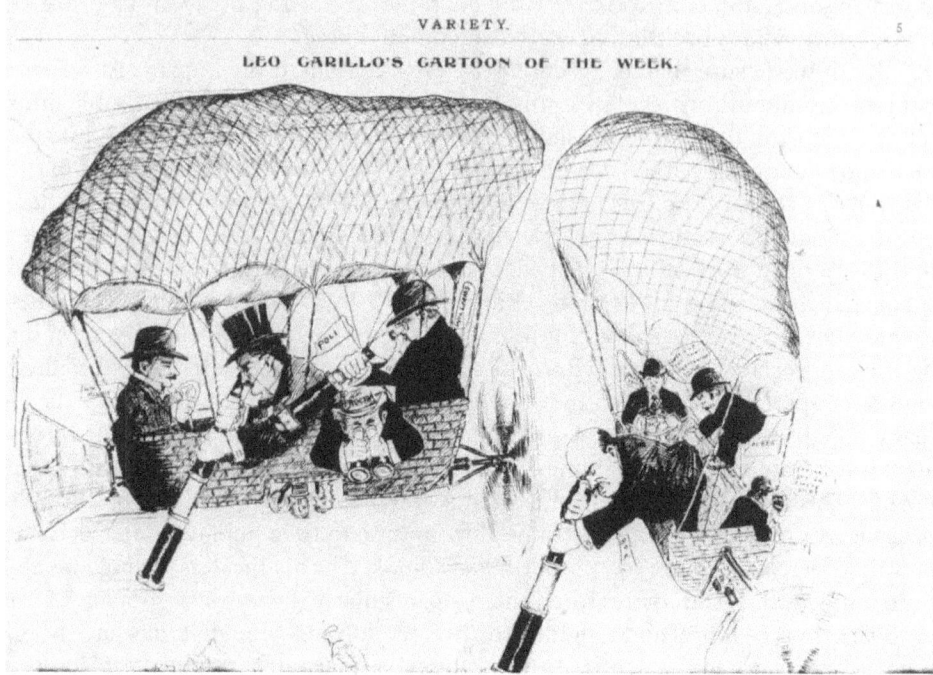

This cartoon from *Variety* (31 March 1906) depicts vaudeville magnates like B. F. Keith—note the "BFK" tag on the bald, hatless character at the right—as hungry, conquering warlords scouting about always, everywhere, for new territory. (Billy Rose Theatre Collection, The New York Public Library for the Performing Arts, Astor, Lenox, and Tilden Foundations.)

which vaudeville must supply," wrote Albee.[53] Never at a loss to craft polemical promotional verbiage, Albee was modern entertainment's first spin doctor.

By the turn of the century, Keith and Albee owned a chain of theaters in New England and the Northeast. But they hungered for more and, like other industrialists of their era, they began to form alliances with other powerful businessmen in their field. What emerged was a syndicate that would further standardize the product, formalize procedures and regulations, create a recognizable national brand that purported to be "clean" and "pure," and, most importantly, develop another income stream for Keith interests in the form of booking fees. Noted Joseph M. Schenk, general manager for a rival vaudeville chain, "What iron and steel are to the industrial market, so vaudeville is to the amusement seeking public of the united forty-nine states." Schenk, subtly yet coercively, urged the performer, if he or she were to succeed, to wake up and recognize that he/she was no longer a prima donna artiste, but rather a "commodity," one "bought and sold for what it is worth, the same as merchandise, steel rails, wheat or grain." [54] This may have been a rude awakening for certain stage artists, but for many, it signified the possibility of regularized employment under a system of legally binding, if not always equitable, contracts. Ultimately, it was of course business professionals like Schenk, Albee, and Keith who determined "what it is worth" and who came to view not just the performer but every fungible element of their industry as an economic commodity.

The centerpiece of the Keith-Albee business enterprise was a conceit called the United Booking Office, a kind of centralized wholesaler of talent, "a switching house that linked managers and performers and directed acts around the circuits" in the words of one vaudeville chronicler, both for its own theaters and for those of other theatrical interests as well.[55] As such, the UBO was the key middleman in vaudeville, giving the Keith empire, in effect, control over many non-Keith theaters via the leasing of talent.

Like any properly run industrial outfit, the UBO developed various formulae for its products. Though vaudeville bills varied in size and content, they typically followed certain guidelines aimed at pleasing the greatest number of patrons. Various recipes and formulae were developed, tested, and refined for what would constitute the most successful bill across the board, in as many venues as possible, giving the enterprise the advantage of scalability. One such scheme had it that an opening act ought to be something "dumb" (meaning, it did not rely on dialogue, per se), like animals doing tricks, so that latecomers to take their seats would be less likely to spoil the proceedings. A good second act was regarded as "anything more interesting than the first act," which might be able to "settle" the crowd in its seats and gear its attention toward what was to come. Third might be a "wake up" act, often comical, to keep customers "wondering what is to come next." Fourth, ideally, would be a big-name performer whose display of talent would hopefully raise audience expectations even further. Fifth: another big name, "something the audience will talk about during intermission." Sixth, the post-intermission slot, was a toughie. This act had to "sustain audience interest without overshadowing the remaining acts," according to vaudeville's professional planners. Maybe a mime; again, something to accommodate the laggards. Act number seven was to be the "on-deck circle" for the headliner. It had to aim big, but offer something different from what was to follow. A one-act play, comic or dramatic, perhaps lifted from the legitimate stage, could do the trick. The penultimate offering was the headliner, the solitary star whom the audience was typically most eager to see. After such a climax, the final item on the bill ought to be something visual, giving the crowd time to decompress and prepare itself to exit. In later years, short motion pictures were used in the final slot, some have argued to "chase" the audience out and make way for a new complement of paying customers.[56]

The United Booking Office grew out of a Keith-controlled syndicate, the Association of Vaudeville Managers of the United States, at the turn of the century. By early 1906, the Keith Vaudeville Booking Circuit consisted of eight Keith-owned theaters and thirteen other venues, largely in the Northeast. That figure grew to twenty-six houses by spring and forty-five by summer. Shortly thereafter, the booking entity took the name "United Booking Agency," and claimed it had "57 good weeks at its command." Less than a year later, other well-known theaters such as Hammerstein's, Shea's, and Poli's joined the organization. In 1907, the Keith outfit extended westward, signing an agreement with the Western Vaudeville Managers Association. Now the combination counted some 180 vaudeville theaters in its ranks.[57] Percy Williams, owner of a successful New York-based vaudeville chain, also linked his fortunes with Keith.[58] By April of that same year, having forged agreements with potential rivals and peers in other markets, the United circuit, in alliance with the Western Vaudeville Managers Association, were "booking together for 200 theaters from Portland, Me. To Portland, Ore.," in the words of a UBO advertisement from the *New York Clipper*.[59] Though to some, the growth of the UBO was a vicious monopoly, a Standard Oil-style trust, it nonetheless, especially from the point of view of individual theater managers, provided a necessary degree of stability in a field never famous for certainty.[60]

In its rapid and aggressive expansion, the UBO was sure to run up against resistance from local managers who did not want to fall under Keith hegemony. Accordingly, "vaudeville wars" broke out in certain markets, such as the one in Rochester in 1907.[61] But, like a powerful organized crime mob—or, more to the point, like the Rockefeller oil combine, which consolidated in 1899—the United Booking Office and its allies usually got their way. In 1912, it threatened to black-list all performers who played dates outside the Keith network. "It Should Be Understood That Acts Booked to Play the High Class Theatres [in rival circuits] Lose Their Commercial Value by Appearing in Other Theatres," read a threatening UBO ad in the *New York Clipper*.[62] On another occasion, the United announced a ban on songs from music publishers who advertised in *Variety* owing to the trade paper's unfavorable coverage of the Keith organization.[63] (*Variety* was founded to champion vaudeville performers and their causes, in distinction to the more conservative trade papers the *New York Clipper* and the *New York Dramatic Mirror*, which tended often to side with management.)

The UBO faced other obstacles and challenges. But under Keith's and Albee's direction, the syndicate either absorbed, defeated, or otherwise dismantled threats to its hegemony. One of the early challenges came from performers. This was understandable. Even before the UBO was formalized, actors were hurting from the fees extracted from them by the Keith booking syndicate. Though the law would eventually set a limit of five percent that could be taken by the UBO,[64] the Keith machine found other ways to siphon money from the hapless artist, such as the Vaudeville Collection Agency, another Keith outfit, that charged an additional two and one-half percent for processing agents' fees. The UBO, according to the *New York Dramatic Mirror*, had once again "drawn the net closer."[65]

Sensing that their autonomy and economic well-being were in jeopardy, a number of performers banded together in 1901 to form a union. Under the leadership of George Fuller Golden, "a curly haired actor who had worked his way up through the theatrical ranks,"[66] the performers took the name of the "White Rats of America," describing themselves as "a social order founded on the same principles of brotherly love as 'The Water Rats' of London," according to a banner advertisement they took out in the *New York Clipper*. Though they formed primarily to safeguard their financial interests, the Rats, like Keith and his peers, advanced a rhetoric of moral purity as another justification for their existence. According to a charter-like public statement which they published in 1900, the White Rats defied the "many coarse and objectionable elements [that] exist in our field of work and play," insisting that "the better members of our profession are entitled to more respect and serious consideration than has as yet been accorded them," due in large measure to performers' "spirit of manhood and morality." Unwelcome, according to the statement, were those "mental unfortunates vulgarly known to the public as 'knockers' and 'grafters,'" whose lowly ethical calculus afforded them no place in "Ratland." [67]

This cartoon from *Variety* (16 November 1907) depicts B.F. Keith as the victor in the mass entertainment war that was vaudeville.

For all their elevated rhetoric, the Rats were really an economic self-protection group. They even tried to form their own booking syndicate in 1901.[68] When they began to feel the pinch of the Keith commission system, they inaugurated a wildcat strike. On the afternoon of Thursday, February 21, 1901, the performers playing all the big circuits—Keith, Proctor, Hyde & Behman's, Percy Williams', M. Shea's, P. F. Shea's, and others—"were suddenly attacked by a variety of ailments and announced that they were unable to continue working—for the present at least," reported the *New York Clipper*.[69]

Despite such tactics, the success of the White Rats as an organized union that could materially oppose management was limited and brief.[70] Before they could consolidate and capitalize on their gains, members of the union began to undercut each other. Also, the tide of public opinion turned against the Rats. When talk of another strike was in the air, in 1911, the *New York Clipper* reminded its readers that the last such work stoppage had "resulted so disastrously to its promoters that it should be a lasting object lesson to them." A vaudeville manager told the *Clipper* that, in his opinion, the striking performers had "done more in one day than we could have done in years" 'to turn the tide of audience sentiment in favor of management.[71] There was never a second strike of the same magnitude, at least not while B.F. Keith was alive.

This cartoon from *Variety* (11 August 1906) suggests the increasing power of theater chain owners and the difficulty it posed for the hapless performer. (Billy Rose Theatre Collection, The New York Public Library for the Performing Arts, Astor, Lenox, and Tilden Founda-

Another specter, that of an antitrust action, eventually loomed, predictably, over the United Booking Offices. This too was initiated by a group of performers. Specifically, they asked the Attorney General of the state of New York to dissolve the UBO's Vaudeville Collection Agency, noting that the UBO controlled "a majority of the first-class theaters throughout the east as far as and including Chicago."[72] But the Keith interests' clever lawyering and legal posturing managed to dodge the threat. Albee, in an article in the *Cleveland Leader*, argued first of all that the UBO controlled only a quarter of the vaudeville houses in the United States. Moreover, he tried to paint the vaudeville industry as a highly competitive one in which agents, producers, and performers were all free entities subject only to the laws of economic contest and free enterprise. In an account eliding any rough edges whatsoever, Albee explained how his fair-minded, pro-competitive, and blindly just booking system functioned smoothly—like clockwork:

> Let us say that John Jones, vaudeville performer, is in Cleveland this week, as shown by the records of the United Booking Offices, and Harry Smith, manager, wishes Jones' services in Buffalo next week, while Frank Brown, manager, wants Jones in Pittsburg [sic] at the same time. They bid for his services. The manager bidding first—according to a slip dropped into a sealed receptacle, and which is stamped on

a time clock which indicates the date and time slip is deposited—gets his service and completes his vaudeville program. Jones, the actor, receives another week's time and Smith, the manager, looks for another act that will attract persons to his theater during the week he is then booking. So much for "restraint of trade" as concerns the effects of our system on the vaudeville players.[73]

Yet Albee's words obscured the fact that it was virtually impossible for an artist to make a regular living without the "assistance" of the UBO Since artists had to travel the circuits in order to work, and since only the UBO and other syndicates, which by this time were operating in unison, could provide an uninterrupted work schedule, the performer was ultimately led to back to the UBO, usually hat in hand, for his or her bookings. After further legal wrangling, a United States District Court judge eventually ruled that the UBO was not subject to Sherman Antitrust Act regulations because, in his view, the booking syndicate did not engage in "inter-state trade and commerce" according to the definition provided in the statute.[74]

More than striking Rats or antitrust legislators, Keith and Albee saw their fellow—nay, *rival*—vaudeville magnates and producers as the biggest problem. Sometimes the turf wars grew heated, as Keith and Albee sparred for territory with other titans of the vaudeville industry. Years after vaudeville's decline, the *New York Times* wrote of the industry's brutal "fights over territories" and the "unjust wielding of power, plotting, betraying and raiding," which grew so terrible, according to the paper, that "for a time it looked as though the vaudeville world would be plunged into a holocaust."[75] The words betray a high drama that few outside the industry understood or empathized with, but it was a drama that the vaudeville magnates felt keenly and in which they played their respective roles most seriously.

Though sometimes there were outright heated disputes, at other times Keith and Albee avoided such unpleasantness by absorbing or signing non-aggression pacts with their chief competitors. An early instance of such tactics occurred when Frederick Proctor began to gain dominance in the New York area vaudeville market. Like Albee, Proctor hailed from Maine. He was the son of a country physician, born in 1851. As a young man, he moved to Boston and obtained work doing errands for the R. H. White Dry Goods Store. Proctor had a fondness for athletics and joined the local YMCA, becoming especially adept at gymnastics. By day he continued to work for R. H. White, but during the evenings he and a partner began to perfect a tumbling and juggling act which they hoped to take on the road. Proctor and his partner, calling themselves the "Levantine Brothers" (the Mediterranean at the time somehow suggesting contortionistic skill), soon realized that goal and were hired at the Theater Comique in Boston for ten dollars a week. Soon, the Levantines joined the circus, "becoming sensational successes in the manipulating of gayley [sic] ornamented barrels and tables and crosses with their feet to the music of the band," according to the *New York Star*. His remarkable success from touring with his gymnastic act permitted Proctor to make the leap from performer to theater owner and producer. He took his capital and bought his first venue, the Green Street Theatre in Albany, in 1880. Several years later, Proctor opened the Twenty-Third Street Theatre in New York City, and from there continued to open vaudeville houses, including the Fifty-Eighth Street, the Eighty-Sixth Street, and the 125th Street theaters in Manhattan, plus additional theaters in the city's suburbs, and ones in Troy, Albany, and other points upstate.[76]

Though a performer at heart—when he died he left over $100,000 to a charity called the Actor's Fund[77]—Proctor was also a shrewd businessman and a force to be reckoned with. For example, he saw the success that Keith had had with "continuous" vaudeville in Boston and initiated it at his Twenty-Third Street Theater in New York before Keith ever arrived. He soon became famous for his advertising slogan: "After Breakfast Go to Proctor's. After Proctor's Go to Bed."[78] Like Keith and Albee, Proctor mastered the rhetoric of moral and physical cleanliness and made it central to his mass market efforts. *A Pictorial Souvenir of the Proctor Entertainments*, a sumptuous promotional brochure his company published and distributed in 1902, stated: "The stage is in charge [sic] of competent managers, and the entertainments are carefully supervised and censored. Nothing is permitted upon the stage which will give offense to the most fastidious. The high moral character of the Proctor plays and vaudeville is universally conceded and commended." In the same publication, the Proctor organization claimed to be "the largest chain under the sole control and individual ownership of one person in the world."[79]

Proctor is said to have eventually controlled some 50 theaters, though this figure is probably inflated.[80] Like Albee, Proctor linked growth in size to a fundamental purity ensured by a class of professional managers manipulating all aspects of the theatrical experience from behind the scenes. But also like Keith and Albee, the promise of purity was largely discursive, a marketing ploy, aimed at creating a commercial brand that, despite its size and scope, was nonetheless safe, even predictable. In 1904, the *New York Dramatic Mirror* criticized Proctor for permitting a sketch rife with "lines in the dialogue which, to say the least, were in shockingly bad taste" to appear.[81] And although Proctor banned smoking from his Pleasure Palace theater in 1898, patrons were still permitted to "sip the insidious absinthe or swallow the foaming beer while watching the merry vaudevillians do their turns."[82] For Proctor, the appearance of wholesomeness was valuable, but not as valuable as the revenues from alcoholic beverages, nor the retention of a hint of saloon culture intended to appeal to a certain class of customer.

Realizing that complete dominance of Eastern vaudeville would be impossible without Proctor's properties, Keith and Albee were faced with two choices. They could either fight the onetime gymnast head-on, or they could form a partnership. Needless to say, they chose the latter, forging a merger of interests in 1906. With Proctor on their side, Keith and Albee were in a substantially better position to make their United Booking Office, soon to be born, a reality. The merged chains only remained so until 1911, at which time they separated. But Proctor continued to book his theaters through the UBO.[83] In essence, Keith and Albee had gotten what they wanted—the enthusiastic cooperation of a potential rival.

Another major potential for war was posed by vaudeville magnate Martin Beck. Unlike the other major figures in vaudeville, Beck was Jewish and foreign-born. He originally came from Czechoslovakia and was educated in Vienna. He performed Shakespeare as a boy in Germany and, at the age of 15, traveled to the United States with a small troupe of actors. After a short tour, Beck found himself in Chicago, jobless. "I needed something to do and up to that time had never been idle," he later recalled. Noticing an advertisement for a manager of the Royal Music Hall on North Clark Street, Beck presented himself as an out-of-work theater manager and thereby bluffed his way into a job. Beck received $12 a week, though this was soon raised to $20. At the Royal, Beck performed a multitude of tasks including "stage manager, cashier, auditor, barman" and, when necessary, "waited upon the patrons who might be in want of liquid refreshments." Beck soon switched to nearby Engel's, acquired a part ownership position and, with a partner, opened another music hall on Chicago's South Side. But an economic downturn ruined the budding enterprise, and Beck eventually had to take a position as a booking manager for the small Orpheum circuit of vaudeville houses based in San Francisco. By 1900, Beck owned several theaters and from there began to expand rapidly, opening up a chain of theaters that spanned the country westward from Illinois to California.[84]

Albee and Keith soon realized that they would have to cooperate with Beck and his powerful Orpheum circuit, since popular performers would want to book a schedule that ranged throughout the entire country. This, naturally, included a good swath of Beck territory. By 1909, Beck, whose venues operated jointly with the hundred or so theaters of the Western Vaudeville Managers Association, also agreed to function "harmoniously" with the UBO[85] by only booking acts who also booked through the Keith syndicate in the east. Beck played tough. He deemed a performer who saw fit to play outside the Orpheum circuit "so deteriorating his value as a high-class attraction that he can never be a desirable offering in [Beck's] theaters," wrote the *New York Star*. The UBO concurred with Beck's self-serving assessment,[86] and the gentleman's agreement between Beck and Keith was in place. "The agreement made between the eastern and western vaudeville managers provides that the Orpheum Circuit shall skip right out west, stick around between Milwaukee and San Francisco, and not come further east under a penalty of another slap on the wrist," wrote *Variety*. Beck also signed up other western chains, such as the Kohl circuit, to work with him and the UBO.[87]

But Martin Beck, a "bald and fat little man" with "his finger in many a theatrical pie,"[88] was not the type to be hemmed in by gentlemen's agreements, and in 1913 he demonstrated his hubris by building the Palace Theatre in the middle of New York City's Broadway district. This "precipitated a war" with the Keith-Albee camp, according to the *New York Times*.[89] But the war was soon ended when Beck agreed to book the Palace through the UBO. Eventually, ownership of the Palace passed to Keith and Albee, where it became the most sought-after venue for the vaudeville artist to play. In 1932, the Palace became the last vaudeville theater to convert to motion pictures, thus symbolically and materially ending the vaudeville era in the United States.[90]

With the inclusion of rival circuits in their vast purview, Keith and Albee had succeeded in creating the first amusement that was truly national in scope. Increasingly, artists came to understand their place in the bigger picture that was vaudeville, opting for "a mass audience over a local" one according to one vaudeville historian.[91] Equally important, a small handful of writers, located mostly in New York, began supplying material to a great majority of the artists touring the circuits.[92] Detailed, almost scientific reports were kept on each act, its performance, reception, and length, and filed with the central booking syndicates. One such report, describing the bill at the Grand theater in Minneapolis on the afternoon of January 18, 1909, listed nine acts and broke each down according to eight separate categories including "style of act," audience reception, and length of play. The report noted that the show began with Bertha Pertina, "toe danseuse," at 2:25 p.m., lasted seven minutes, rated "good" with the crowd, and made use of the full stage. Pertina was followed by Fiddler & Shelton, a musical act that ran twenty-four minutes and scored "big" with the customers. Other acts, such as ventriloquists, gymnasts, and a satirical sketch, followed and were duly recorded.[93]

The concentration of Keith and Albee's power also permitted a putative system of self-censorship—or at least the appearance of such a system—to be installed, aided by Keith's centralization of business operations.[94] However, censorship was far from strict. Rather, a reporting process was put in place to remind performers that they were being watched, though rarely was an act cut or debarred from the stage, especially, as has been noted, if it were popular. In UBO theaters, if a local manager noticed that the crowd found something objectionable, he would have the option of filing a "blue envelope" with the UBO head offices in New York. Only after a number of blue envelopes accrued to an artist's file, though, did the threat of action become real. However, since most decisions on what was permissible and what was not were up to diverse local managers,[95] it was unlikely that a single act would reach its allotted limit of infractions.

Every once in a while, the UBO would send a directive regarding content control or censorship out to local managers. In 1915, for example, the United instructed managers of its theaters to report any "blue" or "mushy" song lyrics to the main office, preferably during an act's rehearsal period.[96] But such actions were rare. By about 1910, the Keith offices were permitting an array of sexually suggestive material on the boards, such as exotic dancers Alice Eis and Bert French, not to mention the vastly popular Eva Tanguay, in whose act sexual allure played no small role.

Keith and Albee from time to time faced challenges from other comers, such as Percy Williams, who sold his successful chain of theaters to Keith in 1912,[97] and Klaw & Erlanger, powerful producers in the world of legitimate theater, who launched their "Advanced Vaudeville" venture with much fanfare in spring of 1907. With William Morris as their talent booker, Klaw & Erlanger boasted that they planned to outspend the Keith chain in production costs per show. "It is the first time that so much money has been spent on a vaudeville show, without a 'feature' securing the major position," wrote *Variety*.[98] Klaw & Erlanger, who had toyed with the names "Refined Vaudeville" and "All-Star Polite Vode-e-vil" before settling on "Advanced Vaudeville," promised to bring in top European attractions that one could not see in UBO theaters.[99] In so doing, the Klaw people were grappling with a basic problem in mass-market economics that had arisen for the first time in the field of staged entertainment: making one's product different enough from that of the competition to be commercially viable, while making it similar enough to appeal to the competition's customer base. For Klaw & Erlanger, the answer to this problem lay in offering a product that was supposedly more alluring than Keith fare but pleasingly familiar nonetheless.

At first, with the help of the ever-ambitious William Morris, things went well for "Advanced Vaudeville," as Klaw & Erlanger managed to open at least 17 theaters "without a hitch."[100] But it soon became clear that competing with Keith and the UBO was perhaps an unrealistic goal, even for seasoned theater veterans like Klaw & Erlanger. In October 1907 the Advanced organization cut ticket prices and announced that yet more money would be spent—up to $4,500—on weekly programs. The strategy failed, and the following month Klaw & Erlanger announced that they would retire from vaudeville entirely within ninety days. In return, they received a one-time payment of $2,000,000 from Keith and the UBO, who took over their theaters and routes. The deal further stipulated that Keith interests would not enter the legitimate theater field.[101] A truce, designed to protect the respective interests of both the vaudeville producers and the legitimate producers, respectively, had been secured. Never again would the Keith camp come under such competitive attack by other would-be vaudeville-hawkers.

Keith continued to buy out potential competitors, such as Chase of Washington, D.C., who not only sold his vaudeville chain to Keith and Albee but saw his twenty-six-year-old daughter marry the aged widower B.F. Keith.[102] Keith and Albee even dealt with the perpetual nuisance of William Morris, the talent agent, who throughout his adult life hatched various schemes aimed at challenging Keith vaudeville. For example, around 1910, Morris came up with the idea of "bargain vaudeville," or some eighteen to twenty acts on a single bill. When this failed, he threatened to "increase the show to 30 acts and run the program until 1 o'clock in the morning."[103] Morris's ambitions were ever ahead of his abilities as a vaudeville producer. Nonetheless, like Keith and Albee, Morris was thinking in the emergent, modern mass-market terms of the era. He once unveiled "a plan to circle the globe with a chain of vaudeville theaters."[104] At his peak, Morris owned or booked far fewer theaters than Keith-Albee and the UBO, whom he never did vanquish. It would have been impossible, for by the first decade of the twentieth century, Benjamin Franklin Keith and Edward Franklin Albee presided over a new phenomenon—the modern entertainment *industry*. They had helped create a centrally run, scientifically managed, commodity-producing entity that would forever alter the field of American leisure consumption. "It is probably the greatest consolidation of money and power in the entertainment world, and ranks with the most important of America's industrial combinations," wrote the *New York Dramatic News* of the Keith interests in 1906.[105] Where staged entertainment had once been an ad-hoc assemblage of localized theaters and short-term contracts, there was now a large, bureaucratic entity that delineated and controlled nearly every aspect of production and marketing.

Keith and especially Albee relished their new cultural status. They were no longer unlettered showmen running a small-time oddity museum. They were powerful national businessmen (Keith having even secured what more recent writers might have termed the present-day male CEO's coveted "trophy wife"), and they built a veritable corporate palace to reflect and galvanize their power. The chambers of the United Booking Offices and related Keith enterprises occupied the top floor of the Putnam Building in Times Square (where the present Paramount building went up, after the Putnam was torn down). In this enclave, loftily above the bustle of the "crossroads of the world," a warren of "walnut desks ranged in close formation" reflected the click-track organizational efficiency of the Keith organization and its ability to exert its systematizing efforts far and wide. "Here are huge ledgers that tell the past movements and the future bookings of every artist deemed worthy of 'big time,'" wrote the *New York Clipper*, whose reporter was also impressed by the bounty of "wonderful card indexes that enable the workers to run down the records of everyone in the business." This was the pulsing heart of the Keith vaudeville business, the brain and viscera, which received detailed reports from hundreds of theater managers each week, assessed those reports, and altered its business dealings accordingly. The reports might tell "just how Bruin's Bears, Nolan and Sweeney, or Millicent Marigold impressed the good people of Providence, Omaha, and every other city they ever played." As with other businessmen building nationwide empires, the telegraph was indispensable. The Keith head office even boasted a law library with over 10,000 volumes, and a general counsel, one Maurice Goodman, "a young lawyer of the highest standing," paid nothing short of a "princely salary" by King Keith.[106]

A journalist visiting the United Booking Offices in 1912 "could not believe they were situated in such a magnificent building as the Putnam Building.... I thought for the moment that I was at 26 Broadway, going to interview Mr. Pierpont Morgan or Mr. John D. Rockefeller."[107] In other words, the Keith interests were not only a major economic and business force, but had become something to be taken most seriously within the enlarging fabric of American commerce. Not only had Keith vaudeville achieved critical mass and cultural legitimacy like banking or oil, but, following logically, so too had the field of entertainment. Along with the United, some twenty-two other circuits and syndicates firmly controlled what happened in the several thousand vaudeville theaters in North America.[108] Some, like Pantages in the northwest quadrant of the country, differentiated their product on the basis of price. Others sought hegemony through mergers, acquisitions, and UBO-like deals with rivals, such as the Sun circuit located in Ohio, Indiana, Virginia, Pennsylvania, and New York. Still others, like the Interstate Circuit of Arkansas, Texas, and Louisiana, operated on a more modest scale.[109] But all looked to the Keith-Albee operation as the model, the chief legitimator of the field. It is significant that the honorary pallbearers at E.F. Albee's funeral in 1930 included Secretary of Labor James J. Davis, Supreme Court Justice Victor Dowling, RCA chieftain David Sarnoff, and Paramount Pictures founder Adolph Zukor.[110] Remarkable for a man who had started off hawking wax figures at a dime museum in Boston.

As entertainment magnates who crafted the cornerstone of the first national mass amusement, Keith and Albee were pioneers. But as businessmen seeking to build powerful national brands, they were very much products of their era. From the pastiche of small, relatively isolated, localized enterprises that characterized American trade in the mid-nineteenth century there emerged large companies that began to successfully market their wares to the entire country or vast segments of it, rather than remaining strictly local or regional. This was perhaps the primary transformation of the United States economy in the late nineteenth century. "[T]he major innovation in the American economy between the 1880's and the turn of the century was the creation of the great corporations in American industry," the esteemed business historian Alfred Chandler has written. Increasingly, these "great corporations" absorbed the role, and business, of small companies that had served the consumer throughout most of the century. The big business operations "appeared suddenly and dramatically on the American scene during the last two decades of the nineteenth century." Prior to that, American commerce was largely determined by "hundreds of thousands of small family firms."[111] In addition to industrial firms, service companies—insurers, banks, utilities, and theater chains—took on large national projects as well.

There were a number of reasons why this occurred. Although the U.S. economy suffered through at least three severe and two mild depressions between 1839 and 1885, by the early 1890s, the country was well on its way toward fiscal health. During this time, a slew of technological advances aided the aims of businessmen who sought to control large bureaucratic firms and sell to a national or translocal market. They included the invention of the typewriter in the 1870s; the cash register in 1879; telegraphy and telephony in the 1870s and 1880s; modern credit-rating techniques from about 1850 to 1890; advanced accounting methods in the 1870s and 1880s; and the proliferation of advertising from the 1880s onward. The government contributed to this phenomenon as well, building a vast number of post offices to serve the growth of national trade. By 1901, there were some 77,000 post offices in the United States, the peak number of the era. Adding to this, standard postal rates for first-class mailings were lowered to two cents in 1883 where they remained until World War I.[112]

Thus, by the time of vaudeville's rise to national popularity in the 1890s, it was possible to conceive of "America," rather than a specific city, state, or region, as a potential market. The nation was no longer a disparate patchwork of regionalized markets, separated by mountains, plains, and rivers. Rather, with the help of an increasing web of railroad and waterway transport systems, and the economic impetus provided by a rapid birthrate and greatly increased immigration, the United States began to function as something of a "national business system," in the words of one economic historian—at least to those businessmen who were interested in seeing it as such.[113] The localized consumer—be it of food products, financial services, or theater tickets—was being assimilated into the mass-consuming public.

The national and super-regional vaudeville chains, while unique among entertainment concerns,[114] arose amid a flurry of national chain development at the retail level as well. By 1900, there were some 60 national chain stores with a total of over 2,500 outlets, including 200 Great Atlantic & Pacific Tea Company (A&P) stores, 59 Woolworth's, and 36 Kroger's. The total number of national chain stores and outlets was to grow ten- and sixty-fold, respectively, over the next quarter-century, with names like J. C. Penney (today "JCPenney") leading the pack.[115] The vaudeville circuits may be seen as the entertainment industry's first retail chains.

The emergence of the "brand," as an historically unique phenomenon, both shaped and reflected the growth of business on a national scope and scale, and pertains directly to the development of vaudeville. Aided by advertising and publicity (not just the respective "science" of each, but the ready availability of vehicles for both thanks to the surging proliferation of magazines and newspapers),[116] the historical emergence of the brand permitted corporations to offer unique products, and thus differentiate themselves from their competitors. At the same time, the practice of branding permitted mass marketers to craft a recognizable universe of consumer goods into which buyers might be lured. Brand-name goods served the potentially uneasy mass-market consumer well, by permitting her to understand, on some level, what she was buying before she paid for it and brought it home.[117]

It has been posited that the growth of brands occurred during the period of business "unification," which began around the 1880s and lasted until the 1950s. In "unification," business leaders, aided by advances in technology and relative political stability, sought to move high volumes of goods and services, often at a low profit margin per item. Using this approach, they succeeded in weaving the country into a more or less united mass market, one in which consumer goods acquired transregional status.[118]

On the forefront of branding was the National Biscuit Company (Nabisco) with its successful "Uneeda" line of the 1890s.[119] Likewise, each vaudeville chain attempted to "brand" itself, in a sense, by presenting star performers on exclusive contracts or by searching "for their attractions in every part of the world," as a *New York Times* article put it, in order to find something truly unique.[120] The owners of the vaudeville chains were ever anxious to have their stages filled with acts one would not see at a competitor's theater down the street. At the same time, the turns they presented could not consistently exceed the conventions of aesthetics or acceptability, for doing so could alienate paying customers. Thus, words like "polite," "pure," "wholesome," and "clean" became closely associated with vaudeville's marketing rhetoric, even if such promises were discursive rather than actual.

By the turn of the century, the landscape of the American economy had been forever transformed. Carefully conceived brands, national markets, and large bureaucratic companies dominated the scene. The age of the large corporation had dawned. "Such organizations hardly existed, outside of the railroads, before the 1880s. By 1900 they had become the basic business unit of American industry," notes business historian Chandler.[121] Ambitious vaudeville impresarios like B.F. Keith, E.F. Albee, Martin Beck, and F. F. Proctor had brought the field of entertainment into the age of big business—or, perhaps, vice-versa.

Yet there was a price to be paid for this dramatic transfiguration of trade and commerce. Whereas individuals had once engaged in economic transactions on a human scale, often being intimately familiar with the shopkeepers and local merchants and businessmen who supplied them their goods, they now had to contend with faceless entities that operated from afar. Whether one was a middleman, an employee, or an end customer, the entire process of transacting business took on a shocking new anonymity. According to one economic historian, the "mysteries of the market" now replaced "an earlier era of face-to-face economic transactions."[122] No longer did individuals have at least the illusion of dealing with their merchants on a one-to-one basis. Instead, much of the power to determine choices of consumption lay out of their hands. People were subjected to what has been termed "the industrialization of daily life." They were recipients in a vast system lorded over by strangers in cities far away. From about 1890 onward, individuals were no longer in direct control for basic necessities; instead, they relied increasingly on an apparatus of mass production, distribution, and marketing.[123]

Jobbers, who served as personal liaisons between local pockets of suppliers and buyers, could not keep pace with the move toward centralized warehousing and standardized price lists. The human element was increasingly replaced by one in which middlemen merely transacted the orders of the head office according to a predetermined set of guidelines. One historian has written that the "old procedure—expensive, uncertain, and inefficient—had at the same time been a human one," for it involved a "glass of whiskey, a few stories, some haggling and promises," whereupon "the local merchant had returned to work certain he was master of his kingdom." Things were different. "Now he transacted most of his business from a price list."[124]

Americans, whether middlemen, retailers, consumers, or employees had to adjust. No longer were they able to believe that they were masters of their own domain. It was in this era that the myth of the "soulless corporation" began to take root in certain precincts of the popular imagination. Hard numbers took the place of softer, interpersonal prerogatives.[125] Even merely earning a wage meant recognizing one's place in a large and increasingly complex economy dictated by outside forces. "An individual's security," writes one chronicler of the so-called Progressive Era, "depended increasingly on the activities of the corporation and the decisions of a few senior executives. Their own efforts and abilities seemed less important."[126] To participate, either as a consumer or a producer, meant to understand how one fit into a large, sometimes arcane scheme of contracts, systems, and hierarchies.

For their part, those increasingly in control of consumption and economics—the Keiths, the Albees, the Nabiscos, and the Searses—did not expect Americans to necessarily make this transition automatically or easily. The potential American consumer had been used to homemade goods, not factory products with identical brand labels. He or she had to be convinced that it was okay to partake in a national market for these kinds of boilerplate products.[127]

The mass-marketers understood that what was needed was more than a simple change in the way business was done. National-level advertisers focused their efforts on easing worries over loss of individual control; their promotional discourse "lubricated an impersonal marketplace of vast scale" and permitted consumers "to comprehend the product on a personal scale," in the words of an historian of advertising.[128] To support their enterprises, large-scale businessmen increasingly marshaled a rhetoric of cleanliness, purity, healthfulness, unity, and honesty to further their economic aims.[129] Presciently, almost brilliantly, they appear to have understood how to counteract concerns about buying mass-marketed products from large, faceless corporations, often located in distant cities.

Take the case of Sears, Roebuck, the catalogue (and later retail) business that dramatically altered purchasing habits in the United States. Richard Sears, who built the company in the late nineteenth century, had a tough job on his hands. Not only did he have to master a process for advertising, selling, and shipping goods to diverse locations around the country, he had to convince the consumer that he was their ally in the same way that general stores and local merchants had long been. Such small-scale purveyors of goods, whom Sears and others would effectively have to supplant, were woven into the fabric of frontier life as much more than mere suppliers of products. Rather, they translated the desires and exigencies of often rural and agrarian small towns to the "manufactories," and vice-versa. The general store was something of a "mecca," its owner "all things to all men."[130]

Richard Sears, who started out selling watches to train riders when he was a railroad clerk, was not the first in the mail order business. Montgomery Ward started up operations in 1872, to be followed by Macy's in 1874, and Spiegel, May, and Stern in the early 1880s. But it was Sears's persistent efforts at winning the trust of the prospective customer, his continual assurances of honesty, reliability, and fealty, that permitted him and his company to rise to a position of unparalleled success in the industry. For, just as much as he searched for a wide assortment of items to sell at modest prices, Sears made it his project to convince middle-class American consumers that purchasing goods from him was as safe and wholesome as purchasing goods from local merchants whose names, faces, and possibly families they knew and trusted. He recognized that many consumers were inherently suspicious about buying from mass marketers. But "Richard Sears set about to break this wall of suspicion," according to a detailed account of the rise of Sears, Roebuck.[131]

To that end, Sears developed a number of clever techniques and tactics. From his early days, he provided copious reminders that his goods were guaranteed to be authentic and fully refundable, no questions asked. For example, in 1892, the diamonds sold through his catalogue carried a "Guarantee and Refund Certificate," which stated: "We guarantee the diamond to be a genuine one and absolutely perfect stone, free from any imperfection whatsoever." Similar claims attended just about every product available through the Sears catalogue, be it crockery, bicycles, guns, fishing tackle, sporting goods, baby carriages, furniture, agricultural implements, buggies, harnesses, saddles, sewing machines, boots, shoes, clothing, pianos, organs, musical instruments, watches, jewelry, diamonds, silverware, clocks, and the numerous other items he sold by the mid-1890s. It actually did not matter. In a sense, Sears was selling the promise of authenticity and the integrity of his business practices every bit as much as he was selling gems or cream separators. It was this discursive entity as much as any material one that he wished the potential consumer to take note of and internalize, such that he or she might shift his or her patterns of consumption and permit himself or herself to become the target of mass-market merchandisers like Sears.

Sears also came up with the process of "Iowaization," whereby he shipped a number of Sears catalogues to one individual and then had that individual distribute them to members of his or her community. For obvious reasons, this built up trust in his concern more readily than if the same individuals merely received the Sears book directly from the company in the mail. Shrewd methods like Iowaization helped transfer the illusion of a caring local merchant, who purportedly knew and understood the buyer, onto a faceless mass-production entity, who may not have.[132]

Sears also included what appeared to be endorsements by outside journalists in his catalogues, signed "Editor." The "editor," of course, was himself, editor of the catalogue. Finally, Sears fetishized the notion of cash-on-delivery. Though he did not invent COD transactions, Sears promoted the idea proudly; it was his way of demonstrating, in dollars and cents, that he had faith in his customers. How could they not, then, develop faith in him?[133]

Through tactics such as these, designed to win the confidence and desires, no less than the pocketbooks, of prospective patrons, Richard Sears installed himself as a towering figure in the shift to a mass-market economy in the late 1890s. Sears, Roebuck, and Co. claimed sales and profits of $2.8 million and $141,000, respectively, in 1897. Thanks to his methods, those figures leapt to $50.7 million and $3.2 million a decade later. Perhaps more than any other individual in the mail order business, Richard Sears paved the way for acceptance of "the great mail order colossi."[134] By

1906, Sears, Roebuck, and Co. was receiving in excess of 900 sacks of mail—mostly orders—daily.[135]

While Richard Sears turned words like "honesty" and "guarantee" into fetishized terms essential to conducting trade, a great many other mass marketers' advertising focused on purity, cleanliness, healthfulness, and freedom from contamination as a way of counteracting any prejudices potential customers may have had toward buying goods and services from impersonal entities based in far-away places. Even a casual examination of advertising copy of the day reveals an obsession with terms like "pure," "wholesome," and "healthy."

A Gillette Safety Razor ad from 1901 told the prospective customer that in addition to "no honing" and "no stropping," he "will know what it means to enjoy a clean, comfortable, sanitary shave." A Chiclets chewing gum ad from the same era not only touted the gum's peppermint flavoring, but actually tried to sell the candy for its supposed medicinal qualities. "[Y]ou need but chew a Chiclet after eating a hearty meal to insure good digestion," read the ad. An advertisement for Mennen's "borated talcum toilet powder" not only extolled the product's healing and soothing qualities but above all else reminded readers, "If MENNEN's face is on the cover it's GENUINE and a GUARANTEE of purity." Ads for Ponds extract, a shaving lotion, warned readers, "Avoid imitations. Many are adulterated with active poisons. Refuse them." Horlick's, a popular brand of malted milk, which, if sold today, might make some claim to tasting good or being low in fat, told readers of its ads (adorned with pastoral scenes of a virginal-seeming young milkmaid and her cow), "Thousands of healthy and robust children have been raised entirely upon it. It is pure, rich milk, so modified and enriched with the extract of selected malted grains as to be easily digested by the weakest of stomachs." Lifebuoy advertised itself as "health soap." The product swore to kill germs and form a kind of protective layer from invading contaminants. Read its ad: "Everyone notices the clean, wholesome odor Lifebuoy has. Its antiseptic properties give it this pure, fresh odor of perfect health.... The cocoanut and red palm oils in Lifebuoy are of great benefit in beautifying and softening the skin. But it is the antiseptic solution in Lifebuoy that makes it so remarkable in cleansing and purifying the skin." Philip Morris cigarettes, in their ad, promised "Pure Turkish tobacco—nothing else," while another ad for the same brand noted that the cigarettes were "perfectly blended in a sunlit, sanitary, Government inspected factory...." Plexo face powder based its entire appeal on its sanitary qualities. "Why use an unsanitary Powder Puff at home," read an ad from 1909, "and carry the still more unsanitary Powder Rag while shopping, traveling, etc., when PLEXO Powder, the kind in a box *with the puff attached* entirely *eliminates* all this danger, bother, and expense?" White Rock, which heralded itself as "The World's Best Table Water," had yet to introduce its trademark nymph perched at a stream. But an ad from 1911 promised that the product was "Put up only in NEW Sterilized Bottles." Lea & Perrins popular Worcestershire sauce not only added flavor to "soups, fish, chops, stews, game, gravies, salads, and cheese," but it also possessed medicinal qualities. "It is a good digestive," noted an advertisement from 1908. A 1907 ad for the famous Cracker Jack candies wasted little copy describing the confection's taste or convenience. Rather, it pointed out that the product was sold "In Sealed 'Triple Proof' Packages" (and this some seventy-five years before the Tylenol cyanide murders led manufac-

68 Blue Vaudeville

THE MORE YOU EAT, THE MORE YOU WANT
A popular 5c. package. Sold by concessionists everywhere. A Winner and Repeater.
The Biggest Popcorn Seller in the World
In Sealed "Triple Proof" Packages. Keeps the contents in perfect condition.
We carry a full line of Package Confections suitable for amusement trade. Prices and samples furnished concessionists who will name the concession they control.
RUECKHEIM BROS. & ECKSTEIN,
CRACKER JACK AND CANDY MAKERS,
247 S. Peoria Street,   Chicago, U.S.A.

White Rock
"The World's Best Table Water"
From
America's Most Famous Spring
Waukesha, Wis.
Put up only in NEW Sterilized Bottles

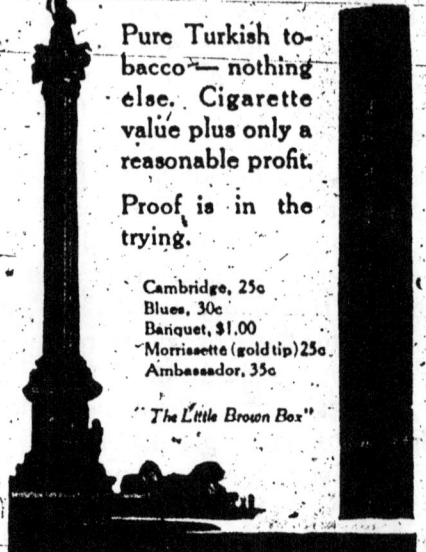

Philip Morris
ORIGINAL LONDON **Cigarettes**

Pure Turkish tobacco — nothing else. Cigarette value plus only a reasonable profit.

Proof is in the trying.

Cambridge, 25c
Blues, 30c
Banquet, $1.00
Morrissette (gold tip) 25c
Ambassador, 35c

"The Little Brown Box"

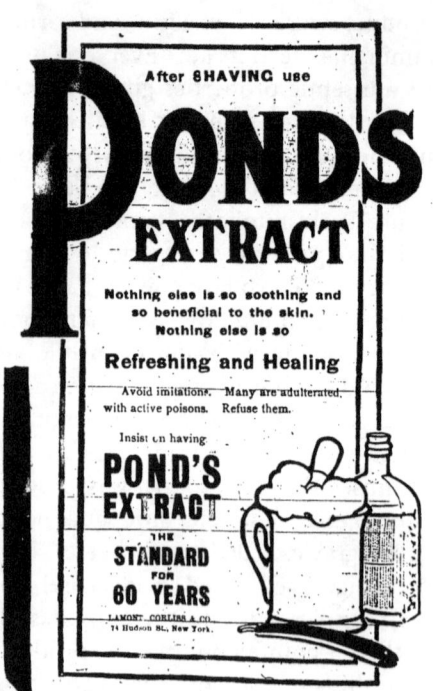

After SHAVING use
POND'S EXTRACT

Nothing else is so soothing and so beneficial to the skin. Nothing else is so
Refreshing and Healing

Avoid imitations. Many are adulterated, with active poisons. Refuse them.

Insist on having
POND'S EXTRACT
THE **STANDARD** FOR **60 YEARS**
LAMONT, CORLISS & CO.
76 Hudson St., New York.

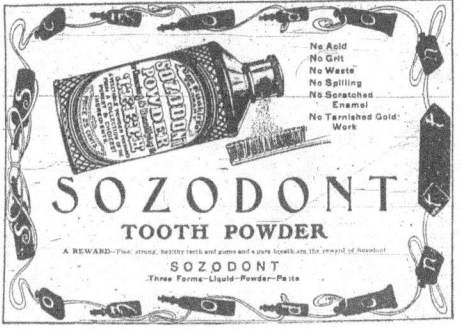 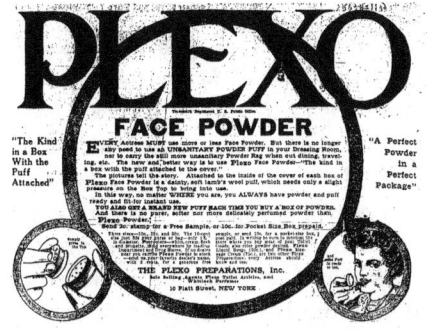

Previous page and above: These advertisements from the opening years of the twentieth century demonstrate a preoccupation, almost an obsession, with purity, wholesomeness, and sterility. In many cases, rather than simply telling us what's in a product, they tell us what's not in it. Oddly similar rhetorical tactics, in a way, helped to sell vaudeville to a mass entertainment audience.

turers to ultra-seal their goods in tamper-proof packaging). The makers of Quaker Rice (Puffed) cereal told potential customers, in an advertisement depicting a rickshaw in the foreground and Mount Fuji in the background, "Quaker Rice has a charm of daintiness and deliciousness that is only equaled by its healthfulness and wholesomeness," while another ad for the same product assured that it "agrees perfectly with even the weakest stomach." Ads for Sozodont, a popular tooth cleaning agent, said nothing about the product's ability to clean teeth. Rather, they advanced the idea that it was free from contaminants of any kind. "Sozodont ... is free from grit or any other substances that would be injurious to the teeth, gums or mouth, and should be the home dentifrice of all who are interested in the welfare of these vital organs, upon which so much depends for the general health of the body." Sozodont's product label said it was "A Vegetable Powder Prepared From A Collection of the Purest & Choicest Ingredients." Royal Baking Powder advertised itself as simply "Absolutely Pure." And Windham canned corn promised a "Pure and Wholesome" product above all else.[136]

Coca-Cola, one of the most successful of the early mass-market products, relied on an advertising and publicity campaign aimed at convincing potential customers that Coke was as medicinal as it was flavorful. Coke advertising copy from 1905 stated, "Coca-Cola is a delightful, Palatable, Healthful Beverage. It relieves fatigue...." (Pepsi ads from the era stated that the soft drink "aids digestion.") Actually, Coca-Cola was originally sold as a headache remedy. In fact, Asa Candler, the man who built up the Coca-Cola company, long resisted selling his product in bottles, believing it should be dispensed in individual glasses at drug store counters, in part to underscore its use a health aid. To Candler, his sweet, fizzy concoction was part pharmaceutical and part fountain drink, to be sipped and enjoyed in the company of others. Candler had been a druggist, and when he turned to brewing up soft drinks, he could never fully shake the idea that he was also mixing a health tonic.[137]

Though Candler later relented, the initial tactic of pushing Coke as "healthful" was immensely successful. Coca-Cola sold twenty-five gallons of its product (which was Coca-Cola syrup) in 1886. By 1906, it was moving some 2.1 million gallons annually, and by 1916, just under 10 million gallons. As late as 1924, Coca-Cola chief Robert Woodruff declared his product succeeded only by maintaining "the highest standards of purity."[138] Other mass-marketers jumped on the bandwagon of promoting their products as medicinal. By the 1920s, the makers of Fleischmann's yeast were advertising their product as a remedy for "intestinal fatigue."[139] In a sense, the promises of moral purity, cleanliness, and a salutary wholesomeness which the vaudeville marketers cast over their product were aimed at a similar goal. In order to sell a mass product to a public unused to it, one had to argue for its safety, its sterility, its freedom from any form of corruption or contamination—even if the truth was often otherwise.

It has been argued that a crucial shift in the approach taken by advertisers occurred as a mass, national market emerged in the late nineteenth century. According to certain social historians, one sees the birth of "therapeutic" advertising, which stressed purity, health, and bodily betterment. This accompanied a change in the dominant culture's moral values, a "shift from a Protestant ethos of salvation through self-denial toward a therapeutic ethos stressing self-realization in this world." Self-realization, in turn, was closely linked to health on all levels, bodily and psychological, "medical with moral standards of well being" becoming equally intertwined as well. [140]

Therapeutic advertising motivated the consumer by "associating products with imaginary states of well-being."[141] Logically, advertisers played on consumers' fears of loss of control in a mass-market society by drumming up "scare copy," which had all sorts of perils, from mechanical failure to bacterial infestation to perhaps the worst peril of all, social disapproval, lying in wait at every turn.[142]

Advertisers and entrepreneurs looking to do business on a mass scale implied that purity and physical well-being were essential components of the modern lifestyle, and that clean, modern, standardized goods were the way to avoid infection and corruption of the self. Bathrooms were redone with new plumbing across the country, the "American carnivore's traditional greasy breakfast" criticized, men's beards and sizeable guts fell into disfavor, while women were increasingly expected to have bodies largely free of hair and faces free of blemish.[143] Thus there emerged, in large measure due to national advertising, an increasingly purified vision of the body, and an ideal of healthful appearance and sanitized living conditions. This diverged from dominant cultural ideals of the early nineteenth century. "What had once been a set of pious maxims about cleanliness," notes one historian, "had become an almost obsessive desire for a sanitary environment."[144]

Important consumer rights groups began to form about this time, and they too attempted to inject an ideal of morality into the otherwise merely pecuniary exchanges between producers and consumers. They did so by equating unsanitary or impure products with immorality and society's lower classes. Middle-class consumers were educated into the belief that, without the imprimatur of this or that socially sanctified consumer group, clothing and other industrially produced goods might well carry with them the taint of deeply feared biological agents, smallpox, diphtheria, etc. The turn-of-the-century consumer was led to believe that products could be either "righteously made and clean" or "degradingly made and unclean."[145] Thus, as advertisers and businessmen were disseminating a rhetoric of purity aimed at assuaging anxieties over mass-market consumption, consumer groups were propagating a discourse of morality that was inextricably linked with healthfulness, purity, and moral soundness.

Another strain of the rhetoric employed by the emergent mass marketers—one related to that which focused on purity and healthfulness—stressed the authenticity, originality, or uniqueness of the product in question. Here it is likely that businessmen were anticipating anxieties over buying products produced en masse by unskilled or semi-skilled laborers in faraway factories. For example, Fatima Turkish, a popular brand of cigarette, used "Distinctively Individual" as its oft-repeated advertising slogan. Hall & Ruckel, makers of Sozodont, advertised their Depilatory Powder with the following lead-in copy: "The first thing one desires to know about a depilatory powder, is, whether it is genuine." It is possible, of course, that the first thing one desires to know about a depilatory powder is whether or not it removes hair effectively. But Hall & Ruckel hung their hopes on a different, and apparently effective, strain of rhetoric. So too did the makers of the "W. L. Douglas $3 Shoe for Gentlemen," whose ads stated: "Caution, W. L. Douglas's name and price are stamped on the bottom of all shoes advertised by him before leaving his factory ... do not be induced to buy shoes that have no reputation. But only those that have W. L. Douglas's name and price stamped on the bottom." Eastman Kodak's famous Land Camera advertised not only its ease of use but the importance of buying only the genuine article. "If it isn't an Eastman, It isn't a Kodak," stated its advertising copy. And Jordan motor cars advertised the virtues of a "personal, individual, intimate car."[146] In an era when the market began to be flooded with goods that looked alike and came from distant, anonymous sources, assurances of authenticity and originality allayed anxieties that one might somehow stray or make a mistake at consumption. The notion of "exclusiveness" had to be reconciled with that of mass production and factory-line standardization. Fittingly, advertisements often assuaged "fears of inundation by the mob." It was the mass scale of the new commercial society, its associated perils and anxieties, that businessmen sought implicitly to address.[147]

One also sees a concern over authenticity and individuality amid the vaudeville producers and performers of the era. As early commodities of mass market entertainment, vaudeville performers went to great efforts to advertise their authenticity or to point out that they had developed a particular routine, dance step, or piece of business. This was especially crucial in an age when intellectual property protections rarely extended to popular culture. Popular vaudeville performer Irene Franklin took out a large, attention-grabbing advertisement in the *New York Clipper* in 1910 after she secured an injunction against Edna Luby who had performed a song called "I'm a-Bringing Up the Family," of which Franklin claimed ownership. "Irene Franklin Wins!," read the advertisement, which thanked "the new Copyright Law" and assailed the "thieving numbskulls who live, like human leeches, by stealing material of proved value." Franklin articulated a sentiment that would become increasingly important to creative personages in the twentieth century, especially stage performers, whose art was so often ephemeral, not solidified in print or cosseted in a gilt frame on the wall of a museum. "Our fight is the fight of every originator, and our object is to drive the bunk mimic and imitator into honest vaudeville and honest applause," her ad declared.

It allowed that one could engage in imitation of her songs, if it were acknowledged as such, thereby not detracting from the aura of authenticity—and, therefore, financial value—surrounding her "original material." Franklin's ad asked for help in adjudicating her cause from fellow vaudevillians, whom she somehow supposed to be on the up-and-up. "Once Again I say, if You Want to Do an Imitation of Miss Franklin, Sing 'RED-HEAD[.]' Brother [White] Rats and Friends will do me a great favor by wiring me of any attempt to use any of Our New Songs [including] 'I DON'T CARE WHAT BECOMES OF ME,' 'I WON'T SEND THE PRESENTS BACK,' 'THE PRIMA DONNA FROM AVENUE B,' 'I'VE GOT THE MUMPS,' [and] 'THE PONY BALLET GIRL[.]'" [148]

The theatrical trade papers of the day contain a torrent of similar advertisements, protests, and warnings about ownership, originality, and copyright infringement. As Irene Franklin's ad indicates, they were usually sarcastic, vitriolic, and bilious. "Maurice Burkhart is the Thief of Vaudeville," read an ad in *Variety*, which claimed Burkhart "GOT CAUGHT at the COLONIAL, NEW YORK this week doing the Most Original Single Act on the stage written by BLANCHE MERRILL." Shortly thereafter, *Variety* announced the creation of its "Protected Material Department," which offered to register "stage dialogue, business, or title" free of charge for the performer afraid of piracy.[149]

Authenticity and originality—or the appearance thereof—were important traits for the commercial survival of the vaudeville artist. This even extended to matters of personal style and dress. One trade paper article criticized "the average vaudeville artiste" for failing to "display enough individuality in dressing," but rather, being "content to go into a ready-to-wear shop and choose what she considers pretty, only to find a dozen others wearing the same dress."[150] Some performers, like Valeska Suratt, achieved distinction and individuality explicitly through the use of clothing. But it was one more burden on the single performer in a huge entity that increasingly treated artists as interchangeable commodity elements—which in essence they were.

If, by the 1880s and onward, mass marketers selling their goods, and vaudevillians, had hit upon the idea of pushing their products' purity, healthfulness, and authenticity, it was a relatively recent development—and one tied directly to reaching a newly galvanized, diverse market that was national, or even international, in scope. As late as the 1870s, according to one history of American advertising, following the lead of patent medicine advertisers, "[E]ither the dishonest or the flippant style of copy" was the predominant mode of mass promotion. But in a short number of years, that approach began to change. Attempting to appeal to a more refined class of customer, certain businessmen began to include not only the appearance of honesty in their marketing schemes, but began to advertise the very virtue of honesty itself. "WIT: If we were giving instructions how to shop, the first thing should be: buy of a merchant who is himself above trickery," stated a late-1870s advertisement by retailers Lord & Taylor.[151] Retailers and catalogue merchants in fact led the charge against specious and sensationalistic advertising. When John Wanamaker began offering guarantees for the quality of his goods, his action has been described as nothing less than "startling" to his peers at the time. By 1900, according to one account, the "showman's tricks on the public were discarded as not suitable for a mercantile business." The Wanamaker model had replaced that of Barnum.[152]

As the market for goods and services began to grow, so too did the modern profession of advertising. Individuals who presented themselves as adept at understanding the consumption patterns of the emergent mass-market customer began increasingly to plan and execute national marketing campaigns. Though the first advertising agency in the United States was founded in Philadelphia in 1845, firms such as N. W. Ayer began to change the goal and function of advertising professionals from the 1880s onward.[153] Whereas earlier agencies had done little more than broker and book ad space in print, there now emerged firms that engaged in analysis and creative planning, and proactively came up with proposals and suggestions for their clientele. They posed themselves as experts, bringing to bear unique knowledge and professional experience that could help solve whatever "special problem" the advertiser might be facing.[154]

Thinkers of a typically more profound ilk began to expatiate on the most effective means of reaching the mass market. In 1903, Walter Dill Scott, a professor at Northwestern University, published the first book ever on the psychology of advertising. In it, the professor argued for "deeper emotional appeals" to the prospective customer rather than merely stating what a product was and why one ought to spend money on it.[155] "If I were to name the qualities that enter into good advertising, I should say, first, imagination; second, knowledge of human nature; and third a little more knowledge of human nature," pontificated an advertising professional in *Harper's Monthly Magazine*.[156] Advertising and marketing professionals had come to see themselves as applied social scientists, delving into the core of culture's collective desires in order to produce measurable economic results. It was their goal to motivate the consumer to buy, rather than simply to inform him of his choices once he had already made that decision. "Half of the customers in any community do not know all they want until somebody tells them," wrote social observer Nathanial Fowler in 1889.[157] With the rise of the mass market came the irresistible project of mass control.

If those in the advertising industry increasingly saw themselves as powerful manipulators of the desires of a great many Americans, they had good reason to. For as the country grew into a cognizable network of consuming patterns, few could avoid the siren call of mass promotion. In the 1890s, social observer Nathaniel Fowler saw "no stratum of society not reached and influenced by advertising." Those subject to influence included even those whose socioeconomic status might have, in a prior age, placed them safely above the fray. "The bluest-blue-blood descendent of the oldest family, who prides himself upon his impenetrability from things common, is affected and proves that he is by saying that he isn't," Fowler pointed out.[158] Advertising professional Lorin Deland estimated in the 1920s that, whereas four decades earlier, newspapers had received just over a third of their revenues via advertising (the rest coming from subscriptions), some of those same periodicals now saw 90 percent of revenues come from the sale of advertising. "[S]o it is evident that advertising and fortunes are related in the public mind," concluded Deland.[159]

Advertising and marketing professionals began to view most Americans as contributing to the "public mind," and it was this entity that they believed themselves able to analyze, understand, and manipulate accordingly. No longer could claims to social status, education, or taste protect one from the discourse of mass marketing.

Wherever a magazine, a newspaper, or a billboard could be situated, the advertiser's war of attrition could be waged. "[I]t is scarcely more than a score of years since magazines were without this feature [ads] that now receives hardly less attention than the text itself," noted *Cosmopolitan* in 1902.[160] In the often chaotic, densely populated world of the American city, exposure to advertising was merely part of the fabric of daily life. The sumptuous copy and illustrations of print advertising alchemically turned mere commodities into objects of genuine desire. Consumption became a desirable thing in its own right, apart from the particular goods sought after.[161]

It was in part to win this war, then, that advertisers and their clients began to rely on the discourse of purity. By stressing the sterility or healthfulness of a given product, businessmen were anticipating and allaying anxieties over the purchase of mass market goods. By 1898, Ivory Soap's marketing copy reminded consumers that it was "99 and 44/100 percent pure," though it failed to say pure *what*. The *New York Times* contained "All the News That's Fit to Print," and nothing else. Cleveland Baking Powder was "Pure and Sure." Shredded Wheat touted the fact that it contained "nothing but the wheat," while Gorham's line of silverware claimed buying its product was "a guarantee for pure metal." And Pear's Soap advertised itself with a short poem conveying its freedom from contaminants: "I will for aye its patron be/And praise its matchless purity." Following the Uneeda Biscuit campaign of the 1890s, there began "constant hammering on sanitation by manufacturers of package goods." The makers of Schlitz beer promoted the fact that each bottle was steam-cleaned prior to being filled with the product. Some businesses linked discussions of purity to questions of taste and refinement. Standard Manufacturing Co. of Pittsburgh, makers of bathtubs and toilets, ran the following advertising copy in 1890: "Ask Your Wife If she would not like to bathe in a china dish, like her canary does. Our Porcelain-lined Bath Tub is a china dish cased in iron. SANITARY, DURABLE, CHEAP."[162] Others linked purity to religion. An 1889 advertisement for Pear's Soap carried a testimonial by famed preacher Reverend Henry Ward Beecher: "If cleanliness is next to Godliness, soap must be considered as a means of Grace and a clergyman who recommends Moral things should be willing to recommend soap."[163]

Understandably, soap manufacturers were in a logical position to advance the promises of purity and non-contamination. In England, the makers of Sunlight Soap offered £1,000 if users found "any impurity."[164] In America, in 1900, the makers of Sapolio soap, through rhyming verse and whimsical illustrations, crafted an imaginary world that was utterly and completely free of contamination of any kind. They called their pretend hamlet "Spotless Town," whose libretto, worth reproducing here in part, seemed worthy of an opera house or other lofty cultural venue:

> This is the maid of fair renown
> Who Scrubs the floors of Spotless Town,
> To find a spec when she is through
> Would take a pair of specs or two
> And her employment isn't slow
> For she employs SAPOLIO

The "Spotless Town" epic goes on to include versification by the mayor of the blindingly scoured burg, the "brightest man for miles around," and a look at the butcher, whose "tools are bright as his renown"—and a man who, thanks to Sapolio, was never so "indiscreet" as to leave his various cleavers and meat axes caked with blood and offal.[165] (Keith and Albee would loved to have operated a vaudeville theater in Spotless Town.) Not only had they appealed to a fetish for cleanliness and sterility, but the makers of Sapolio had linked such preoccupations to wisdom, virtue, and intelligence.

Soap makers were not the only ones who created a fictional world of cleanliness. To emphasize its locomotives' use of clean-burning anthracite coal, the Lackawanna Railroad advertised its services with the character "Phoebe Snow," a maiden in a pure white dress who rode the rails. "Said Phoebe Snow/About to go/Upon a trip to Buffalo;/My gown keeps white/Both day and night/Upon the Road of Anthracite…. When nearly there/Her only care/Is but to smooth/her auburn hair./Her face is bright,/Her frock still white/Upon the Road of Anthracite."[166] The Lackawanna ads conflated cleanliness with notions of maidenly virtue and beauty—a tactic that had surfaced elsewhere.

Other advertisers seized upon the idea of feminine beauty and modesty as their iteration of purity. A *Cosmopolitan* piece on fashion advertising noted a trend toward the use of "pretty faces and graceful figures" in advertisements of "a highly superior order of merit because of beauty of face and raiment." But, the article noted, there were certain lines that had not to be crossed in the creation of successful mass marketing campaigns, namely the use of "indelicate drapings." Instead, the article opined, "it came to be understood that good taste required that everything offensive should be eliminated, and that that advertisement was most effective which attracted all and offended none."[167]

Inevitably, the advertising industry began turning the discourse of purity and honesty inward, promoting its own operations as august, square-dealing, and above reproach. One authority on the history of advertising observes that N. W. Ayer, one of the first successful national advertising agencies, presented itself as "chaste, dignified, and solemn" in ads for its own services. By 1911, the Advertising Federation of America, a group comprised of the leading companies in the industry, publicly "declared" that they were "for ethical advertising."[168] About this time, the Curtis Publishing Company, which put out *Ladies' Home Journal* and the *Saturday Evening Post* and was the recipient of a great sum of yearly advertising dollars, created its vaunted "Advertising Code," which was soon to be copied by many other major publishing concerns in the United States. In its Code, Curtis publicly stated that it would "exclude all advertising that in any way tends to deceive, defraud, or injure our readers," including "[e]xtravagantly worded advertisements," and ads "of an immoral or suggestive nature" including "representations of the human form" clad in "any suggestive negligee or attitude." In addition, Curtis swore to forbid advertisements for medical or alcoholic goods, ads which "knocked" other products, and ads from real estate speculators, and tried to discourage promotions for goods that could be bought on installment plans.[169] (Of course, to survive in the early twenty-first century, Curtis would have had to abandon all of these vaunted guidelines.)

The message was clear: behind the organs of the emerging mass media supposedly were men with standards and integrity, men who could determine the rules of consumption better than the consumer herself. Like the vaudeville impresarios, it was suggested that they pulled the strings and kept the typical consumer safe from the potential pitfalls of the mass-marketed product. Little wonder that Columbia bicycles trumpeted the fact that its vehicles were "inspected in every detail by 21 engineers and mechanics."[170] The more engineers, mechanics, scientists, designers, and patriarchal protectors working together the better.

Promises like those of the Curtis and Columbia companies played well in a culture increasingly preoccupied with the potential hazards of mass consumption. Such concerns ran highest in urban markets where denizens were particularly dependent on faceless mass-market goods. As might be predicted, worries over mass consumption often took the form of worries over disease, impurity, and contamination. "Bacteria exist by millions in every pinch of dust of the city street; they swarm in dust that the whole family inhales when the housemaid sweeps or beats a carpet. They settle on bread as it comes from the bakery. We cannot possibly hope to escape ingesting a certain number of them," warned a *Cosmopolitan* article from 1913 titled "The Battle of the Microbes." The message was clear: life in the city, a manner of existence inextricably linked to depersonalized mass consumption, was also a life replete with the threat of toxicity. Those least able to fend for themselves, those most innocent, were at the greatest risk. "At every other tick of the clock a baby dies, most of them killed by carelessness. Give the baby pure milk, and he will almost certainly live," warned the same article, taking an urgent tone foreshadowing that of the anti-marijuana rhetoric of later ages. The germs, poisons, and toxins inherent in the world of the urban consumer were seen not merely as arbitrary agents of nature but instead as rapacious invaders, possessed of an ill will all their own. *Cosmopolitan* wished to break the news to readers that there was indeed a war afoot, and filled with more casualties than any military conflict, such as one "a few weeks ago [in which] ten thousand Turks were reported to have fallen in a single battle with the Bulgarians." The newspapers had reported that story to all the world, noted *Cosmopolitan*, but "no newspaper thought to mention that many times ten thousand victims had fallen on the same day before microbic foes that are far more relentless than Turk or Bulgar." The magazine, its correspondents apparently on the front lines, wrote of even seemingly benign germs as "treacherous ingrates; for, even as they bivouac under a flag of truce on your bodily surfaces, exterior and interior, they are forever on the lookout for an opportunity to invade your blood-stream and lymph-spaces; and when the opportunity comes, they will wage a guerilla warfare." Thus, the microscopic contaminants that especially haunted urban locales, were cunning, deceptive, and hostile; they sought to fight a ruthless war, one based on "guerilla" tactics. These threats, like those of Communism in a later era, were labeled variously, "The foe that is always with us," and lethal "invaders" that had no trouble rounding up "recruits" with which to storm "[t]he barriers that hold them at bay—the walls and barricades of the human fortress...." Maintenance of the pure, the fresh, the wholesome was the key weapon humankind had to win this war—for example, "perfectly fresh milk (which is obviously impossible for the city dweller)." Unless such *matériel* were deployed, the infectants latent in store-bought goods would almost certainly overwhelm, in the enormity of their numbers, those least prepared to do battle: "Some market milk has 5,000,000 bacteria in a single drop—and a baby dies at every other tick of the clock."[171]

Others blamed those already sick, in addition to an urban environment of mass consumption. "The expectoration of a consumptive," wrote one C. D. Zimmerman in a letter to *Scientific American*, "may contain millions of germs." Said expectoration, if it were to land on a city sidewalk, would soon be tracked over a wide area, mixed with dust, ground down to "the finest powder," kicked up by passing motorcars, streetcars, and carriages, and then "sent into thousands of healthy lungs." The burgeoning urban clime itself participated in permitting the polluted to corrupt the pure. Accordingly, it too had to be kept in check, its streets and alleyways "kept scrupulously clean by hand labor, preferable to machines, and thoroughly sprinkled from four to ten times a day."[172]

On the one hand, with the potential for influenza and tuberculosis outbreaks in a highly contagious urban clime, concerns over public health, to be sure, may have reflected a very realistic fear of disease.[173] Yet on the other hand, the burgeoning urban environment was perceived as a fearfully chaotic and potentially lethal place, out of the control of traditional social forces. To combat its myriad inchoate dangers, the strictest vigilance, sanitation, and human "hand labor" were needed. In promising cleanliness, bowdlerization, and censorship, the promoters of vaudeville—*the* emergent mass-entertainment product of urban America—were similarly engaged in a timely and appropriate war of propaganda.

In addition to being perceived as medical threats, those stricken with illness were blamed for their maladies, the belief being that the microscopic disorder must reflect some underlying moral or psychological shortcoming. "When a person is sick," noted *Cosmopolitan*, "it is a sign that the laws of nature, i.e., the laws of God, have not been complied with.... The causes usually—lack of will, and ignorance." In some cases, the villains were vices such as "much tobacco ... alcoholic drink, drugs, pickles, and all other queer things...." But the net result was the same, in that the world was "full of weak, unhappy miserable, people—people who are sick or who think they are sick."[174]

If sickness reflected vice, then health was naturally the result of virtue. Women who strove after beauty and household industriousness, for example, would be less likely to fall ill to microscopic invaders, some believed. Dr. Louise Fiske Bryson, a reformer of the 1890s who lectured to girls and young women, "affirmed that systematic efforts to be beautiful" would insure "a fair degree of health and that happiness is the best safeguard against vice," according to an article in *Scientific American*. Dr. Bryson also argued that bathing, proper breathing, and good circulation would result from and produce further beauty. Exercise could be helpful as well, and there was "no exercise more beneficent in their results than sweeping, dusting, making beds, washing dishes, and the polishing of brass and silver." Such household aerobics were, in the doctor's estimation, more salutary than "all the lotions and pomades that were ever invented."[175] Lotions and pomades, after all, were just the sort of widely advertised, early mass-market goods that many reformers distrusted, despite the products' repeated claims of purity and freedom from contaminants.

Cultural concerns over the purity of mass-market goods found their greatest discursive and material expression in the federal Food and Drugs Act, usually called the Pure Food and Drug Act, which was signed into law by President Teddy Roosevelt on June 30, 1906. But it was not Roosevelt who was the driving force behind the Pure

Food Act, despite his attempt to take credit for it later in his career.[176] Rather, it was Harvey Wiley, chief chemist of the U.S. Department of Agriculture and zealot in the struggle against "adulterated" foods produced by corporate concerns and sold to a supposedly naïve public. It was Wiley more than any other single figure of the era who devoted himself to "the whole matter of wholesomeness and unwholesomeness of ingredients in foods," as he put it in his enigmatic, self-published tome, *The History of a Crime Against the Food Law*.[177]

Harvey Washington Wiley was born in the countryside near Kent, Indiana, in 1844. His father was a farmer and lay preacher. Religion, self-discipline, virtue, and moderation were stressed constantly in the Wiley household. As a boy, Wiley taught himself to read, taking to the Bible, Shakespeare, the *Atlantic Monthly*, *Uncle Tom's Cabin*, and John Abbott's *The History of Napoleon Bonaparte*. Wiley entered nearby Hanover College in 1862 where he remained for two years until he joined the 137th Regiment of the Indiana Volunteers, though he never saw active service in the Civil War.[178]

Upon returning to civilian life, Wiley began developing an interest in health, nutrition, and vice. For Wiley, the body was a delicate and well-balanced machine, but one that waited to betray its owner should she or he ingest impurities or toxins of any kind. Life, in Wiley's view, was "no idle gift.... Man must be careful to preserve it." The "gross intemperate man," he wrote, would find himself with a body "made up of foul bundles of impurities, a miserable mass of tobacco, pork, and grease" should he treat his physical being idly.[179] Though never an openly religious man, Wiley seems to have transformed the sectarian zealotry of his childhood home into a kind of scientific and biological sectarianism. Certainly, self-righteousness resonated loudly in everything he did. "I had the good fortune to be ranged on the side of right in every important contest I can remember," he once said.[180] Others noted Wiley's penchant for fanaticism and prognostication. "I have referred to Wiley as a prophet," wrote a journalist in the *Nation* in 1916, "and it is no mere figure of speech. He is never at a loss for a prophecy...." The same journalist dubbed Wiley a "preacher of purity."[181]

In 1868, Harvey Wiley began an apprenticeship in medicine with several local country doctors. The following year he started a (somewhat more) formal medical training by enrolling at the Indiana Medical College. Inspired by visits to local bath houses, a bit like Ibsen's Dr. Stockmann in *An Enemy of the People*, he began formulating theories on sanitation and diet. Despite his growing interest in science, though, Wiley was also a keen student of literature and the arts, teaching courses in Latin and Greek at Northwestern Christian University in Indianapolis in 1869.[182] But it was poetry that interested him most among the humanities. Throughout, his life, Wiley penned numerous poems about food adulteration and contamination. They are both entertaining and revealing, suggesting a man moderately interested in letters and wildly preoccupied with the possible toxicity of factory-made foodstuffs. Among his work are these verses:

> We sit at a table delightfully spread,
>   And teeming with good things to eat,
>   And daintily finger the cream-tinted bread,
>   Just need to make it complete

> A film of the butter so yellow and sweet,
>   Well suited to make every minute
> A dream of delight. And yet while we eat
>   We cannot help asking "What's in it?"
> Oh, maybe this bread contains alum and chalk,
>   Or sawdust chopped up very fine,
> Or gypsum in powder about which they talk,
>   Terra Alba just out of the mine.

In his Shakespearean disquisition on food contamination, Wiley wondered if, perhaps, the "pepper perhaps contains cocoanut shells;" and suggested that the "coffee, in sooth, of baked chicory smells/And the terrapin tastes like roast veal." Meanwhile, the "wine which you drink never heard of a grape/But of tannin and coal tar is made," and "you could not be certain, except for their shape/That the eggs by a chicken were laid." The poem, which may look to the modern eye like a cross between Homer and Dr. Seuss, suggested an adversarial relationship between the eater and his food, a world in which no diner could ever sit at a table, even at the fanciest of banquet spreads, without sighing, "Oh, I wonder, I wonder, what's in it."[183] To view ingestion this way, and to argue that others do so as well, was Wiley's particular gift—or curse.

When Harvey Wiley looked at the cornucopia of mass-produced foods, despite its diversity and convenience, he saw the potential for harm lying everywhere just beneath the surface. But food in its pure, Platonic state was not *inherently* harmful, in his philosophy. When compromised for economic and commercial reasons, however, it turned into perhaps mankind's greatest threat. For Wiley held that the "food of man, as prepared by the Creator and modified by the cook," was acceptable. But when mass-market middlemen intervened in the purveyance of foodstuffs, adding "a burden to any of the organs, or any change which diminishes their normal functional activity," then such intervention was perforce "hurtful."[184]

By his late twenties, Wiley had become a devout Darwinist and student of the dictates of rationalism and empirical science. He enrolled at Harvard and earned a Bachelor of Science degree in 1873 and, following this, took a teaching position at Purdue. During his tenure at that university, Wiley traveled to Berlin where he familiarized himself with European research on impurities in food and drink. (By the 1870s, England, Germany, and Sweden had all enacted food purity statutes.) But it was in 1883, the same year that Keith and Albee formed their famous partnership, that Wiley's life was to take a fateful turn. For in that year he began working in Washington, D.C., as a chemist for the Department of Agriculture, eventually heading the Department's Bureau of Chemistry.[185]

Upon arriving at his new post, Wiley undertook to resolve the great "sorghum question." It was his belief that the crop sorghum could yield sugar more cheaply and in greater quantity than either cane or beet. Developing a process for doing so would permit America to foster a robust domestic sugar industry. Political struggles and changes in administration sandbagged his efforts, however, and he turned his attention to the matter of food purity. Wiley broadly termed it the problem of food "adulteration." He saw adulteration as "not merely the debasement of a product but broadly as any purposeful change that altered its composition or the meaning of the name under which it was sold," according to a Wiley biographer. In Wiley's eyes, "[a]dulteration followed commerce and manufacture."[186] It was that simple.

For Wiley, then, concerns over food impurities were really anxieties over a new market in which trade was largely anonymous, solely profit-driven, and increasingly focused on an urban mass market. In the modern, industrial world, the matter of food quality and purity, a concern since the dawn of civilization, took on an entirely new dimension. The shift from home kitchens to factory lines and the onset of interfirm competition saw manufacturers' "ethical standards dulled by the impersonality of their function," leading them to "debase" their products to survive the ravages of the market.[187] It is possible, even likely, of course, that small-scale manufacturers and merchants operating in an earlier, less depersonalized era, cut corners and "adulterated" the products they sold as well. Therefore, it was the anxiety of industrialization, urbanization, and the move toward mass selling that may have underscored the concerns of Wiley and others like him at the time.

In 1887, Wiley issued his first report on food impurities, titled *Food and Food Adulterants*. In it, he and his fellow chemists at the Department of Agriculture declared that they had found milk to be watered down; butter to contain large amounts of margarine; spices rife with husks, dirt, crumbs, and charcoal; wine watered-down; lard extended with cottonseed oil; baking powder cut with salt; coffee inflated with chicory, acorns, and sawdust; and canned vegetables dressed in harmful coloring agents. In some cases, the foods contained adulterants that held the potential to make a person genuinely sick. But in others, the adulterants were really harmless additives that detracted only from the trade value of the item in question, such as water in wine or, in another instance, table sugar or molasses in maple syrup.[188] Thus, to Wiley, "impure" came to mean not only deleterious but misleading, misadvertised, or misbranded as well. In other words, the struggle against food impurity was as much a struggle against emergent modes of industrial mass production, promotion, and selling, supported by an anonymous discourse that publicized *en masse* without being responsive to the individual customer.

By 1900, Wiley had his sights set on forcing the government to enact sweeping food and drug legislation. Beginning in 1902, he began an experimental procedure aimed at advancing this end both through the accrual of knowledge and for the publicity it would garner. Wiley gathered a group of young men, all volunteers, and fed them only foods, for months at a stretch, adulterated with a number of substances Wiley thought especially pernicious and commonly employed by food manufacturers. The substances included borax, formaldehyde, and saltpeter. These volunteers "signed a pledge to eat nothing or drink nothing excepting what we gave them at the table." The pledge further stipulated that they lead their lives as normal—go to work, sleep at night—with the only deviation from "normal" consisting, perhaps, in the fact that they were kindly to "collect and present to us every particle of their secreta," as Wiley explained to Congress during the Pure Food and Drug hearings. They also agreed not to overindulge in alcohol, tobacco, or any other kind of excess. Wiley later wrote that no experiment so extensive had ever been conducted on human subjects anywhere at any time. The public was immediately fascinated with Wiley's undertaking, no matter that it used living human beings as its guinea pigs. George Rothwell Brown, a reporter for the *Washington Post*, dubbed the group of volunteers the

"Poison Squad."[189] The name quickly caught on. Wiley's public relations project was advancing with the same aplomb as his scientific one.

Vaudeville and music hall performers began to write songs about the famed "Poison Squad." In 1903, Lew Dockstader's famous minstrel company could be heard singing the following in a Washington, D.C., theater:

> If you should ever visit the Smithsonian Institute,
> Look out that Professor Wiley doesn't make you a recruit.
> He's got a lot of fellows there that tell him how they feel,
> They take a batch of poison every time they eat a meal.

Breakfast for the recruits, according to the Dockstader lyric, consisted of "cyanide of liver, coffin shaped;" lunch, a serving of "undertaker's pie, all trimmed with crepe;" and for "supper, arsenic fritters, fried in appetizing shade;" all washed down with a nice "prussic acid lemonade." (Prussic acid is a compound that can produce cyanide when properly catalyzed.) Similarly, S. W. Gillian's ditty, "The Song of the Poison Squad," described "the merriest herd of hulks the world has seen," who were "on the hunt for a toxic dope that's certain to kill, sans fail." The "Pizen Squad" was said to "dine with a matchhead consommé, drink carbolic acid brew" with a side of "tyro-toxicon condiments." Gillian's tune dubbed the Poison Squad "death-immunes."[190]

Despite the opposition of large trade groups, such as the Food Manufacturers' Association, the "Poison Squad" experiments and the Bureau of Chemistry's several bulletins on food adulteration swayed the government in favor of passing food-protection legislation. The bill passed the Senate in February, 1906, by an overwhelming vote of 63 to 4, and the House did the same four months later by an equally astounding 241 to 17.[191] No doubt the publication, also in February, 1906, of Upton Sinclair's *The Jungle*, with its "vivid accounts of the disgusting, depraved practices that prevailed in the [meat] packing plants,"[192] helped greatly to sway public and governmental opinion in favor of such a statute.

The statute, under Harvey W. Wiley's urging, aimed itself as much at economic as chemical practices, specifically seeking to eliminate "any article of food or drug which is adulterated or misbranded." Accordingly, authority for enforcing the law would fall not only to the secretary of agriculture, but to the secretaries of commerce and the treasury as well. The statute debarred the misuse of "terra alba, talc, chrome yellow, or other mineral substance or poisonous color or flavor, or other ingredient deleterious or detrimental to health, or any vinous, malt or spiritous liquor or compound or narcotic drug." It further inveighed against "any substance [that] has been mixed and packed ... so as to reduce or lower or injuriously affect its quality or strength," and also any product from which "any valuable constituent of the article has been wholly or in part abstracted," or one "mixed, colored, powdered, coated, or stained in a manner whereby damage or inferiority is concealed." Of course, if a product should "contain any added poisonous or other added deleterious ingredient" it too would fall under the statute's injunction. The text here is fascinating, for it not only demonstrates an obsession with the toxins and contaminants that might be lurking in factory-produced items, but it also envisions the manufacturer and seller of food as an enemy of the common good, both economic and biological. Appropriately, the Pure Food and Drug law contains specific provisions for mislabeled goods and products that are "an imitation of or offered for sale under the name of another article."[193] The goal was to protect the public from naive consumption practices as much as from poisons and impurities in food.

Having seen the food law passed—and having made his share of enemies in Washington—Harvey Wiley left the government service in 1912. A headline of the day read, "Women Weep as Watchdog of the Kitchen Quits After 29 Years." Wiley took a post at *Good Housekeeping*, where he helped run their product-testing laboratories. He also continued to conduct his own private scientific research and crusaded for further matters of public health, such as infant care.[194] To the end, he remained a staunch advocate of the public weal, never fully separating biological shortcomings from what he saw as moral ones. "[I]t is a sin to be sick," he held.[195] He joined the "Hundred-Years-Old Club," whose members took a pledge "to live a whole century or consign his memory to everlasting disgrace." In this pledge, Harvey Wiley Washington was to come up short. He died in 1930 at the age of 86.[196]

Harvey Wiley and his Pure Food law are perhaps the foremost examples of an obsession with purity and cleanliness present in turn-of-the-century American culture. Such worries in fact betrayed deep anxieties over the emergence of mass commerce—its scope, its anonymity, its insatiability. Those increasingly at the helm of America's new commercial culture, whether lawmakers like Wiley or businessmen like Richard Sears, Asa Candler, B.F. Keith, or E.F. Albee, met, and further fed, such concerns by propagating a discourse focused on contamination and sterility, microbial infestation and health, unwholesomeness and wholesomeness. They were products, and yet they were also among the chief authors, of their age. They were, in short, historical figures in every sense of the term.

| three |

"Of Pleasing Face and Form"
The Sexual and the Sensual

We have seen how vaudeville theater developed as a pioneering form among nationally-oriented, mass-market forms of corporate entertainment in the United States, and how it marshaled a rhetoric of purity and cleanliness in order to do so. Developing such a marketing discourse, as we have also seen, permitted the vaudeville chiefs to build a mass audience, within a society animated and often divided over questions of morality and sexuality, all at a time when businessmen in other industries were engineering their own mass-market experiments with blossoming success.

The strategy employed by these entertainment entrepreneurs permitted the vaudeville stage to win popularity as a space where sexually titillating or less-than-wholesome fare could be deployed and explored. The vaudeville stage was a highly sexualized space, especially compared to the relative norms of the day, where unclad bodies, provocative dancers, and singers of "blue" lyrics all vied for attention. It was a site in which the female body was posed as an emergent sexual commodity within a burgeoning urban climate of commerce. In this climate, consumption, sexuality, and mass-marketing efforts overlapped and interacted dynamically, each impacting the vector of the others, and vice-versa. Because of acts like these, furthermore, a new degree of sexual liberalization emerged—if the objectification of the female body may be viewed as an example of liberalization. In any case, there developed, in the realm of popular amusements, a marked departure from earlier, Victorian mores and norms.

Historians and scholars have begun to explore how the female body became an object of particular sexual delight during a specific era and for specific reasons. Some have observed a distinct fetishization of the female body emerging in the mid-nineteenth century. The onset of this, the argument goes, was tied to a number of other developments, including the respective and interrelated rises of consumerism, modern state administration methods, surveillance, and the "disarticulation" of sight from touch (with sight gaining cultural privilege). Such fetishization, at least one scholar has argued, resulted in "the spectacularization of the female body"—that the female form became, in other words, desirable as a sexual spectacle in and of itself—in a way that it had never quite been before.[1] As we will see, the vaudeville stage was one important locale for the "spectacularization" of the female body—that is, its presentation as a viewable commodity gravid with visual erotic content.

In order to fully appreciate the emergence of this "spectacularization," one must also understand that it was accompanied and abetted by important changes in the way the modern nation-state began to monitor and exert control over many people's daily lives. That is, some have claimed that the state's new interest in, and adeptness at, delving into and controlling the lives of its citizens, pre-Orwellian though it sounds, was a decidedly male or masculine project. Put another way, the "male"-characterized apparatus of government began to regulate people's lives just as the female body was itself becoming an object of desire and control.[2]

This period—the mid-to-late-nineteenth century—saw the development of not only the mechanics of modern state governance but also of its close cousin, the mechanics of modern corporate governance with its bureaucracies, hierarchies, and rationalized organizational structures. It was vaudeville that more than any other economic project brought such developments to the field of entertainment, providing a key nexus of male administrative authority and female sexual objectification—"spectacularization," in a sense. In other words, modern industries like vaudeville played a critical role in regulating, defining, and offering for sale the female body as a visually consumable sexual product.

As the American city, the modern market par excellence, continued to grow in the late nineteenth century, ever becoming the center of the nation's cultural landscape, the sexualized female body itself became ever more enmeshed within the practices of marketing, promotion, and consumption. Whether window shopping for clothing or stopping into an urban eatery for a quick meal, one was increasingly confronted with the alluring female body. Shapely and suggestive mannequins in department store windows, many "wearing" only undergarments, sexualized the experience of walking down the street, conflating such sexualization with consumption. This constituted a radical change from earlier selling practices in which, according to one expert on the rise of retailing, "merchants tended to pile up goods on shelves or mass them into architectural cones or arches." The same expert points out that novelist John Dos Passos took note of the new sexually charged nature of the urban clime in his novel *1919*. Even mundane interactions could get one of his characters "terribly agitated," Dos Passos wrote, "so that it was hard not to show it. The wobble of the waitresses' hips and breasts, while they were serving meals, girls' underwear in store windows."[3]

In the American city of the late nineteenth and early twentieth centuries the female body was on display as a sexual object as never before. However, it was either on display for a price as a consumer good, or was somehow connected to the act of purchasing. It was dressed up in underwear in department store windows to underscore its sexual power and it was often treated similarly on the geographically and culturally contiguous vaudeville stage. By the late nineteenth century, points out one historian of American advertising, promotional cards for consumer goods regularly showed women, as if seen through a peep-hole, in various states of undress, as a means of attracting attention to various products.[4]

In many ways, the female body was the act surest to please a vaudeville audience, with audiences preferring "a mediocre sister act [to] a good brother act (they were better to look at)," in the words of one vaudevillian.[5] A list of women who did little more than appear on stage in close-fitting or form-revealing outfits could go on and on. When a performer calling herself "Mardi Gras" appeared at Keith's Fifth Avenue theater in 1913, *Variety* wrote, "Mardi Gras looks fine in tights and could be booked on her figure [alone]."[6] Some years earlier, another theatrical newspaper wrote that "Pauline Hall sang several songs and showed her fine figure to advantage in tights" at Keith's Union Square.[7]

Understandably, female vaudeville performers began to conceive of acts that were little more than excuses for them to get on stage in tights, clinging gowns, or other revealing attire. The actress known as Patrice put on a "fairy" sketch at Proctor's Fifth Avenue in 1900, in which she showed "the full figure of a gal" and "made a very pretty picture in her clinging gown," while performer Josephine Hall went on at Koster & Bial's two years earlier "in a tight-fitting suit of knickerbockers which showed that her figure had lost none of its trimness."[8] Gibson's Bathing Girls, a popular attraction during the 1907 season, offered up a dance number set at a "seaside resort" in which the title performers naturally had to appear in "bathing costumes."[9] When the Louise La Gai dance company presented a mini-ballet called "La Tigresse" at Keith's Fifth Avenue theater in 1913, the lead female dancer "forgot to put on tights in the final scene, wearing but a leopard skin."[10] Appearing "almost in nude form," according to the *New York Clipper*, La Gai proved "one of the hits of the long program" and rated "numerous encores."[11] Increasingly, middle-class American audiences were learning that the female body could be publicly revealed rather than cloaked in successive layers of matronly modesty and dignifying finery.

Many actresses, it seems, could easily counteract a lack of talent with a surplus of bodily exhibition. When the "Ladies' Comedy Quartette" appeared in vaudeville in 1907, the *New York Dramatic Mirror* noted that "their attempts at comedy were very sad... [but] when the four young women made their appearance at the finish in snugly fitting military costumes, the enthusiasm was pronounced."[12] Some years earlier, performer Julie Mackey took the innovative approach of doing "The Lost Chord" in tights. "Just think," wrote the *Dramatic Mirror*, "of Sullivan's masterpiece coming before an audience in a pair of pink fleshings."[13] So common were tactics like these that critics occasionally expressed surprise when a female vaudeville performer actually possessed artistic talent in addition to sensual wiles. Singer Alexandra Dagmar chalked up a crowd-pleasing success, not only because of "her beautiful face and stunning figure, but on account of her superb rendering of some well-chosen songs," mused the *Dramatic Mirror*, mildly stunned, in 1899.[14]

Still, though talent could be admired, it was not always essential. Mlle. Guerrero created a pantomime act concerning a robbery, but was nonetheless "heavily advertised as 'the most beautiful woman in the world,'" according to the trades, rather than for her miming skills.[15] The New York critics noticed a similar tendency with actress Isabelle Urquhart. In 1897, Keith's Union Square theater was "filled to the

Lillian Herlein used alluring gowns and tight-fitting clothes to sculpt her body into a sexualized commodity par excellence on the vaudeville stage. (Billy Rose Theatre Collection, The New York Public Library for the Performing Arts, Astor, Lenox, and Tilden Foundations.)

brim" to see Urquhart enact a sketch of her own devising. In the act, Urquhart, well aware of her much-publicized "statuesqueness," did "little more in the sketch than display her form in a handsome gown to the utmost advantage," according to the *New York Clipper*.[16]

Lillian Herlein was one of the female vaudeville performers who became most adept at supplanting bodily display for either vocal, kinesthetic, or dramatic talent. Her gowns were "cut particularly low in the back," while her bathing costume was deemed "risqué." Altogether, according to one critic, it was not her songs but her abbreviated costumes that "had apparently the desired effect upon those [openly enthusiastic men] in the gallery."[17] Several months later, when Herlein appeared at Keith's Fifth Avenue, *Variety* wrote that she was "bound to make talk" owing to her "appearance in full tights during her final song called 'Swim, Swim, Swim.'" As has been noted earlier, this was the primary aim—"display of her 'figger'"—of Herlein's stage turn.[18]

If the display of female bodies proved appealing on the stage, certain theater managers realized they could be used to increase revenues elsewhere about the theater. When Ted Marks took over as manager of Koster & Bial's vaudeville house in 1900, he replaced its "stolid German waiters," despite their years of loyalty and experience, with "three buxom barmaids" in the theater's café.[19] Dos Passos might have found such a sight familiar.

Sometimes, the proliferation of scantily-clad female bodies in vaudeville drew the moral ire of reform-minded onlookers. When "French dancers" the Dartos appeared at Koster & Bial's in 1898, one journalist found that "the display of legs and lingerie is startling."[20] Similarly, a critic at Tony Pastor's found the Washburn Sisters musically talented, but also worthy of rebuke: "The new member of the firm is an excellent substitute for her predecessor, being of pleasing face and form, but her stock of 'ginger' far exceeds the demands of refined variety audiences."[21] The following month, another singer at Pastor's, Maud Nugent, was also deemed "much too spicy to admit of commendation" by the *New York Clipper*'s critic.[22] A sketch called "Mrs. Radley Barton's Ball," which was produced at Hammerstein's Olympia in 1897, drew similar outrage, committing, in the words of one spectator, "many offenses against good taste" not the least of which were the "costumes of the four girls who first appear in bathrobes [which] are fully as suggestive as they are intended to be."[23] Still, comments like these had little effect on acts that, though controversial, were popular. Even E.F. Albee, vice-principal of the Keith "Sunday School Circuit," once made known his belief that the folks (read: men) in his theaters "ought to have a little fun" from time to time.[24]

Female vaudeville performers not only perfected the art of exhibiting their bodies in revealing or form-fitting costumes but they actually improved upon it by working costume changes, in full view of the audience, or the shedding of raiment altogether, into their songs, dances, and dramatic sketches. Fannie Fondelier, a violinist, "discarded a cloak she wore at the opening and performed in tights,"[25] while the "clever French singer" Liane D'Eve changed "her costume several times in view of the audience" making her act "a decided success."[26] Similarly, singer Gertie Van Dyke possessed a "pretty figure displayed in neat tights [which] was very effective," and put on display thanks to a "couple of changes made in view of the audience," which helped the act score big.[27] Veronica Jarbeau "changed into tights" in order to sing "a song which was tinged with indigo…."[28] Zelma Rawlston made her changes of garb, speedily and in full view of the audience, the key feature of her performance. The program at one of her performances asked the audience's forbearance for forty-nine seconds while she changed, but she delighted her crowd even more that evening by stripping and re-clothing herself in half that time.[29]

By executing tantalizing costume changes in full view of the crowd, performers like these were in effect making the private public. In an era governed by restrictive mores, they permitted male theatergoers a voyeuristic glance behind the Victorian dressing screen. Spectacles that had previously played largely on the burlesque stage, with that venue's all-male, working-class connotations, were now brought into wider public view. This was indeed a privilege worth paying for.

Some went to the trouble of fashioning a sketch or short play that would result in a woman changing, stripping, or otherwise shedding her raiment. In a skit called "The Lady and the Pugilist," which went on at Tony Pastor's in 1904, the leading woman "removed her walking suit to try on [a] new gown."[30] Several years later, in a sketch called "The Billiard Room" at Percy Williams's famous Colonial theater, actress Liane De Lyle's character wore a long gown, only to be "discarded to reveal the shapely form of the young woman in tights."[31] In "Sam Todd of Yale," the title character, a proper Yale crew sculler, gives his clothing to "bathing Bessie Terry, whose clothes are stolen by a lunatic."[32] Certain men in the audience no doubt cheered the lunatic, though in the becalmed, "respectable" manner authorized by the vaudeville magnates in their playhouses.

An extremely popular sketch called "Au Bain" or "Suzanne at the Bath" advertised the fact that it contained a young woman changing out of her clothes in full view of the spectator—and perhaps little else in the way of plot. "The audience notices for the production in this city led to the belief that it would be broadly Gallic," wrote the *New York Clipper*, and suggested that it appealed primarily to theatergoers who held "hopes of seeing the full 'limit' reached." Probably afraid of arrest or censure, the producers of "Au Bain" cleverly kept the actress's act of disrobing in view of a pair of all-seeing, voyeuristic male eyes, without revealing too much to risk legal action. For Suzanne began to strip in front of the audience, "but after taking off her waist goes behind shrubbery and the 'man in the moon' alone sees the completion of her preparations." Standing in for both the voyeur and the prude, the moon-man, emerging from behind a bank of clouds, "by rolling his eyes, making various grimaces and looks of astonishment leaves the audience little to surmise as the progress of Suzanne's disrobing." The message was clear: even if spectators were denied a full view of the unclad female body, it was nonetheless on display for pleasure, perusal, and judgment. By the following month, "Au Bain" had emerged as "the salient feature" of the bill at Koster & Bial's "with Adele Ritchie doing the disrobing."[33]

Some enterprising female performers exhibited their bodies by combining circus or gymnastic feats with the removal of clothing. Again, the point was to end up displaying a nearly naked body rather than virtuosic physical coordination. Female "acrobats' disrobing scenes were often identified as salacious displays for male patrons," notes a recent scholar of the vaudeville era.[34]

Show women of this sort—those who did athletic stunts while also shedding attire—appeared relatively early on the vaudeville stage. In early May 1898 Adgie, "who combines the talents of the lion tamer and disrober" impressed spectators at the Olympia theater in New York. A critic who saw her show had little good to say about Adgie, wondering "where this boudoir business is going to stop." The disapproving critic relayed fancifully that "even the lions, which were supposed to be very fierce, and ready at a moment's notice to chew the lady up, turned away in disgust," humorously projecting his own unease onto the big cats.[35] Later that year, Virginia Aragon walked the high wire at Koster & Bial's. But it was not her balancing abilities that drew the attention of the crowd. Rather, it was Aragon's figure, replete with "superb lines," that made for "a splendid appearance, which, as the old-time managers would say, is 'alone worth the price of admission,'" in the words of one viewer.[36]

In 1907, the team of O'Rourke and Marie improved on Aragon's formula. The latter of the team was a "young woman of lively spirits and exuberant personality who can

Like other vaudeville actresses, Adele Ritchie used a combination of unique, luxurious costumes and her own sexual allure to please audiences. Her character disrobed in a controversial short play called "Au Bain," or "Suzanne at the Bath," in 1898. (Billy Rose Theatre Collection, The New York Public Library for the Performing Arts, Astor, Lenox, and Tilden Foundations.)

undress on a slack wire and sing a song at the same time," wrote someone who saw the show at Pastor's.[37] In 1910, a performer calling herself "Venus on Wheels" also framed the display of her figure in an act containing circus-like feats of physical prowess. Venus on Wheels boasted a "well rounded figure," her "black union suit showed every curve in the girl's possession." As if that weren't ginger enough, Venus got rid of her "loose-fitting suit early on while thus garbed—if one can call such a costume a garb," wrote a reviewer for the *New York Clipper* who saw Venus perform bicycle stunts for the crowd.[38]

Other female disrobers attempted to couch their striptease in the trappings of high art, such as "The Girl With the Dreamy Eyes," a woman who "offered her violin playing while garbed in scant attire, going down into the audience and wandering halfway down the aisle, while thus dressed—or undressed—playing the violin meanwhile." The near-naked fiddler was "bare-armed and bare-legged, save for little sandals on her feet, and her body was draped simply in black lace, which fell about the knee." As a "joke," according to one man present at the show, the program "said the 'costumes were designed and executed by Lady Duff Gordon.'"[39] Whether playing the violin or walking a high wire, these performers successfully pleased male theater patrons by giving them a version of the burlesque hall striptease made respectable by the use of culturally clever framing devices. They also appealed to patrons by serving up the sexually titillating in the guise of circus, a form of entertainment already popular with a middle-class clientele. Indeed, the mere existence in public view of the active and exposed female physique could itself be a provocative sight, as "women's incursions into athletics and public amusements were tied to women's sexual spectacle," in the words of a recent vaudeville scholar.[40]

Stripping the female body of clothing on the stage could transform that body into a kind of sexual commodity—just one act in a succession of similar acts that a patron was certain to get for the price of admission. However, the female body could just as easily be commodified through the *use* of clothing. Rather than taking *off* their clothes, a number of female vaudeville personalities achieved success by draping themselves in luxurious apparel, alluring, desire-provoking, sometimes flimsy, sometimes exotic or wild. They became, in a sense, walking arguments for consumerism, flesh-and-blood mannequins, every bit as much the objects of desire as their clothes-shedding peers, but objects of consumption rather than sexual fetishization. "Miss Walters displayed a magnificent new gown beautifully trimmed with lace that caused women in the audience to buzz for several minutes after she came on," wrote the *New York Dramatic Mirror* of an actress who appeared at Keith's Union Square in 1903.[41] A week earlier, Florence Bindley had created "a sensation with a new costume she wears called the 'diamond dress'" alleged to be the "most expensive gown ever worn on the vaudeville stage," glittering with some "4,000 brilliants, giving it the appearance of a ball of fire," according to one clearly impressed spectator.[42]

Performers like Walters and Bindley cleared the way for other women whose apparel proved their chief attraction. When Carrie Perkins appeared in a sketch called "Have You Seen Bill" at Tony Pastor's, the *Dramatic Mirror* wrote, "Her gown was a superb creation and it displayed her ample figure admirably."[43] Perkins had achieved the double success of presenting both her clad body and the alluring figure beneath it as desirable objects, somehow phenomenally inseparable. With richly-adorned gowns grabbing attention in vaudeville, it was only a matter of time before the "dress display" or "fashion show" took to the vaudeville boards. *Variety* staffer Sime Silverman lamented that "This 'Fashion Show' thing" was less likely to appeal to many of the men in the house, than to their wives: "To a henpecked husband watching this thing with his wife it must be like living in a death cell. There are now two kinds of 'girl acts' in vaudeville, with and without clothes. One will draw the men the other will keep them away." Silverman was suggesting that the stripper or scantily-clad female on the stage provided a kind of spectatorial satisfaction that, while a form of regularized consumption, nonetheless offered relief from life's day-to-day burdens. In his view, it would seem, the women of high fashion provided a similar pleasure for those women in the audience. As one chronicle of the vaudeville era put it, "The male patrons came to get some laughs and look at the beautiful women and the lady patrons came to see the latest styles in clothes and hair-dos."[44]

In some ways, the female performers who fared best on the vaudeville stage were those who combined sexual allure with elements of pure visual spectacle. As at least one historian of popular culture has argued, vaudeville audiences were drawn to performances based on "visual novelties" rather than an abundance of narrative content.[45] Performers who wanted to combine sexual titillation with visual effects could do so by quantity—offering, say, a gaggle of undraped female bodies to overwhelm the senses—by special effects like water and light, or by a combination of these two elements. In 1902, the Fadettes, "an orchestra composed of good-looking and clever young women" took the first of these approaches. "[T]he fact that the eye is pleased while the ear is tickled with sweet sounds makes the orchestra an irresistible attraction," wrote the *New York Dramatic Mirror*. Accordingly, the Fadettes enjoyed a healthy run of three weeks.[46] Similarly, when Keith's Fifth Avenue presented a female-only bill in 1912, *Variety*'s Dash observed, "There were many men in the house, unquestionably drawn by the 'All Women' billing."[47] Other producers followed suit. Two years later, Hammerstein's theater scored big with "13 Girls in Blue," which was based on a popular burlesque act of the period, "22 Girls" in tights.[48]

In addition to sheer numbers, female performers could improve their sexual cachet by making their bodies the center of a technological or special effects display on stage. "In these dances," notes one cynic, "all the gals did was practically pose in transparent gowns and a guy from the orchestra pit would throw different colored slides on them."[49] As early as 1899, Letta Meredith conjured up an act consisting of little more than "a series of colored effects projected upon her shapely form."[50] Those who combined numbers with spectacle achieved even greater success. At Keith's Union Square in 1901, the Eight English Roses, "an octette of uncommonly pretty young Britons," danced in frames using light and mirrors to create optical illusions with their bodies. "The girls were exceedingly good to look upon," noted a reporter for the *New York Dramatic Mirror*. But, he fretted, because each Rose's name was not listed in the program, "Just think of how many 'mash' notes they will miss."[51]

By 1910, the combination of electrical illumination and the female form had become so commonplace that some critics doubted audiences would still respond. Following the appearance of Loie Fuller's "Ballet of Light" at the Fifth Avenue theater, *Variety*'s Rush argued that the New York public had become "sated with barefoot dancing," having endured "so much of it under the full glare of all the lights that the exhibition of six girls unclad as to the legs is not particularly startling."[52] Rush's distaste may reflect his professional requirement to attend many more vaudeville shows than the average ticket-buyer. For Rush, familiarity may have begun to breed contempt.

Using water was another way to heighten the spectacle and sexual allure of a woman's body on the vaudeville stage. Whereas electrical effects conflated female sexuality with notions of technology, industry, and progress, water carried connotations of arousal, fertility, and procreation. An act at Proctor's Pleasure Palace in 1898 called "La Pluie et la Neige" brought forth "a number of very pretty girls in a dance beneath showers of real water."[53] Some years later, Odiva, "the Living Mermaid," developed an act where she disrobed and performed other tasks while entirely submerged. According to the *New York Telegraph*, Odiva was born in London but was shipwrecked at age three "in the South Pacific and got ashore in the Samoans to grow up among the soft-voiced Kanakas that Robert Louis Stevenson loved."[54] The story of her prove-

Odiva, the "Living Mermaid," performed underwater feats of strength and agility in vaudeville. That she did so in a tight, formfitting bathing suit did not hurt. (Billy Rose Theatre Collection, The New York Public Library for the Performing Arts, Astor, Lenox, and Tilden Foundations.)

nance is unlikely; it was probably fabricated by vaudeville promoters accustomed to selling freak acts to dime-show spectators. What is certain, though, is that Odiva could hold her breath for long periods of time and looked pleasing in a bathing suit. After being introduced by an announcer, Odiva, "wearing a light color walking dress," approached an enormous water tank, placed well downstage amid the blaze of the footlights, and "surrounded by a pretty forest set with springboards on both sides."

After plunging into this sort of human fish tank, Odiva "strips to a black union suit," according to a reviewer. Underwater for two full minutes, Odiva engaged in "sewing, eating, and acrobatics" without once having to come up for air.[55]

Odiva may not have been truly "Samoan," but she was presented as such and her appeal was thus tinged with an air of the exotic. Similarly, the female body on the variety stage lent itself to images of colonial fantasy and historical curiosity. In 1901, "50-Beautiful Ladies-50" appeared at Keith's Union Square in a "pageant of the nations," with each woman flying the colors of a different country. In addition to "two Amazonian marches and a dance," one woman put on an "Egyptian scarf dance" while another demonstrated the "Drill of the Red Hussars."[56] A decade later, the "Dance Dream" at the Colonial theater featured "reveries" of "dancing girls of different periods, wearing the costume and doing the popular dance of the day."[57] If a shapely female form under the stage lights offered one kind of voyeuristic fantasy, the same body posed as a geographic or historic—or in the case of Odiva, physical—oddity provided yet another.

Odiva and her seemingly exotic peers may have been popular for a time, but no water-frolicking woman proved more successful in vaudeville than Annette Kellerman. Kellerman billed herself as the "Diving Venus," and engaged in displays of diving, swimming, and water ballet. Although she had been swimming since early childhood and had, at age 16, swum "almost the breadth of the English Channel," according to the *Philadelphia North American*,[58] her main appeal was her bathing suit-clad body. E. F. Albee himself, as has been noted, set up an elaborate system of mirrors behind Kellerman on the stage to provide ample views of her tightly-clad rear.[59] In 1908, the *New York Dramatic Mirror*, reviewing her vaudeville act, described how "her superb figure [is] shown to particular advantage," and also remarked, "Much has been written of Miss Kellerman's figure but mere words fail to do the subject justice. [She] inspires painters and sculptors to do their best work."[60] The *New York Clipper*, writing of Kellerman's show at the Victoria Roof Garden, observed, "Her graceful dancing and fine physique call forth enthusiastic applause at every performance."[61] New York's vaudeville reviewers seem not to have had plaudits enough to heap onto Annette Kellerman—or her curves.

When the Diving Venus appeared at Keith's Fifth Avenue theater in 1909, one enthusiastic male spectator rushed the stage and tried to snap pictures of the performer who was wearing a "short-skirted bathing suit." Spotting the eager photographer before he could expose any film, Kellerman dove into the tank of water before her and proceeded to strip and change her attire, like "a sort of submarine Charmion," in the words of *Variety*'s Rush who compared her to a popular vaudeville striptease artist named Mlle. Charmion (of whom more will be said later).[62] Despite this purported modesty, the papers were filled with photos of Kellerman, not to mention numerous other paeans to her bodily beauty. In 1909, the *New York Star* ran a poem entitled "A Midsummer Rhapsody to Annette Kellerman," with a verse reading, "O, girl, your form makes all artists stare/O, girl of curves that please the cultured eye."[63]

Whatever skills Kellerman possessed in swimming or diving were eclipsed by her appearance. "She had a beautiful figure and when the water hit that tight-fitting black suit ... B-R-O-T-H-E-R," wrote a onetime vaudevillian.[64] Perhaps more than

Anette Kellerman impressed vaudeville audiences with her aquatic displays—as well as the expanses of bare or barely-clad skin she *also* displayed. (Billy Rose Theatre Collection, The New York Public Library for the Performing Arts, Astor, Lenox, and Tilden Foundations.)

any other single woman in vaudeville, Annette Kellerman and her producers and promoters helped forge an emergent notion of the woman as viewable sexual commodity. It was her observable body displayed in scant or tight-fitting attire, arrayed on the stage in a spectacle of light and water—"spectacularized," to employ the neologism described earlier in this chapter—that made her a huge hit. She was called "a rare jewel among women who expose their 'figure' to an audience's gaze," and it was further argued that there could be "no more perfect figure than Miss Kellerman presents as she appears in her diving costume of black silk tights ... It fits snugly to the skin ... a perfect figure neither sex would tire [of] seeing." Though Kellerman found great success in the vaudeville theater, the era's primary form of corporate urban entertainment, she was promoted as a "natural" beauty who owed her feminine allure to a freedom from the urban locale. Kellerman's "suppleness" was said to be that which "no hothouse beauty could develop in an atmosphere of cigarette smoke and press agents," according to one account.[65]

Kellerman herself advanced the idea that the trappings of civilization were injurious to a woman's beauty potential and sexual allure, decrying the notion that "frills and gewgaws of raiment which serve rather to conceal than to set off the figure are becoming." Kellerman felt that no matter how nice the garment, "it cannot but look out of place on a woman who is compelled to tight-lace herself to an agonizing degree to wear it"—or so she once wrote in the *New York Journal*.[66] "Clothes ruin us! They do harm to our bodies. But they do worse to our souls," she once insisted. In Kellerman's calculus, "There would be no fat people ... if we wore only a little chiffon."[67]

Kellerman's attitude (and that of her producers) presented most women with a conundrum. On the one hand, they were encouraged to display their natural form; yet on the other, that natural form was implicitly to be compared to Kellerman's and those of other "perfect women" in the eroticized public sphere of performance and consumption. Kellerman and her backers cleverly tried to capitalize on this position by forming "The Annette Kellerman Health and Physical Development School of Correspondence for Women." For a fee, subscribers could receive health and beauty advice allegedly written by the Diving Venus herself. "Every Woman Should Have a Beautiful Figure Health and a Clear Complexion" read the banner headline of a 1910 advertisement for the Kellerman School. "The attainment of beauty and health is not a matter of luck or of being born so," the ad assured nervous women, and advised them to take heart: "If you are too thin—too fleshy—underdeveloped or unshapely—if your complexion is sallow—if you are weak, ill, tired or languid, or in any respect not as Nature intended you to be, I can be of great help to you," read Kellerman's testimonial copy. On the one hand, Kellerman suggested that "Nature"—and not clothing or make-up—could render a woman thin, beautiful, tan, or whatever she fantasized with regard to her appearance. Yet only by spending money could Nature's beneficial effects be unlocked. And Kellerman, owner of a "perfect" body, claimed to hold the key. Performers like Annette Kellerman, while liberalizing mores about the body, were also feeding women's anxieties about their sexual allure and bodily perfection. Advertising images of about this time were busy doing much the same, urging women to "look at themselves as things to be created competitively against other women: painted and sculpted with aids of the modern market," in the words of an historian of American advertising.[68] Like the claims of purity and wholesomeness that often belied the truth of factory-produced goods, but yet greased the wheels for their acceptance, the Kellerman school paradoxically sold women "Nature" and a return to the natural via a commercial product subscribed to from afar.

Unlike many other female vaudeville performers, Annette Kellerman made the successful transition from stage to motion picture screen. Her first film, released in 1914 and produced by Universal, was called *Neptune's Daughter*. The movie was shot on location in Bermuda, a rarity during the silent era when studio sets which could be recycled for film after film were the norm, and ran to seven reels (approximately 150 minutes), also unusual when feature pictures typically ran three or four reels. *Neptune's Daughter* boasted impressive special effects, elaborate costumes, and a cast with hundreds of extras. The plot was an arcane mix of fairy tale, melodrama, romantic fantasy, and farce. Kellerman played a mermaid fittingly named Annette who seeks revenge against King William whom she holds responsible for the death of her sister at the hands of a fisherman. Predictably, Annette falls in love with William whom she had met when he was disguised as a woodsman. Antagonists come in the form of Olga, William's fiancée, and Boris, Olga's scheming lover, who together manage to stage a coup and throw the rightful King William in prison for a time. However, Annette returns, "slays William's adversaries, and upbraids the people for their injustice to him."[69]

Neptune's Daughter was a huge success. Upon its premiere, the *Chicago Tribune* reported, "For hours some of the people waited, standing in line to see the pictures of Annette Kellerman in 'Neptune's Daughter'... The seats were so precious that theater parties were willing to be separated scattering about inside from the first row to the balcony," while the *Cincinnati Times Star* wrote that "a theaterful of humanity eagerly watched the long film through two and one-half hours Sunday night in heat that made an icy plunge more appropriate amusement.... Had Annette Kellerman herself appeared on Keith's stage in all her personal glory, she would have had no larger audience than her film presence attracted Sunday."[70] Indeed, as these news reports suggest, Kellerman's objectified form was perhaps the perfect item to transplant from the live stage to a cinema increasingly concerned with the eroticized gazing pleasures of the male spectator.

Not everyone was enthusiastic about Kellerman's onscreen image, though. Upon seeing *Neptune's Daughter*, one woman complained to the mayor of her town that Kellerman's movie was potentially harmful. A sequence in which Kellerman, clad in flesh-colored tights to give the appearance that she is skinny-dipping, was deemed "suggestive and not good for boys and girls of high school age to see." And as for "that part where the mermaid is turned to an earth maiden and comes out of the woods seemingly clothed only in her flowing hair," that too was decidedly inappropriate for the "impressionable youth" of the irate woman's home town.[71] Similarly, Mayor V. A. Schreiber of the hamlet of East Liverpool, New York, found posters of Kellerman in "flesh-colored tights" to be "beyond all bounds of decency," though there is nothing to suggest he moved to have them taken down.[72]

Despite moral burbles like these, Kellerman was given another film to star in, this one even more elaborate, pretentious, and risqué than *Neptune's Daughter*. It was the Fox-produced *A Daughter of the Gods*, whose title suggests that its creators were

Vaudeville star Annette Kellerman made several movies. This still is from her 1917 picture *A Daughter of the Gods*. The film, which featured an apparently unclad Kellerman, caused one woman to assault her husband after he had gone to see it three times in three days. (Billy Rose Theatre Collection, The New York Public Library for the Performing Arts, Astor, Lenox, and Tilden Foundations.)

trying to capitalize on the success of Kellerman's first picture, as sequel- and franchise-makers do in the present day. The film took eighteen months to make, boasted a cast of 19,744, and cost over $1,000,000 to produce. Like *Neptune's Daughter*, *A Daughter of the Gods* was a collage of fantasy, fairy tale, melodrama, and sexual display for the leering patron. In it, Kellerman plays a girl who, disconsolate after the death of her bird, hurls herself into the ocean only to be reborn as "Anitia, a daughter of the Gods," also described as "a mysterious beauty." A convoluted plot involving characters with names like "Chief Eunuch," "Fairy of Goodness," "The Sultan," and "The Arab Sheik" results in Anitia vanquishing the "Witch of Evil."[73] Though the film, like *Neptune's Daughter*, had a complex narrative and bewitching visual effects, it was Kellerman's unclad figure that formed its centerpiece. "Beauty is the keynote of the film. Beauty and symmetry of the female form," noted *Moving Picture World*.[74] Male spectators sought out this very quality. A West Virginia woman made "four deep gashes in her husband's head" with a potato masher following the release of *A Daughter of the Gods*. "That scoundrel went to see that Annette Kellerman movie three times in three days, and he'd tell me every night what a pretty form she had," complained the angry, masher-wielding wife.[75] The lifting of Victorian sexual mores clearly presented new difficulties for many an American housewife, not to mention her vulnerable spouse.

Kellerman also made the 1918 Fox picture *Queen of the Sea*, which, as its title suggests, fit the boilerplate formula of her other films. In this fantasy film, Kellerman plays Merilla, queen of the sea. A fabulous plot mixing romance and melodrama has Kellerman falling in love with Prince Hero, rescuing Princess Leandra from the treacherous "Tower of Knives and Swords," and saving the lives of several lucky sailors. The picture ends happily, and Merilla ends up with her Prince Hero.[76]

Perhaps more than with any other single female performer, the imperatives of consumer capitalism and the fetishizing gaze of the heterosexual theater patron found their surest inscription on the body of Annette Kellerman. Indeed, others tried to copy the Kellerman formula. When Joe Smith and the Louise Alexander dancers appeared in a routine called "The Devil Tempting Innocence" at Keith's Fifth Avenue, *Variety*'s Dash reported that the lead female performer wore an outfit "cut extremely low, and for color this pale yellow thing has it all over the pink for appearing flesh like … after the pattern of the bathing suit worn by Annette Kellerman."[77] Similarly, when Kellerman signed with the Keith interests, rival William Morris engaged Rose Pitnof, "a fifteen year-old girl who swam from Charleston Bridge to Boston Light" and had a figure to rival Kellerman's.[78] In the standardizing system of corporate entertainment, few things signaled success as clearly as being copied.[79]

Another performer who capitalized on her appearance in a bathing suit was Lalla Selbini, who created an act called "the Bathing Girl." Compared to Selbini, Annette Kellerman displayed the athletic skills of a true Olympian. In fact, despite her attire and the name of her act, there is no evidence that Selbini ever went near the water, on stage or off. "It isn't so much what the young woman does as what she wears that will attract attention," wrote *Variety* editor Sime Silverman. Selbini enacted a few simple juggling tricks and then discarded her costume, "appearing as nature intended her with only a skin-tight piece of cloth separating her natural color from the gaze of audience." Like Kellerman, Selbini offered a view of sexually forthright womanhood unencumbered by Victorian notions of acceptability. "Without the aid of corsets she presents a figure that excites admiration," offered Silverman, who felt several of the performer's other quasi-acrobatic stunts left "little to the imagination." Despite having become inured to many an openly racy vaudeville routine, Silverman

A still from Annette Kellerman's 1918 movie *Queen of the Sea*. As usual, she wears little other than a revealing bathing suit. (Billy Rose Theatre Collection, The New York Public Library for the Performing Arts, Astor, Lenox, and Tilden Foundations.)

judged Lalla Selbini "frankly indecent," though he also conceded that her very indecency would probably render her "a drawing card thereby."[80]

Sime Silverman was right. Selbini drew large crowds and inspired "gasps of astonishment" when she went on.[81] When she appeared out West on the Orpheum circuit, the *Los Angeles Times* too noted that Selbini's act was little more than an elaborate striptease, a "classic beauty almost au natural" whose shows were nothing short of a "sensation." While reporting on her success, the paper also frowned on Selbini, regarding her act as "very much of nothing" and paving the way for less performing skill on the vaudeville stage in favor of greater bodily display. This was the essence of her routine: "There is a little ordinary juggling, a little singing in a small parlor voice, a little bicycle riding, an act on a single wheel—and, suddenly, as she stands at the top of her pedestal, there is a single hook unfastened, a quick swirl of draperie, and Selbini a la Eve—save for that tight-clinging, filmy blue—finishes her act." [82]

Lalla Selbini went on to appear in her "startling bathing suit" on the vaudeville stage for over half a decade, trading on "the meager clothing of her body and the generous expose of her shapely form, perfect in its beauty," according to a Cincinnati newspaper which referred to her as "Lula Salbini."[83] "She was a beautiful gal with a beautiful form, so who cared if she juggled or not," adds one familiar with her act.[84] When questioned in the Midwest about the propriety of her act, Selbini told the *De-*

Lalla Selbini was another vaudeville actress who capitalized on a pretty figure—which she showed off to great advantage after dirobing onstage and cavorting about in skintight, flesh-colored outfits. (Billy Rose Theatre Collection, The New York Public Library for the Performing Arts, Astor, Lenox, and Tilden Foundations.)

troit *Free Press*, "It is just what they wear on the other side [of the Atlantic] at all the fashionable bathing beaches and nothing ever is thought of it."[85] Like other disrobing performers, Lalla Selbini tried to tie her erotic behavior to European taste and fashion in order to lend it an air of class and acceptability. She played the sophisticate in the face of critics who found her shocking, sometimes promoting herself as "La Belle Baigneuse."[86] But it did not always work as she intended. In 1906, Selbini was arrested on indecency charges in Pittsburgh following complaints by a number of women.[87] Nonetheless, such run-ins were rare.

Eventually, Lalla Selbini put together an elaborate and expensive stage setting to frame, and thereby further legitimate, her bathing-suit-clad antics. When she came to Keith's Union Square in New York in 1913, she sported a "carload or more of scenery ... thirty European artists, including a band of fifteen, several horses, a real live lion, and numerous other accessories." The theater was packed at each show, with patrons hoping to catch a glimpse of "one of the prettiest figures on the stage."[88]

She helped further advance the notion, too, that the female body was capable, and indeed made for, the attainment of physical perfection. "Be good if you would be beautiful," she told the *New York World* in 1906. Also, advised Selbini, take three cold baths a day, eat a breakfast consisting of "plenty of fruit, a soft-boiled egg and a glass of milk," and get lots of sleep and exercise. Reporting her weight and height— 121 lbs. and 5'4"—the *World* noted that the Bathing Beauty boasted the precise measurements as those of the "prototype of all perfect forms, the Venus de Medici."[89] Whereas images of feminine perfection in prior ages had been idealized in artistic renderings of immortal beings, the modern era increasingly placed this onus on ordinary women of flesh and blood—women who consumed, went to the theater, and inhabited the mercantile landscape of turn-of-the-century urban culture.

Works of art were also used in vaudeville as the basis for scores of "posing" or "classical statue" acts, who costumed themselves in the high-brow rhetoric of cultural refinement—and little else. Posing acts in the form of tableaux were popular in New York from about 1840 onward. Though promoted as chaste and morally uplifting, many living pictures were in fact designed to be sexually titillating in their presentation of feminine beauty and perfection. No wonder they fell afoul of the law and reformist efforts several times during the nineteenth century.[90]

In vaudeville, though, by presenting themselves as "artistic" and therefore rarified, many posers and statue-imitators got away with giving eager audiences a generous serving of nudity while avoiding the moral censure of authorities and anti-vice crusaders. Clara Betz was one of the earliest performers to ply her trade as a poser. She appeared at Koster & Bial's in 1898 "in a full suit of tights" and "gave an exhibition which on the bills was called 'classic poses.'" The same reviewer felt it essential to point out, "She is pretty and well formed."[91] The *New York Dramatic Mirror* was a bit more cynical about Betz's "posing in the make believe 'altogether'" [meaning, presumably, altogether *naked*]. Betz struck poses under "a strong calcium [light]" which, in the *Mirror*'s opinion, "held the breathless attention of the gentlemen who are long on applause and short on hair." Even those in the cheap seats reportedly "put the elastics in their neck to a severe strain trying to get a good view of the lady with the curves."[92] It was not rarified artistry the patrons were interested in glimpsing so much as a display of the unclothed female form that trod the fine line between voyeurism and exhibitionism.

Other producers of "living pictures" and posing acts made a greater effort than Betz to link their presentations to the world of fine arts, such as one might see at a museum. Professor Brengk's "Parisian Statues" offered "three men in bronze" and "three women in porcelain" in such poses as "Venus," "The Vase," and "The Atlas Group."[93] Robbie Gordone, a "beautifully formed woman," took a similar approach to great avail, reproducing famous statuary to the sound of rousing approbation. "Hers is an act that appeals only to the eye, and is intensely interesting," wrote one critic. Gordone's stances included, "Persecution of a Virgin," "The Awakening of Galatea," "The Lion's Bride," and "The Death of a Dancing Girl." The crowds at both the Keith and Proctor theaters supplied "liberal applause" for Gordone.[94] Mlle. Loraine won similar plaudits when she appeared at a Keith theater "posing as bronze statues ... artistically presented," while Nirvana's living pictures specialized in views of the life of Ukrainian separatist Mazeppa, many on horseback, suggesting shades of Lady Godiva.[95]

Although some observers felt that living picture acts were simply transplants from the burlesque stage,[96] the cover of refinement in which they shrouded themselves often protected them from rebuke or censure. After a posing act produced by Ray Beveridge appeared in New York in 1908, the *New York Dramatic Mirror* opined that nothing "could possibly be taken as questionable," because "the golden dust coverings of the models served as a better veil than any amount of draperies could possibly have done."[97] Other acts, which did not employ much in the way of covering or "draperies" or the purported dust of precious metals also avoided criticism, by dint of their supposed cultural refinement. When "Art Studies" appeared at Keith's Union Square, one critic felt that the sixteen pictures it offered, including several nudes, were "so artistically posed that even the most fastidious could not help admiring them."[98] In all likelihood, heterosexual male theatergoers accustomed to burlesque shows admired them the most. Similarly, Jean Marcel's Living Pictures, perhaps the most consistently popular of all such posing acts, won high praise from critics and spectators for its artistic allure. Despite tableaux such as "In Italy," which proffered "a reproduction of the sensuously painted scenes of the women of the Latin country,"[99] Marcel was held in high moral regard. In addition to being "artistically posed"—or perhaps because of it—"the absence of vulgarity and suggestiveness is also a thing that calls for high praise," felt one reviewer.[100] Again, the façade of European allure supplied both a necessary exotic distance and sophisticated refinement to what was basically a display of exposed flesh.

What worried onlookers was not necessarily nudity, but nudity purveyed in an atmosphere dictated by mass-market demand rather than the authority of cultural elites. Unclad bodies were not in and of themselves evil, but when placed in a mass amusement venue and sold for the price of a cheap ticket, they suddenly became threatening. As we have seen, the nude was seen by many as permissible when in the studio of a painter or sculptor. But the appearance of the same models, in the same state of undress, on the stage for mere public amusement, where neither education nor socioeconomic status, but rather the mere price of a ticket, determined entry, was cause for alarm.[101]

Thus, the nude or semi-nude artistic posing act could occasionally fall afoul of critics and onlookers, usually when it began to resemble popular amusement fare—

such as that of the burlesque hall—more than an artistic or educational project. After seeing Charlotte Davies do her posing act at Hammerstein's theater—an act that included "Statue of a Maiden," "September Morn," "The Bath," "The Dancer," and the suspect-sounding "The White Slave"—*Variety*'s "Jolo" dismissed the routine as "merely a vulgar display of robust undraped femininity."[102]

As the titles of Davies's poses indicate, her appeal may indeed have been more prurient than aesthetic. Jolo's *Variety* colleague Sime Silverman had already observed that the word "classical" in a vaudeville act typically meant that its players were not "fully dressed," and furthermore that "the usual posing number [relies on] nudity."[103] Sime was ever a shrewd, if sometimes irascible, observer of the vaudeville stage.

Accordingly, very little eluded Sime's analytical skills or wry commentary. When Mervin Morgan put on "Visions D'Art" by posing on a stone block in her underwear, he wrote, "Merv has some figger [and] figger goes a long way toward getting salary from the box office."[104] Others were less sanguine when it came to posing acts. When Maud Odell, "the English prize beauty," brought her posing act of "living pictures" to the vaudeville stage, which included "a startling view of Miss Odell's figure from the rear" in a stance entitled "Spring," one drama critic felt it was "too strong for audiences that have stood the various Salomes without protesting very loudly. The art of undress can go no further than this, which in the language of the day is the 'full limit.'"[105] Odell, in one account, "would pose, and after each pose she would wear less clothes, and didn't start with much." Eventually, it got "pretty bad and the police made her put on more clothes."[106]

The posing act that promised absolutely to reach "the limit" came to the vaudeville boards in 1898. It was known as "An Affair of Honor," and it featured two nude female duelists in a dramatic sketch based on two paintings, "Une Affaire d'Honneur" and "La Réconciliation" by Emile Antoine Bayard.[107] But the dramatic content was not the act's main appeal. Rather, word got out (probably intentionally leaked to the trade press by the theater's management) that the women, in an effort to precisely reproduce the paintings, would appear naked to the waist. Indeed, in rehearsals, observed by several journalists, this was the case and the resulting buzz drew huge crowds to Koster & Bial's. Fearing police action, though, the managers decided to tone it down a bit for public presentation—at least temporarily. The "Affair of Honor," whose private rehearsals had been publicized in the press, was altered such that "the fair duelists wore pink fleshings." The managers of the vaudeville house found their venue "jammed with an expectant throng of sensation-seekers," but the thrill-seekers "departed in a gloomy mood when they found that their hopes had been dashed to the earth." Several days later, perhaps believing the storm had passed, and no doubt relishing the idea of another house "jammed with an expectant throng," Koster & Bial's featured the women "naked to the waist." Alas, the storm had not passed. There were protests, and the "fleshings" returned. One might think this would have caused the managers to learn their lesson. One would be wrong. Two weeks later the "Affair" performers were arrested "on a charge of violating a section of the code relating to offenses against public decency." Following a "police-court brawl expensive and disorderly," the case was subsequently dismissed and "An Affair of Honor" was permitted to continue to the relief of those ringing up the box office receipts.[108] The vaudeville managers' perseverance (not to mention greed and, perhaps, thickheadedness) had finally paid off.

Capitalizing on the relative freedom afforded nude acts that wore the "classical" or "artistic" mantle, some vaudeville performers began offering "classical dances" to audiences eager to see the unclad female body in motion. Upon seeing classical dancer Thamara de Swirsky's act, "Dash" of *Variety* concocted the following "[r]ecipe for the making of a classical dancer." It was simple: "Strip the subject, wind three and half yards of gauze around the body, not allowing any below the knees, then have the subject hop on her right foot, leaning slightly forward at the same time giving a short backward kick with the left."[109] The "classical" dancer, who probably owed more to the modernist styles of Ruth St. Denis, Isadora Duncan, and Maud Adams than to Greco-Roman antiquity, became popular on the vaudeville boards for her exposed flesh and her flaunting of Victorian sexual mores. "[O]ne of the pastimes of youth in these days is looking for bare-legged girls [and] bare-legged young women in 'classical' dances," remarked the irascible but all-knowing Sime Silverman.[110] The trappings of high art also reminded vaudeville patrons that powerful, patriarchal figures were in charge behind the scenes, carefully, even scientifically, regulating the amusement fare for mass consumption.

Many early modern dancers in high culture were often described as "classical" or "barefoot." These descriptors suggested "a sense of liberation from artistic and social constraints and a hearkening back to ancient models," in the words of one dance historian.[111] The scantily-clad "classical" dancers on the vaudeville stage took a page out of high culture's notebook, and then popularized, commodified, and sensationalized it. Indeed, many vaudeville dancers may have been trying to mimic Isadora Duncan who, on stage, "presented a 'natural' body," without corset and "loosely draped in her signature form-revealing tunics of floating silk or chiffon, hair flowing freely."[112]

Like her cousin the posing act, the classical dancer in vaudeville could invoke censure if she pushed the accepted limits of respectability. The "classical" dancer Mlle. Mernereau, according to the *New York Clipper*, displayed "about as much of her undraped form as she possibly can without incurring the displeasure of the authorities." The *Clipper* found her act "distinctly out of place in a family vaudeville theater."[113] Of course, her act was quite *in place* in a theater heavily attended by men seeking a new form of entertainment—the mass-marketed eroticized spectacle.

Though male "classical" dancers were few and far between, they too occasionally appeared in vaudeville. Rather than providing visual pleasure or provoking rebuke, they typically earned little more than the scorn of (patriarchal male) onlookers, similar to unclad male athletes and strongmen in vaudeville. *Variety*'s Sime Silverman offered that Paul Swann, a "wholly classical" dancer who appeared at Hammerstein's vaudeville theater, would appeal to women more than men, and the "older the woman the more they will like to see him float about the stage with his arms moving snakewise and his body twisting, almost squirming." Like his female "classical dancer" counterparts, Swann sported scanty costumes, rendering him, in Sime's estimation, "almost as naked as some of the women who have danced around for different reasons."[114] Players like Paul Swann presented a conundrum, for the unclad male body was a kind of counterfeit currency in the sexual economy of mass amusement at the turn of the century. His referent was the unclad female dancer, but phenomenologically he put forth a masculine corpus, thus confusing codes of spectatorship based on female objectification and the erotically charged male gaze.

Performers who put on classical dances, or reproduced well-known scenes from art and mythology, posed the female body as an alluring sexual commodity. It is not surprising then that sketches in which women played artist's models or other objects of visual pleasure were common on the vaudeville stage. In some cases, these sketches and short dramatic playlets, most of which were set in an artist's studio, featured little in the way of plot. Merely, they were an excuse to have a woman pose for, or impersonate, a work of art. Actress Frankie Bailey appeared in "My Lady's Picture" at Proctor's Twenty-Third Street theater, an art studio scene which made ready display of "the contour of her lower limbs," leading to Bailey's regard as "having the most perfect figure on the American stage," in the words of one spectator. Her "costume consisting of black tights and a close fitting jacket" made for "a most alluring picture."[115]

In "The Silhouette Girl," a woman enters an artist's studio, discards her clothing, "leaving the girl in her little union suit," against a background which "threw the woman's figure into sharp relief."[116] Similarly, Mlle. Rialta brought a sketch called "The Artist's Dream" to Keith Theatres in 1910. Set, as per usual, in an artist's studio, the model posed inside a frame while the artist slept, dreaming about "Rialta's very shapely build [which] is shown to capital advantage."[117] Acts like "The Artist's Dream" wove male fantasies of being able to summon scantily clad women on demand with the reality of woman as purchasable sexual object. Logically, these performances sometimes suggested a form of relief from the strictures of marriage and husbandhood. In an act called "The Goddess," from 1907, a sculptor chisels a rendering of Diana (in Greek mythology, Artemis, goddess of the hunt and the moon) on which he puts a $10,000 price tag. But no sooner has he finished and stuck a for-sale label on his work than his Diana "comes to life in his studio, and demands that his wife be slain so their lovemaking may proceed without interference."[118] Here, the image of woman not only affords the man who has made her a financial boon, but also an escape—if through rather indelicate means—from the drudgeries of marriage.

Artist's studio sketches usually suggested that the model, a woman useful solely for her bodily allure and willingness to take her clothes off, was inevitably the object of the artist's forbidden lust. In a "comedietta" entitled "My Husband's Model," a suspicious wife disguises herself as the model in her artist husband's employ to find out if her suspicions are based on fact.[119] (They are. But, like most of the myriad vaudeville sketches dealing with infidelity, the married couple is reconciled at the end. This stock ending was not merely intended to stave off moral criticism but, moreover, to allow the sketch to contain a healthy quantity of cheating husbands, secreted lovers, and surreptitious trysts without actually seeming to condone it all.)

In an interesting variation on the artist's model sketch, one such playlet had a woman playing a wax mannequin "smitten with the window dresser who manipulates her arms and—er—limbs and also dresses and un—well he prepares her for public view anyway [in] a pretty negligee."[120] Here the woman is offered up as not only a sexual object but a totem of consumption as well—the department store mannequin—not to mention a being who falls in love with the man who controls her every position while managing to manipulate her into a decided state of pleasure.

Perhaps the most famous solo vaudeville performer who posed herself as an artwork was known simply as "La Milo." Once referred to as the "famous poseuse of

Great Britain," La Milo covered her body in "alabaster whiting for the marble effect" and, thus coated, impersonated numerous famous statues and characters from classical mythology. Though some "looked for a sensational disclosure of the nude in art" in La Milo's show, her act was said to be free of "all taint of immodesty and any appeal to coarseness."[121]

La Milo was actually an Australian woman named Pansy Montague who had achieved great success in vaudeville by the time she was twenty-two years old. "She wears no clothes but the drapery necessary to make her poses resemble the original statues which she imitates," reported the *Detroit News*, which added that La Milo's body was clad only in "an enamel preparation that gives the appearance of marble." The paper opined, "Nobody who is not ashamed to take his wife to inspect the classic statues of an art gallery should be ashamed to see La Milo."[122]

Not every onlooker felt La Milo's appeal was purely artistic and devoid of the sensual, though. "Tom, Dick and Harry, each armed with opera glasses, the lenses of which are almost powerful enough to pierce the enamel that alone protects the stage goddess from the world," filled theaters on both sides of the Atlantic when La Milo appeared, reported the *New York Telegraph*. Despite her artistic pretensions, La Milo was every bit as much a voyeur's fantasy. According to the *New York American*, La Milo chose to impersonate statues of Venus, Diana, Phryne, Lady Godiva, Monna Vanna, "and other mythological and historical women renowned especially for their virtues, pulchritude and utter disregard for prevailing modes," especially where sexual mores were concerned. La Milo was "the talk of the town." [123]

As if to underscore her voyeuristic appeal, and publicize her exhibitionistic tendencies, La Milo simulated Lady Godiva's ride by galloping on horseback "through the streets of Coventry" in England in 1907 clad only in several lengths of chiffon and a long, flowing wig. "[E]very man in the thousands who jammed the streets was a 'Peeping Tom,'" wrote the *Chicago Tribune*.[124]

In addition to her sexual appeal, La Milo was yet another example of a female vaudeville personality promoted as a "perfect woman," a lionized ideal of feminine sexuality to which ordinary women were to compare themselves. "She is perfect in every measurement. Artists say of her she is a new Venus de Milo. Even her flesh is marble," commented the *New York Star*.[125] A newspaper advertisement promoting La Milo in 1907 called her renderings of Venus, Psyche, Hebe, Io, and other women of classical antiquity a "valuable educational treat." But it went on to construct the posing beauty as a kind of Platonic archetype of the female body, one with "proportions [that] are said to be perfect," all together a "splendid specimen of mature womanhood who has been compared inch by inch with all the beauties of mythology and has not been found wanting." La Milo's proportions were supplied with topographical precision—"Height, 5 feet 8 inches; Bust, 37½ inches; Hips, 42 inches; Waist, 26 inches; Upper Arm, 12 inches; Forearm, 9¾ inches; Wrist, 6 inches; Throat, 13½ inches. She weighs 162 pounds, is 21 years of age, has a clear complexion, blue eyes, and nut-brown hair." The advertisement brought up, and then summarily dismissed, one criticism of La Milo for being too "marble cold" in her poses; her popularity outweighed such gripes, noted the ad copy, and her body was thus discursively constructed as a veritable blueprint of feminine perfection. Her beauty, it was implied via its dis-integration into a series of measurements and fragmented traits, could be reduced to a formula and was therefore obtainable. Of course, most women could never hope to look like La Milo. It helped little that "her message to the American woman is 'do not sag.'"[126]

Posing acts like that of La Milo and others also capitalized on the increasing popularity at the time of artist's models, some of whom began to achieve notoriety around the turn of the century, not unlike fashion "supermodels" of the late twentieth/early twenty-first century. "In her way, too, she is an artist," wrote *Cosmopolitan* in a 1901 article on the subject of the professional art model—a woman who, like the actress, "must have the histrionic temperament." *Cosmopolitan* pointed out that many models "like queens content themselves with one name." Hence posers like "La Milo" or "Le Deodima."[127]

As a genre, posing acts were eclipsed in popularity by the so-called "Salome" dancers who appeared suddenly on the vaudeville scene in 1907–08. The Salome dancers cooked up their own variations on a common theme: a wild, gyrating interpretive dance number based on the Biblical story of the young woman who dances for King Herod, its rendering by Oscar Wilde, its operatic iteration, or some creative combination thereof.

Artistic representations of Salome go back at least as far as the Middle Ages. Some medieval artists rendered Salome as "a minstrel doing handstands or sword-juggling," according to an expert on English minstrelsy of the Middle Ages.[128] By the nineteenth century, the story of Salome had become of great interest to authors, composers, dancers, and painters. Writers Heinrich Heine, Gustave Flaubert, and Oscar Wilde, and composers Alexander Galzunov, Jules Massenet, and, of course, Richard Strauss, all adapted the tale of Salome in their respective works. The nineteenth-century artists "focused on Salome's sensuality, perverseness, and seductive powers," writes an historian of the Salome genre. Salome may have also symbolized an older, outmoded, and declining social order, one "on the brink of radical reform or dissolution."[129]

Many give credit to Maud Allan for starting the "Salomania" fad of both the high and popular stages, beginning about 1907. Inspired by Wilde's play and Strauss's opera, Allan developed an act that has been deemed a hybrid of "sexuality and pseudo-spirituality, apparent innocence, a transparent skirt, and thinly disguised lust, the whole package wrapped up in the rhetoric of High Aesthetic Purpose."[130] This appealing combination of sexuality and the artifice of high culture would soon make Salome dancers the perfect commodity for the mass amusement needs of the vaudeville circuits.

The Encyclopedia of Vaudeville argues that Gertrude Hoffman was the first to bring a Salome dance before the vaudeville public, in 1908, and that she was not inspired by Maud Allen's Salome dance. What is clear, though, is that by the fall of 1908, Hoffman was just one of an onslaught of women bringing various versions of the Dance of the Seven Veils to the major circuits. The Salome craze was so pronounced that even the United Booking Office was unable to keep up with demand.[131] As *Variety* noted, "Even the 'rubberneck' ballyhoos have changed their cry. Now it's 'Take the automobile and go Saloming.'"[132] In 1908, Hoffman's Salome number "smashed several Hammerstein [box office] records to smithereens."[133] Eva Tanguay, Ada Overton Walker, La Sylphe, Millie De Leon, Pilar Morin, and numerous others successfully posed themselves as Salome dancers during the act's brief, but intense, period of popularity. Mlle. Dazie, who dance historian Richard Bizot states was the first to perform Salome before an American audience in Florenz Ziegfeld's *Follies of 1907*, had even opened a "school for Salomes" which by the summer of 1908 was graduating no fewer than 150 aspiring Salome dancers per month.[134]

The typical Salome dance depicted the famed Dance of the Seven Veils, for which Salome, instigated by her mother, Herodias, is given the head of John the Baptist. According to *Variety*'s Sime in 1908, the Dance of the Seven Veils symbolized the "surrender of Maidenhood, [and] may be for no man's eyes other than the bridegroom's." Following the dance, Salome is "[b]roken, lost in the horrors of remorse, her Spirit an outcast, her body a reproach."[135]

Salome dancers added various touches to personalize and differentiate their routines. For example, some traipsed about with the cleaved-off head of John the Baptist, while others omitted this gory detail. But almost every Salome dancer traded on the scant attire, sensual abandon, and frenetic movement she brought to her act. By offering live-motion images of a woman possessed, the Salome dancers suggested sexual climax, rebellion against restrictive moral norms, and, like the "classical" posing and statuary acts, vestiges of the objectified female body of the burlesque stage. "In burlesque is the proper place for it," wrote one journalist. The Salome dancer, in his opinion, typically displayed what he called "a 'cooch' undulating movement," and noted audiences preferred it when, after "the last of the seven veils is removed, even less than a veil" remained.[136]

Certainly, it was essential for the performer to expose as much of her body as possible, either directly or filtered through the insinuation of gauzy fabric. "Truly, there seems to be no stemming the tide of nearly naked dancers of this description," wrote the *New York Clipper* late in the summer of 1908. The theatergoing public, noted the paper, was far from "satiated with the terpsichorean novelty, judging by the business done at all the houses where that feature is put on."[137] Eva Tanguay's Salome act featured a costume that was judged perhaps the most risqué, "if a strip of cloth may be described as a costume," in the words of one reviewer.[138] She was hugely popular.

As with any act demanded by the public, competition was fierce. Each Salome struggled to make herself unique from a pack of rivals, while providing enough erotic predictability to "put over" her act successfully. Ada Overton Walker, the only African-American Salome dancer in mainstream white vaudeville,[139] attempted to refine her Salome act, not by covering up or toning down her dance steps, but by eliminating some of the scene's gore and carnage. Unlike other Salome-ers, Walker did not carry the severed head of John the Baptist about the stage with her, but rather, merely touched her lips to it as the curtain fell. Kissing a severed head may not strike one as especially tasteful, but apparently it was—at least compared to what else was out there at the time. [140]

Others tried to claim ownership of their respective Salome numbers. Dancer Millie De Leon took out an advertisement which proclaimed:

SALOME DANCERS
—ATTENTION—
MILLIE DE LEON...
CHALLENGES

All Salome Dancers that she can outdance her imitators, in style and execution, for any amount of money.[141]

With characteristic pluck, Eva Tanguay too attempted to claim sole right to the Salome number.[142] Tanguay's version, entitled "A Vision of Salome," with original music by Melville Gideon, premiered at Keith's Alhambra in New York City in the summer of 1908. Her routine also featured impressive set pieces, including a river, blazing torches, and an altogether "massive stairway"[143] all of which hearkened back to the extravagant stage settings of nineteenth-century melodrama. In Tanguay's Salome act, though, it was more the actress than the role which drew the crowds. As usual, Eva Tanguay merely used a popular trend to frame her unique personality and unpredictable stage antics. When spectators went to see Tanguay's Salome, it was "was really Miss Tanguay whom they saw, clad in Biblical garb—or what there was of it," according to the *Brooklyn Citizen*. The paper's theater critic thought it a shame that the *real* Salome probably wasn't as "cute and pretty and lithesome" as her imitator, known to audiences as "the cyclonic one" for her frenzied dance movements. In Tanguay's act, the head of John the Baptist peeked out of a well, like a curious voyeur, as the near-undressed Tanguay twisted and stepped in lively fashion, "the audience going wild with a sea of opera glasses trained where they will do the most good."[144] John the Baptist, it seems, may not have been the only voyeur.

Some critics actually lauded Tanguay for *cleaning up* the Salome craze. The *Brooklyn Times*, for example, found "absolutely no vulgarity to it," nor anything "suggestive or offensive unless one be hypocritical." But other critics were not so encouraging. The *Brooklyn Daily Eagle*, in many ways the most well regarded Brooklyn paper,[145] assailed Tanguay not just for her lewdness, but for what seemed to be her utter disregard for, or complete ignorance of, the underlying story. "[A]s to artistic results there are absolutely none," argued the *Eagle*, the overall product being "merely ludicrous and grotesque." But the critic could not separate Tanguay's brazen sexuality from the act's perceived artistic content. Tanguay as Salome, "wearing apparel to a point just within the ban of the law" and gyrating freely, wildly, for a crowd decidedly different from what one might expect to find in an opera house or other site claiming the status of high-art venue, was a threat and a contradiction. Her Salome, like others, differing probably more in degree than in substance, wrenched a narrative from the groves of rarified art and brought it to a mass audience, aided by a superb and complex marketing system and, symbiotically, daring attire and no shortage of sexualized heat.[146]

Tanguay may have attracted the ire of moral reformers, but she was not alone in doing so. A number of critics and crusaders saw Salome acts as a base form of pandering. The Salome numbers inspired New York pastor John Wesley Hill to proclaim that "amusements to-day are as bad as in the old days of pagan Rome."[147] But it was not just clergymen, perhaps as a group predisposed to distrusting theatrical entertainments, who spoke out. So shocking and transgressive were the Salome performers, it would seem, that they inspired at least one actress to inveigh publicly against them as well. Marie Cahill, according to the *New York Times*, made "a frank attack on the vaudeville managers for giving 'Salome' dances" and declared "that they have thrown discretion to the winds and have forfeited the privilege of judging what the youth of the country may be permitted to see." According to Cahill, Salome dancers clothed "pernicious subjects in a boasted artistic atmosphere," really little more, in her estimation, than "the most vulgar exhibition that this country has ever been called on to tolerate." Cahill went so far as to write a heated letter to the New York State Republican Party arguing for "legislation that will put a stop to this willful poisoning of that great teaching institution, the drama," in her Horatian conception of the stage. The actress and would-be reformer insisted that one "plank" of the party's platform should favor "the establishment in the State of New York of a commission with powers of censorship over the dramatic stage" since, as she saw it, the vaudeville managers and executives had "thrown discretion to the winds." It should be pointed out that Cahill saw vaudeville as especially dangerous because, in her estimation, its relatively modest admission price made it more easily accessible to the "multitude of our young people who cannot go to school because they must work" and who "have acquired little or no taste for reading good books."[148] An inexpensive, mass-market entertainment, available for the simple price of admission, which had little use for the elite arbiters of taste, looked especially threatening to Cahill and others of her ilk.

Marie Cahill was not alone in suggesting that Salome performances clothed "pernicious subjects in a boasted artistic atmosphere," much like the posing and statuary acts of vaudeville. One journalist, who termed the fad "the Salome infection," felt this kind of routine made especially clear the fact that vaudeville clothed itself in a rhetoric of cleanliness that permitted it to get away with manifold offenses against moral decency. Joseph I. C. Clarke wrote in the *New York Times* in 1909 that vaudeville had made a name "vaunting itself as a safe and elegant resort for middle-class families, providing clean but entertaining performances that the feeblest intellect could enjoy," observing that the vaudeville chains had spread "guileless stories in the papers how certain reckless performers or 'teams' had had to omit even the mildest cuss-words from their 'acts' under the threat of having their contracts canceled." But nonetheless, here were "Pearian [sic] Salome's cavorting in undress all over their 'safe and elegant' stages." Clarke seems to make clear that the vaudeville chiefs were more concerned with the appearance of impropriety, and with the propagation of a marketing rhetoric aimed at advancing it, than with impropriety itself. Incorrectly, Clarke thought such a project would ultimately fail: "It is as normal for American audiences to demand clean plays as clean shirts. The mind of America is morally, sound."[149]

Even Martin Beck, who controlled the powerful Orpheum chain of vaudeville theaters, ostensibly objected to the Salome craze. Beck was accepting of modern dancers like Isadora Duncan who may have pushed the limits of respectability; but for Beck, the Salome dance was "degrading," and he affirmed that his Orpheum Circuit would be "diverting its energies to the higher and loftier plane of entertainment," rather than lowering itself to that of the Salome craze.[150] In this pronouncement, Beck was doing just as Clarke implied—telling the organs of public discourse that his theaters were wholesome in order to get away with the presentation of acts that were not. In response to public outcry, usually instigated by members of the clergy, Salome dances were, for a time, banned in Brooklyn and New Jersey, and placed "under observation" by the police in New York.[151]

Martin Beck may have thought near-naked dancing acceptable if proffered by a highbrow artist such as Isadora Duncan, but a number of practitioners of refined, high-status art dancing like Duncan embraced "Salomania" just as enthusiastically as their popular culture counterparts, perhaps because they too had been chided as indecent rebels. Moreover, these dancers, possessed of loftier artistic spirits, nonetheless appealed to audiences with a healthy dose of nudity and sexual suggestiveness. Ida Rubinstein, who prepared a Salome dance accompanied by a custom-written score courtesy of St. Petersburg Conservatory Director Alexander Glazunov, generated considerable buzz in Moscow by intimating that she would cast off all seven veils and "appear completely naked." Despite threats of closure by Russian authorities, the show went on in December 1908. Legendary Russian acting coach Konstantin Stanislavsky, who saw Rubinstein's Salome show in Paris the following year, inveighed against her act, saying, "I have never seen anyone more naked, and vapidly naked. How shameful! The music and ... staging of the Dance of the Seven Veils are very good. But she is without talent, and naked." But nudity did not bother Ida Rubinstein. Her bodily sensuality was central to her identity and she posed nude for a number of well-known artists.[152]

Despite occasional outcries in America, Salome dancers continued to draw huge crowds in vaudeville and inspired the greatest evidence of its success: parody. Ada Overton Walker, who had done a straightforward Salome dance for a while, was later thought to do the best burlesque of Salome, though Jessica Preston ran a close second. Julian Eltinge, the famous cross-dresser, would have pleased Oscar Wilde himself, by creating a popular Salome act.[153] Blackface comedian John Hymer composed a wryly hilarious and dead-on "coon song"—a bastardized white-culture abstraction of what were thought to be "authentic" African-American folk tunes—on the Salome phenomenon entitled "De Sloamey Dance." It went:

> If yo'se got a little act
> An' yo' can't git any time,
> Don't go an lay de blame
> On Mistah Rush or Sime [*Variety*'s critics].
> Tho' 'way yo' clothes—wear a smile,
> Read hist'ry an' den take a chance;
> Git a piece uv skeeter bar [mosquito netting]
> An' go do de Sloamey dance...
> I seed a lady do dat dance
> I was kinder disapp'inted,
> She didn't weah much clo'es at all
> An' she sho'ly wuz loose j'inted.
> Dey say its classic—I don't know,
> But from all that I can see
> Dat thing dey call de Sloamey dance
> Looks like old Hooch a kooch to me.[154]

Lubin, the motion picture producer, even committed a version of the Salome dance to film. It promised "in vivid scenes, the drunken feast given to the Senators by Herod" and, following the famed Dance of the Seven Veils, "the hurried entry of Salome's mother, throwing a leopard skin around her daughter." Exhibitors could pay $44 for the 400-foot reel.[155]

Even after the public craving for Salome dancers died down somewhat, performers experimented with untamed dances in form-revealing outfits that owed a clear debt to the Dance of the Seven Veils. In 1910, Adeline Boyer brought an act called "The Princess of Israel" to the vaudeville boards. The number, like the Salome, was set in a mythic-Biblical locale, specifically "the Royal Palace of King Solomon's brother" and contained dances with cymbals, daggers, and at least one seduction scene. The *New York Clipper* felt that Boyer's routine was "much on the order of the 'Salome' dances seen so much of late." During one dance, Boyer unwound a scarf that had been covering her figure, and in so doing, "disclosed herself in a costume that was scant, to say the least."[156]

Simone de Beryl and Emile Agoust drew on another well-known Bible story to create an act that featured enough disrobing and sinuous choreography to make it just as much at home on the burlesque hall stage as on vaudeville's. It was called "The Temptation of Adam and Eve," and was, in the words of *Variety*, as "near the naked truth of the Biblical incident as they dared follow it." De Beryl played Eve, the "few clothes woman." The man who played Adam may have managed his role a bit less deftly, appearing, according to the reviewer, "like an unshaven miner who had come up from the bowels of the earth in a fairy's outfit."[157] But as we have seen, men unclad in vaudeville were treated as sexual counterfeits, ciphers, or even as effeminate. It was the leered-at woman who could make herself all the more womanly by performing in little that would conceal her spectacle of bodily form.

Other performers discovered that titillating acts like these need not rely on Western religious myths. The performer "Princess Sita Diva" concocted an act called "The Diva Dasi" set in a "Hindu temple." Sita Diva, in the words of one critic, was "a shapely woman who had no compunction about showing her figure." Her act, some mélange of pantomime and burlesque turn, was branded "a first cousin of the gone-before Salome or coochee-coochee."[158] In addition to owing an obvious debt to the Salome-ers, Sita Diva also reprised an act by "Radha," who some years earlier had toured with a dance also set in a "Hindoo temple" in which she displayed "the nudity of the body between the skirts and bodice."[159] If the trappings of high art could permit an unusually liberal display of the female form (by the standards of the day), so too could a semblance of the exotic, the non-Western, and the anthropological.

Of all the Salome dancers, perhaps the best known—and certainly the one whose career withered most lamentably after the fad was over—was a woman who called herself "La Sylphe." Like many female vaudeville performers who relied on the sensual, a mysterious, European-sounding name lent her an air of refinement and legitimacy. La Sylphe was actually Edith Lambelle, born in New York City in 1882. The *Blue Book Magazine* reported that Lambelle/La Sylphe was "the first of the Salome sisterhood to arrive in New York," and that she initially danced with "limbs and feet bare" until the police ordered her to wear "tights at least." Eventually, she settled on a "transparent skirt and a small bodice" to ply her trade.[160]

In addition to showing a great deal of skin, La Sylphe put together an impressive stage setting of special effects and astounding visuals. In her act, according to one paper, "The rise of the curtain displays a scene of gloomy, ghostly interest in which passing clouds and lightening flashes spasmodically obscure the moon. In the midst of this elemental tumult Salome makes her appearance, a dejected, remorseful, desolate being come to an even more desolate spot to cast her self in a despairing effort of soul sacrifice at the feet of the monolith."[161] The "monolith" was a stage element called the "Monolith of the Dead Faiths" and seems to have been unique to La Sylphe's act. "Seldom has Broadway witnessed a more weird, wild, and ecstatic dance of abandonment [sic]," wrote the *New York Dramatic Mirror*.[162]

Still, the main appeal was La Sylphe's unclad body, on display up on the stage. "Public interest in the 'Salome' undressed dance has risen to a fever pitch," observed *Variety* after La Sylphe's appearance at Keith & Proctor's 125th Street theater.[163] La Sylphe (and her managers) never lost sight of this fact. It was hinted by the producers that La Sylphe's costume would dwindle as the week went on; the stratagem brought in people in "droves." The only unhappy personage may have been the beleaguered Keith & Proctor treasurer who was "as busy with the pasteboards as he ever had been during his life," according to the *New York Clipper* during La Sylphe's engagement at the Keith & Proctor house. Not surprisingly, La Sylphe flirted with touring the burlesque circuit, or wheel, following her United Booking Office engagement.[164]

Gertrude Hoffman, who is credited by some with having started the Salome craze, also put together an act that relied on scant clothing and untamed dance steps, which conflated modern dance and the burlesque hall. Her "Vision of Salome," which debuted in July 1908, caused a "mob" scene of "mid-summer madness," thanks in part to her "gauzy" shirt and "transparent black skirt." Hoffman's "dance full of abandon" climaxed in a moment wherein she flung her body to the floor and kissed the severed head of John the Baptist.[165] *Variety* called the dance number, which contained "a most perceptible wiggle" and "several corkscrews with her arms" little more than "dignified 'cooch.'"[166] Despite such scathing remarks, Hoffman's Salome was a decided success. The week of her Salome number proved the biggest ever for Hammerstein's box office.[167]

While others went on to copy Salome, Hoffman experimented with different exotic dances and further pushed the limits of acceptability. Her presentation of "Radha," a "Hindoo Temple dance," in 1909 featured Hoffman in filmy skirts writhing about on stage in a depiction of "the five senses."[168] A similar dance earned her arrest in New York for "violating a section of the penal code, which relates to an offense against public decency," according to the *New York Clipper*.[169] Hoffman was eventually released, but continued to present shows which got her in trouble with legal authorities. In 1911, she starred with a troupe of Imperial Russian dancers at the Winter Garden theater in a ballet based on the life of Cleopatra. Letters complaining of Hoffman's scanty dress as Cleopatra poured into the mayor's office.[170] A certain B. Ogden Chisolm of 66 Beaver Street wrote in a letter that Hoffman's Egyptian queen was not the high-class dance recital it purported to be but was instead simply "lewd and disgusting, with very little to redeem it." Chisolm urged the mayor to order the show cut or shut down entirely. Mayor William Gaynor, who had actually ruled in favor of motion picture interests some years earlier when anti-vice crusaders threatened to close the city's nickelodeons,[171] swayed with the political current. Gaynor wrote back to Chisolm, "I thank you for your letter.... There are certain people here who are doing all they can to degrade the public stage in this city. I am sufficiently assured that the play is disgusting."[172] Gaynor ordered the police to have a look at Hoffman and the Russian ballet and, perhaps because the managers of the ballet had reportedly toned it down, the police found "nothing indecent in the show as it is now being given."[173]

Still, Gaynor had a political career to think about, and those in charge of the performance were presented with a summons to appear in the West Side Court on charges that the Cleopatra dance given by Miss Hoffman and her dance troupe was "not proper for the stage." Legendary producer and dramatist David Belasco came to the hearing to testify on behalf of Morris Gest, Hoffman's manager-director, and J. F. Cass, manager of the Winter Garden. Belasco, perhaps concerned about the negative economic impact that censorship and show closings might eventually have on his own enterprises, tried to defend Hoffman by pointing out that standards of decency can change across cultures and historical periods. He also tried to frame the event as artistic and dignified rather than base and popular. Belasco held that "ever since the time of Christ we have had dancing in fleshings, and if they complain about this dance they will have to complain against every dance at the Metropolitan Opera House this coming season." Belasco equated scant dress with beauty, and pointed out that yet-more-scantily-clad dancers entertained royalty in Europe. If such artistry were good enough for monarchs across the Atlantic, surely it was fit for public consumption here.[174]

For their part, the Russians too expressed shock at the narrow-mindedness and ethno-cultural ignorance of the American authorities. They could not believe that in America they were regarded as "immoral" and "salacious." The Russians claimed they had been subjected to surveillance and harassment by local authorities, and felt that it was merely their status as social and political outsiders which led certain Americans to allege that they had somehow "degrade[d] the art which we love." They learned that art in "imperial schools at Moscow and St. Petersburg." If the Americans were so base, ill-educated, and xenophobic as to regard their imperially-authorized art as smut, then perhaps they would not return.[175] It was a threat that went over poorly. Their bluff having been called, Hoffman's Russian ballet never came back to New York.

Another vaudeville performer who followed closely in the footsteps of the Salome trend was Princess Rajah. Rajah combined scant attire with unconventional choreography and a display of bodily strength impressive enough to put her over with the crowd. The *Milwaukee News* reported that Rajah was a "black-eyed, dark-skinned beauty from the banks of the river Nile" whose movements on stage were "wild, barbaric, and graceful." The *Louisville Post* on the other hand saw Rajah's compendium of "wriggles and gyrations of the body" as no different "from those of the various Salomes."[176] *Variety* called Rajah's work a "'cooch' thing" characterized by a "seductive wiggle."[177] No wonder that several Midwestern cities, including Chicago and Pittsburgh, imposed a temporary ban on Salome and Salome-like dancers following Rajah's appearances in those cities.[178]

Rajah, whose dance numbers have been described by at least one recent scholar as having been "sexually expressive,"[179] not only offered burlesque-like dance fare, but added a circus element by bringing a live snake on stage for her climactic Cleopatra-and-the-asp number. The serpent, in fact a Mexican adder, was produced from a box, whereupon the dancer "fondles it as if it were a kitten," in the words of the *Toledo*

Blade. Rajah's efforts inspired imitators. "We must judge all snake dancers now by Princess Rajah," noted *Variety*.[180] The snake, a kind of phallic symbol and emblem of alleged female sin and seduction stretching back at least as far as biblical antiquity, must have pleased many a male theater patron immensely. Like other vaudeville performers, Rajah helped accomplish the form's delicate balancing act: she staked out new sexual territory for the female body while simultaneously permitting powerful businessmen to help dictate the commercial terms of that body.

In addition to the thrill of having a supposedly poisonous snake on stage, Rajah possessed remarkable physical strength which she showcased in her "sensuous muscle dance" in the words of the *New York Dramatic Mirror*.[181] After the snake bit, Rajah tacked on a turn in which she somehow grasped a chair "firmly in her teeth, holding it aloft while she is in a reclining position, and then rising and whirling about like a top, still gripping the chair in her teeth." The crowds at Hammerstein's loved it.[182] If Rajah's act, with its live snake and unorthodox use of a chair, seems like it fit better among the curios of a Barnumesque "museum" than on a vaudeville stage, then perhaps it once did: Rajah had been discovered by Willie Hammerstein as she performed at Huber's Dime Museum.[183]

Other performers capitalized on the appeal of exotic or seemingly non-Western dance numbers to provide the audience with a sexually provocative show. Chief among them was Millie De Leon. At Koster & Bial's vaudeville house, De Leon put on an "Oriental" dance "commonly designated by the expressive term 'coochee-coochee,'" according to the *New York Dramatic Mirror*. It is unclear just what was "Oriental" about her performance, but what is certain is that it consisted of gradually stripping off layers and elements of clothing. "At the end of it, Mlle. De Leon further borrowed Charmion's specialty by removing her garters and tossing them out to persons in the audience," reported the *Mirror*. But whereas Charmion had flung only one pair of garters, Millie De Leon upped the ante and deployed three pair. Not surprisingly, De Leon was eventually arrested for presenting a dance considered "indecent" at one New York venue.[184]

As the passage above from the *Mirror* indicates, Millie De Leon, like Rajah, Hoffman, and the slew of Salome dancers all owed a debt to Mlle. Charmion, who was among the first to bring burlesque elements to the vaudeville stage. Charmion, who pioneered the approach of using a European name and identity to push the limits of respectability, successfully posed herself as a sexual object in a production system that nonetheless billed itself as clean. In that regard, the vastly popular Eva Tanguay would also be indebted to Charmion.

Mlle. Laveria Charmion burst onto the vaudeville scene in the final years of the nineteenth century. She called herself "the Parisian Sensation" to add an air of exoticism to her persona, and to allow herself greater leeway in the presentation of sexually suggestive material. At the time of her death in 1936, the *New York Evening Post* reported that her legal name had been "Mrs. E. Marion Bird" and that she had been born about 1880.[185] By that time, Charmion had long since faded from the public eye. Her act was little more than an excuse for "the Parisian Sensation" to take her clothes off in a provocative manner on stage, aided by some flirtation with trapezes and other acrobatic measures.

Charmion's act flew in the face of Victorian values, and the performer drew ample criticism as a result. One critic found Charmion "vulgar" and felt that "it is certainly to be deplored that any part of the public demands acts of this kind." A critic at the *New York Clipper* felt similarly. He conceded that although Charmion was a clever performer, she was nonetheless "disgustingly suggestive." Somehow, Charmion avoided legal entanglements and turned up the heat at her show by flinging garters "one at a time" into the cheering crowd. It worked. Charmion was retained for an extended run at Koster & Bial's shortly thereafter. When she played New York several years later, her "disrobing act" won "frequent bursts of applause" from the enthusiastic crowd. In fact, around 1900, Charmion could more or less legitimately argue that she was "the greatest drawing card in existence."[186]

Like other female vaudeville performers who relied fundamentally on sexual appeal, Charmion made her body the site of parallel desires: consumerist for the women in the audience, sexual for the men, donning "an immensely stunning gown" at the beginning, which was then "removed by degrees," revealing beneath it "fearful and wonderful lingerie that, of course, passeth the understanding of mere man," in the words of one who caught her show.[187]

Charmion's sexualized display may have drawn rebuke, but it was also a powerful tool. It excited many even as it disgusted some (and these two groups undoubtedly overlapped in places); it became a purchasable commodity while it suggested the purchase of other consumer goods like gowns and lingerie. The seeds of fetishism Charmion planted grew healthily as Victorian society and its restrictive mores loosened. By the time of her 1909–10 tour, critics and observers took her act in stride, rather than viewing it as a disruptive force, gently lauding her generous "display of her curves." [188] And the *New York Clipper*, which had found her "disgustingly suggestive" a decade earlier, also had a few nice things to say, finding Charmion "decidedly fair of form and feature," and able to execute what the paper considered to be impressive feats of physical strength and coordination. Still, the paper noted, it was her disrobing that seemed most to "enhance her value as a vaudeville attraction." As further evidence of cultural legitimacy, Charmion had also graduated to playing Keith-owned and UBO-booked theaters.[189]

Charmion's body, like that of other female vaudevillians, was itself the subject of intense interest even off the stage, becoming an early-twentieth-century example of the ideal for women to emulate and men to possess. An article called "Ladies How Does Your Figure Correspond with the Measurements of Charmion" ran in the *Denver Post* in 1904. The piece listed Charmion's every measurement in obsessive detail: Height, 5'1"; weight, 125 lbs.; length of face, 7½"; wrist, 6½"; calf 14"; figure, 36–22–36. The article noted that she was "admired by all men and most women for her beautiful form and generally considered the most perfect type of physical culture in women." Though Charmion was perhaps "perfect," her athletic body also posed vexing questions for a society accustomed to repletion in its women. "[H]er arms, … when she performs any feat of unusual strength, show the muscles of a Sandow, rather than the lovely curves one likes to see in a woman's arm," wrote the *Denver Post*. Charmion's muscular build, necessary for her stage antics, rendered her neck and shoulders decidedly unwomanly according to what some understood to be the dictates of the day, while "violent and severe exercise" had resulted in shoulder blades that stood out "like knobs." The paper provided a copy of Charmion's diet, suggesting the "perfect" body lay within reach of any woman inclined to make the effort. For breakfast, some grain mush and milk, plus fruit. No pastry or coffee. No intoxicants of any kind. For dinner, soup, steak or roast beef, and vegetables. A cold bath every morning completed the regimen.[190] Charmion liked to suggest that her physical allure was the result of a temperate and modest life. "Any woman—almost any, at least—could be as I am if she would stop eating pudding and pie, exercise on the trapeze and dine twice a day," she told the Des Moines Register. She never smoked or drank, she said, and posited that when a performer injured or killed himself, the fault could nearly always be laid on "the way he has been living."[191] Thus, Charmion whose act was decidedly unwholesome, flaunted an air of wholesomeness about her persona nonetheless. Her figure was within reach, she argued, and therefore ordinary women might be expected to have "perfect" figures as well. Throughout her career, Charmion rarely failed to please.

Charmion's act relied in small measure on the use of sumptuous gowns and in large measure on the use of a sumptuous figure. Valeska Suratt, another perennial favorite in vaudeville, reversed this formula to great effect. She displayed her body and often crossed the fine line between acceptability and censure. But perhaps more than any other single performer, she made herself an icon of fashion and personal adornment. From her early days on the vaudeville stage, Suratt created an act in which sex appeal and fashion fetishism were inextricably bound. When her "snake dance," a number not unlike Princess Rajah's, played Hammerstein's in 1908, *Variety* wondered which was the more alluring, the snake or the clingy gown, for one showed "as many curves as the other."[192] Suratt also devised a sketch called "Hip, Hip, Hurrah" in which she played a character called the "Queen of Fashion." *Vogue* magazine took notice and described her gowns in almost lurid detail, treating her raiment as others had treated Charmion's or Annette Kellerman's "perfect" bodies: considered in its most infinitesimal elements, like an explorer's cartography of exotic wilds. The fashion magazine called Suratt "one of the best dressed women of the stage." *Vogue*'s editors were clearly wowed by her garb which consisted of an "unlined smoke gray silk Brussels net worn over an evening gown of dull rose satin." The effect was classy, yet obviously seductive, the Asian-style attire being "loose, yet revealing the lines of the figure." The sleeves were long and possessed of soft lines, silk appliqué, hand-painted detail, and embroidered in "soft tones of old rose, pinkish heliotrope, and dull mauve." Gold thread trim completed the effect.[193] The *Vogue* article, which described a number of other Suratt gowns in equally obsessive detail, recalls the text of the brochure describing every refined and luxurious nuance of Keith's New Theatre in Boston. Like *Vogue*, Suratt was trying to appeal to an audience of modest means who aspired to greater wealth and were increasingly mobilized as consumers in a market society.

Suratt brought images of finery to a new level in 1913 with a fantasy sketch in which she played a damsel who is "found chained to woe" and, at last, "awakened by Love who takes her from crepe to diamonds."[194] It is interesting that in Suratt's allegorical playlet, Love is useful in as much as he leads her to the heights of fashion and luxury. According to one news report, Suratt wore $20,000 worth of jewelry, clothing, and accessories. The audience was "amazed" at the "silk scenery" she worn on her person in the form of her own fashion creations.[195] Journalist Alan Dale (who also wrote for *Cosmopolitan*) described Suratt as a "riot of clothes" and stated that her routine demonstrated "how to crowd five acts full of clothes into a twenty minutes' sketch!"[196]

But Suratt was no mere mannequin. She was also adept at weaving sexuality with fashion, the body exposed with the body adorned. In her 1909 musical-comedy act "The Belle of the Boulevards," Suratt wore her usual striking gowns, but they were constructed so as to leave generous expanses of her bare back exposed for all to see. "So much 'back' to be seen all at once has never presented itself before in vaudeville," wrote Sime Silverman of *Variety*.[197] The show, in which Suratt played the title character, "a profligate Parisian chum of a degenerate spendthrift who puts modish gowns and brilliant gems on her, while she in return inducts him into the reckless life of Paris," drew the censure of the police in some parts of the United States.[198] By conflating material desire with sexual desire, Suratt was in some ways anticipating techniques that would later become commonplace in mass-market advertising.

Suratt pushed the sexual envelope in other ways as well. Her sketch "The Girl with the Whooping Cough" was shut down by New York's Mayor Gaynor in 1910 because he had found it "salacious." Gaynor had been informed ahead of time that Suratt's show might be sexually suggestive, so he obtained a copy of the script, but found nothing especially troublesome in it. Undaunted, the mayor sent one of his stenographers to the theater to transcribe the act as it occurred on stage, believing perhaps he had seen a bowdlerized version of the playscript. The resulting document revealed that "the lines which had been complained of were due mostly to 'gagging' that is [how] the players interpolated them." On this basis, the mayor of New York shut down the show, though he never actually saw it.[199] Suratt fared equally poorly in other cities. The *Philadelphia Times* called "The Girl with the Whooping Cough" "coarse" and "vulgar." "It was a performance which no self-respecting person would care to see," argued the paper.[200]

For Suratt, though, fashion was useful in as much as it helped create that most desired and yet elusive good in mass-market culture: personal style. In an article called "Personality—That's Me," which she wrote for *Green Book Magazine* in 1915, Suratt outlined her philosophy. "It's my personality that wins for me. I'm no singer. Heaps of people can beat me dancing. Precious few of them, though, get the salary I do. Why? Because I'm *me!*" Suratt said that she never copied or took inspiration in any form from others, especially other performers. Her clothing, her hairstyle, her adornment, which she reckoned others would not dare copy, were uniquely attention-grabbing not so much on their own merits, but because they were mere outward manifestations of Suratt's inner specialness, her *me*-ness. She decried "the great majority of women who never go beyond the style in choosing their gowns," and she even claimed that she had once capriciously torn the neck off a dress to alter its appearance, an act of fashion transgression that marked her "emancipation from the bondage of style."[201]

In a sense, Suratt was expressing, and trying to deal with, the fundamental paradox of an emergent mass-market culture: the art of retaining one's individuality through the consumption of mass-produced goods. For Suratt, and for so many others (notably Eva Tanguay), the answer lay in the evanescent notion of personal "style." She performed the role of one who had resolved the paradox by making a personal

Valeska Suratt was popular in vaudeville as much for her sleek figure as for her unusual and distinctive stage fashions. (Billy Rose Theatre Collection, The New York Public Library for the Performing Arts, Astor, Lenox, and Tilden Foundations.)

imprint on goods that would otherwise cloak her in factory-produced anonymity. Though her approach may have had its problems, Suratt was acutely aware of a truth that individuals in her era and onward had increasingly to recognize: that consumer goods and their contribution to personal style were the primary tools people had at their disposal to navigate a complex social world. "Where images and things had once connoted one's place within an immutable network of social relations, they were now emerging as a form of social currency in an increasingly mobile commercial world," notes a cultural historian of the period.[202]

Men were rare in disrobing or sexually suggestive acts, because the commodified sexuality of the vaudeville stage, as in many other areas of an emerging commercial culture, was inscribed on the object of woman. Like the posing and artist's studio acts, a vaudeville routine that offered up a woman for the (presumably male) voyeur's gazing pleasure had a good chance at success. Consider the work of Charlotte Wiehe, who specialized in creating "mimodramas," a pastiche of drama, dance, and pantomime. Her most well-known mimodrama was "La Main," in which Wiehe, known for her pretty face and impressive figure, played a dancer named Vivette who, having rejected her too-forward date earlier in the evening, was now taking off her clothing as she prepared for bed. But as Vivette progressed toward nudity, a burglar lurked in her room, initially unbeknownst to the dancer. "He cannot refrain from watching her—who could?" wondered the *New York Times*. Partway through her denuding, Vivette catches a glimpse of the burglar holding some curtains apart that would otherwise have obscured his gaze. She continued undressing nonetheless.[203] Here was a woman who set her own rules, or so it would seem. Wiehe improved upon the voyeuristic-gaze scenario by creating a piece that was itself centered around a voyeuristic gaze. In other words, spectators looked at another spectator looking, thus authorizing the primary, spectatorial act of looking.

Men who wanted to participate in the performance of sexually suggestive vaudeville acts had often to team up with a woman. Such was the case with Bert French, who created some of vaudeville's most popular, and sexually titillating, numbers with his partner Alice Eis. French and Eis gained notoriety in big-time vaudeville around 1909 with a creation called "The Vampire Dance," which was loosely based on Rudyard Kipling's poem, "The Vampire."[204] The number dealt with a Parisian prostitute and her feminine wiles, but was really an excuse to have Eis cavort about the stage in various degrees of undress, striking seductive poses. The *New York Dramatic Mirror* assailed Keith's United Booking Office and argued that to call it a legitimate dance piece would be to perpetrate "a libel against the name of art." *Variety* reckoned that "The Vampire Dance" featured "a degree of vivid detail that is almost medical." What is certain is that Eis wore "a tight-fitting dress" with "a skirt slashed almost to the waist," and little underneath save for a thin film of flesh-colored silk, giving the appearance of nudity. Moral critiques did not impede and may in fact have helped "The Vampire Dance" in its path to major success, drawing capacity houses even in the heat of summer and earning "vociferous applause."[205]

In 1913, Eis and French concocted an act called "Le Rouge et Noir," an allegorical dance routine with Eis similarly dressed in a fancy corsage, a high-slitted skirt, "and very little else." After playing for a remarkably long stint in those days, six weeks, they were arrested on obscenity charges. Later that year, the Kalem studio shot Eis and French for motion picture audiences.[206]

Perhaps chastened by their run-in with the authorities, Eis and French developed a new number in which costumes were neither revealing nor shed. "It's funny to see the French-Eis people all dressed upon the stage" mused *Variety*'s Sime Silverman of "The Lure of the North."[207] But not long thereafter, the two were up to their old tricks. In "The Dance of Fortune," Eis romped about the stage "clad in scarcely more opaque raiment than adorned Mother Eve before the fall," according to one present at the show. The two were summarily arrested. Their lawyer, Arthur Hamm, defended it as "a work of art."[208] In doing so, he was merely following the pattern established by others who sought to bring sexually provocative material to vaudeville while avoiding social or governmental censure. If a naked body or a suggestive dance could be placed in the category of "art," it was no longer within the purview of the appetitive and threatening mob. "Art" could be controlled, delimited, defined, and disseminated by culture's elites. But mere entertainment obeyed only the strictures of the marketplace—and therein lay its power and its danger.

When men appeared by themselves in states of undress they were rarely defended as engaging in "artistic" creations, like many of their female counterparts. Rather, they were presented as examples of athletic accomplishment. They were promoted solely on their strength, musculature, and physical prowess—if not, curiously though predictably, their masculinity—divorced from any hint of sexual allure. When Max Unger appeared at Koster & Bial's in 1900 he lifted men on bicycles and permitted a board holding eight people to see-saw across his "massive chest," earning him the descriptor, a "magnificent specimen of physical development."[209] Indeed, undressed men in vaudeville, be they weight lifters or oarsmen, were almost seen as a distant relation of the freak act, or perhaps something fit for the scientist's lab—but never the bedroom.

Eugene Sandow, the muscle-builder and strongman, was perhaps the best known of the men who appeared solo and nearly naked on the vaudeville stage. Clad in a toga (which was presently discarded), Sandow offered "displays of the apparently superhuman power that is his" in 1902 at Keith's Union Square Theatre. One critic observed that Sandow's acts of exhibition, if done by a female performer, might be "promptly suppressed." Clearly, Sandow was not meant to be perceived as overtly sexual, even though a great many women, and certainly a few of the men, in the house must have appreciated the scantily clad muscle man in just such a way. "Sandow's attire, or rather the scarcity of it, suggests that he might do well to give out, besides his dissertations on how to develop the physique, a few friendly tips on how not to develop pneumonia," wrote the *New York Dramatic Mirror*.[210] But Sandow was seen as an oddity—an impressive oddity, to be sure—but an oddity nonetheless. Unlike Charmion or Annette Kellerman, men were not expected to try to emulate Sandow, but rather to observe him from afar and offer up droll commentary. This despite the fact that he was, quite literally, put up on a pedestal during subsequent tours.[211]

Even when unclad men offered themselves up as works of art, they were rarely objectified sexually in the same way that their female peers were. Treloar, a former star of Harvard's varsity crew team, executed various poses at Keith's Union Square in a giant frame "in which his really superb muscular development was shown to great advantage." But despite this objectifying motif, the ex-Harvard man was described as an "exponent of modern physical culture" rather than a sexually alluring body who might draw censure. Similarly, Francis Gerard put on a muscle show while enclosed in "a cabinet brightly illuminated." The audience ooh'd and aah'd, but for Gerard's athleticism and posing skill, his impressive "physique," rather than for his near-nakedness—or so felt one observer at the time. Unclad men in vaudeville offered up their "physique" for public inspection, a non-sexual, physiologic entity, while women put their "figure" on display, an item tied closely to their erotic allure and sexual objectification. Only Jimmy Britt was called "the handsomest fighter in tights," which was the mildest of appellations.[212]

Almost-nude men could also be viewed with impunity if they were non-white or non-Western. As in so many other locales within the weave of turn-of-the-century culture, the non-white or non-Western body was emptied of its potential for sexuality by dominant culture onlookers. To do otherwise would be to risk the threatening anxiety that accompanied viewing the "other" as fully human and, therefore, a potential sexual rival. Toon and Moung Thit, "two Burmese jugglers," appeared in 1899 "in nature's habiliments save for a breech cloth and tattooing on their nether limbs." No objection was made to their nudity.[213] Indeed, the Burmese performers must have offered a kind of colonial or anthropological pleasure for Western audiences. After Fatma and Smaun, billed variously as "Burmese Midgets" and "Indian Pygmies," put on a show consisting of acrobatics and slapstick comedy, their manager took them through the audience where spectators could wrinkle their brows and gaze closely upon their perceived bodily strangeness. "They are very small people and they scored largely for their diminutive proportions," noted one present at the show.[214] Even more than the undressed male physique, the non-Western body constituted a site of fascination like that of the freak act. And like the unclad female body, it could be posed as well as an object of consumption.

The right sort of naked body on the vaudeville stage—white, female, well-proportioned—provided erotic pleasure. But it also permitted a kind of temporary escape from the exigencies of marriage and family life. By gazing at a disrobed woman other than his wife, a man might experience the artificial thrill of sexual adventure or infidelity. Nude-seeming acts were not the only routines that provided this kind of excitement. A vast number of vaudeville sketches centered around cheating husbands, jealous wives, cases of mistaken identity involving spouses, and comic turns that mercilessly lampooned the institution of marriage, seeking, presumably, to provide similar pleasures (for many men).

One species of sketch featured men fantasizing about past loves, who appeared conveniently on stage as they sprung to mind. In "A Dream of Fair Women," following a fight with his wife, a man sleeps while "his former loves pass in review." In "All in the Family," a young man, in bed with an illness "and rather delirious, falls asleep and imagines he is visited by four or five different women, each claiming to be his wife."[215] Both pieces envision marriage as a fluid and voluntary state, and the male as never fully possessed by the woman. A sketch from 1901 called "The Bridegroom's Reverie" is perhaps the best example of such an entertainment. In it, a bachelor retires to his den shortly before his wedding day to "smoke his last cigar as a bachelor." A picture frame then reveals to the audience what he is daydreaming about: "a succession of comely girls," all former sweethearts of the groom-to-be, variously posing, singing, dancing, and playing musical instruments. After a most pleasant reverie, the bachelor eventually realizes that the girl he is to marry is "the best ever."[216] Sketches like these nearly always pretended to redeem the notion of marriage and typically ended with an estranged couple happily embracing one another, any misunderstandings felicitously cleared up. But they did so more to avoid criticism, and to present fantasies of infidelity within a framework of acceptability, than to proffer a moral lesson. "The Bridegroom's Reverie" in particular combined several elements that must have appealed to men in the audience at the time: women as objects of visual beauty, fantasies of bachelorhood and all that it could seem to entail, and the man as able to call forth at will an abundance of attractive females.

A similar sketch, which also incorporated the oft-used trope of the jealous wife (as if to paint all wives as burdensome nags) was called, appropriately enough, "My Wife Won't Let Me." It centered around "a hen-pecked husband ... brow beaten by a jealous wife," who ends up giving refuge to a female acrobat clad in little more than a few tights, proper for the stage perhaps but questionable in the private chambers of a married man. The wife, naturally, finds her husband with the tantalizingly exposed acrobat and the comical crisis comes to a head until it is resolved.[217] But the appeal of this sketch was based on the fact that a scantily-clad woman ends up in the private quarters of a hen-pecked man. That is, she invades the very space marked by marital tyranny—in a "risqué" outfit designed to elicit "shock," in the words of one present at the performance of "My Wife Won't Let Me."[218] Her uncensored sexuality acts as a challenge to that burdensome restriction.

Sketches like these delighted in showing women disrobing in private quarters, especially when such women were around men other than their husbands. In "The Order of the Bath," two strangers at a boarding house, a military captain and a young woman "in her petticoat," end up locked in the bathroom together ready to take a bath, while the sketch "A Duplicate Husband" featured a robber who inadvertently sneaks into his brother's apartment whereupon the woman of the house, taking the robber for her husband, "calls upon him to unfasten some mysterious nether garment." In "Bob Rackett's Pajamas," a young man and a woman are accidentally assigned the same hotel room. The woman, arriving while the man is in the bathroom, puts on his pajamas and pretends to be a man. Upon seeing her dressed up as such, he threatens to "remove her pajamas by force." She confesses and it turns out the two are estranged sweethearts who reconcile with one another at the end of the sketch.[219] In this piece, some male spectators may have derived pleasure from the androgynous sexuality of the woman-in-man's-clothes and the prospect of her being made to disrobe in his private chamber.

While strange women disrobing provided one kind of fantasy scenario, this was not the only vice associated with freedom from the married state. Smoking, drinking, poker-playing, and similar diversions were also presented as guilty pleasures in which most married men were presumably no longer permitted to indulge. In "How to Get Rid of Your Mother-in-Law," which played Keith's Union Square in 1901, a man named Dr. Rich "makes violent love to [an] old lady," only to have the doctor's wife catch them "embracing [and] mamma smoking and drinking with" her philandering husband.[220] Similarly, in "Dangerfield '95," Madge Primrose is engaged to Jack Dangerfield, of Harvard's class of 1895. Primrose is shocked to learn that her Ivy Leaguer fiancé is "in the habit of gambling and drinking, and has other vices common to the rich men's sons contingent in every college." To foil him, she plays at indulging herself in these vices as well, and the two end up "wrapped in each other's arms."[221]

Though wives and fiancées typically ended up reconciled with their men at the end of a sketch, such was not *always* the case. In "Who's Safe," a sketch from 1898, a jealous wife who suspects her husband has been carrying on with his typist disguises herself as "an Irish scrubwoman, and, in this way, manages to watch the billing and cooing of her husband and his fair clerk at close range." The disguised wife eventually beats up the typist and demands a divorce and alimony from her cheating husband.[222]

Monologists'—that is, stand-up comics'—jokes at the expense of marriage were ubiquitous on the vaudeville stage. A famous vaudeville couplet held, "Marriage is an institution. So is a lunatic asylum." Another comic monologist once quipped, "I believe every man should take a wife, but be careful whose wife you take," and "None of my folks attended the wedding; they said they wanted to remember me as I was in life."[223] Routines like these made marriage a perpetual scapegoat and object of insult; they implied that marriage was an unpleasantness to which most men eventually surrendered. For many men in the audience, routines like these must have been empowering—reaffirming and justifying fantasies of independence and irresponsibility. Surely, they served this function for women vaudeville-goers too, though they may have been more modest in the outward manifestation of their delight.

Depictions of vice also held a certain appeal for vaudeville spectators, both male and female, because they too provided a kind of voyeuristic escape from the strictures of respectable middle-class life. Acts set in opium dens, brothels, and athwart society's sundry margins facilitated a theatrical version of slumming. Consider a musical sketch called "The Smoke Queen" from 1913, which was set amid the innards of "a Chinese hop-joint" and featured the title character singing "in a delicious soprano that made us all yearn for one of those 'pills.'"[224] A variant on this type of act had "a poor, half-dead 'dope' fiend of a girl" brought into a district attorney's office. The lawyer dangles some "koke" before the strung-out woman in order to ascertain the whereabouts of a missing boy. In a touch straight out of melodrama, the investigating attorney discovers the doped-up girl to be his long-lost sister-in-law and agrees to let her go without pressing charges.[225]

Though skits like these could be used to convey the evils of drugs on one level, at another they provided a highly contrived glimpse of the city's seamy though fascinating underbelly. Accordingly, vaudeville performers developed numerous variations on the genre. Singer Gladys Vance developed an act in which she sang a tune that she claimed had been penned by a "reformed dope fiend." In it, she held forth on the drug's insidious effects, and counterbalanced them by "raving" about the goodness of motherhood and home life. A milder permutation featured impressionist C. W. Littlefield imitating a boy puffing on his very first cigar," a routine that at least one observer found to be unfit for a theater "frequented by refined people." Still, as has been noted in an earlier chapter, respected and respectable stage impresario Tony Pastor invited Littlefield back a few months later to reprise the impression.[226]

Acts which claimed to provide a view of slum life were similarly popular with vaudeville audiences. "A Romance of the Underworld," a "playlet" by Paul Armstrong which came to Keith & Proctor theaters in 1911, was a substantial hit and saw its run extended on at least one occasion. "Underworld" succeeded, in large measure, because it drew aside the "curtain" that normally shielded the respectable middle class from the seedy "slum characters" of the streets. It appealed to theater patrons because it traded on what one theater critic felt was the bourgeoisie's "strange fascination about the criminal types." Vaudevillians Aurelio Coccia and Mlle. Amato devised a pantomime along similar lines, but possessed of an international flair, called "A Night in the Slums of Paris" featuring Amato in a wild "apache" dance—so-called "apache" (pronounced "uh-POSH") routines being closely associated with certain African-American performers whose supposedly relaxed morality made them objects of safe fascination for middle-class white audiences.[227] In an urban world with increasingly defined economic and cultural boundaries, acts which purported to open a window onto life on the other side, however artificial, must have been thrilling.

The vast majority of acts depicting drug use, slum life, and the like were not chiefly meant to confer moral messages, but a few were. On occasion, vaudeville managers and producers would offer up turns with a distinct progressive or reformist philosophy. Usually, this was done for the public relations value, because routines like these were not consistently popular with vaudeville audiences. Every once in a while, someone would suggest that vaudeville was a good venue for moral instruction. "The good theater is a good physician that works wondrous cures, without the taste of bad medicine," argued J. J. Sullivan, Cleveland's district attorney. In his view, "clean, pure vaudeville" could function as "the brilliant spark that flashes light into the shadows of the soul and sings sweet songs to the soul that needs rest."[228] But most onlookers knew better than to make such statements—or at least believe them.

Short plays and skits inveighing against excess, particularly drugs and alcohol, appeared in vaudeville from time to time. A sketch at Keith's Union Square from 1903 dealt with a rural couple who move to the city, whereupon the man begins dreaming of extravagant wealth and narcotics. But, to be sure, he comes to his senses upon waking up and decides to go home to his wife. Presentations like these that cast city life in a bad light were destined for scant success in vaudeville, the quintessential form of urban mass entertainment at the turn of the century. Others enacted the perils and pitfalls of drink. "A Daughter of Bacchus," which one critic described as "an eloquent temperance lesson as well" as being funny and entertaining, showed a woman who renounces the bottle and subsequently patches up her ailing family relationships.[229]

Legendary temperance activist Carrie Nation also saw in vaudeville the potential for moral instruction. When an actress at a theater in Butler, Tennessee, sipped a glass of iced tea meant to look like liquor, Nation, believing the prop to be in fact the genuine article, stormed onstage and smashed the bottle. "You can't make this little girl do any drinking when Carrie is around!" she announced to a dumbfounded audience. The crowd failed to applaud.[230]

Vaudeville sketches occasionally tried to teach the lesson that doing charity work was one's duty, especially if one was a child of privilege. In "The Awakening," an allegorical skit that went on at the Palace in 1915, the character "Miss Millionaire" learns from her fiancé, Kirk Fairplay, that the workers in her father's factory are starving and underpaid. Presently, she goes to sleep whereupon she succumbs to a prophetic dream in which she is startled by such personifications of degradation as "Miss Starvation, Mr. Crime, Miss Redlight" and other characters that look like the latter-day relatives of medieval morality drama personages. Miss Millionaire awakens enlightened, and determines to undertake settlement work. The cultural onus to do charity was strong in the Progressive Era (and thereafter), but not if it meant disturbing more deeply held hegemonic beliefs. A "comedietta" entitled "For Reform," which played Keith's Union Square in 1899, offered a valuable, if diverting, lesson to wives who "think they are doing noble work by neglecting their homes for fashionable charity work", in the words of one critic. Another morality lesson in vaudeville was called "Hanged," a "sensational sketch" that simulated a hanging and inveighed against capital punishment.[231]

Finally, some suffragists tried to use the vaudeville stage as pulpit to preach equal rights for the sexes. Singer and violinist Jeanette Lowrie used her act to deliver a veritable "dissertation" on women's rights featuring musical numbers with names like "I Want to Vote" and "I Guess I'll Please Myself." Hammerstein's even announced "Woman's Suffrage Week" in 1912, inviting suffragists to come watch sketches and songs on the topic of women's right to vote. Unfortunately, the mere presence of suffragists "drove away the regulars" and the experiment was not repeated. Though Keith and Albee were never outspoken on the suffrage issue, they too saw in it the potential to increase box office revenues, and in 1913 they banned "jokes at the expense of suffragists, even the militants," according to the *New York Times*.[232]

In general, though, acts that tried to teach moral lessons or hold forth on reformist issues were rare in vaudeville. Even sketches and short plays that ended with a couple in a happy embrace were hardly arguments for the sanctity of marriage. Endings like these, as has been suggested, were really just palliatives tacked on to titillating sketches about cheating, jealousy, and promiscuity. If the good name of marriage was marred by such acts, it was further bad-mouthed by numerous comics whose acerbic jokes blamed on the married state all of malekind's, and many of femalekind's, daily woes. In any case, acts with any kind of message, good or bad, never gained the popularity of acts featuring women in scanty outfits, suggestive dance numbers, or, preferably, some combination thereof. As the businessmen who controlled vaudeville were beginning to discover, the sexualized female body was a valuable, if somehow reproducible, commodity. Accordingly, they made plenty of time for Salome dancers and other women willing to put their "perfect" bodies on display. In so doing, they were effecting a brilliant balancing act. On the one hand, they were helping to liberalize (a certain kind of) public acceptance of the female body; on the other, though, they were gaining control over the female form as a commercial entity. To some extent, women throughout the twentieth century would try to recover control of their bodies from the patriarchal forces that claimed ownership of them around the turn of the century.

four

Wild Woman
Eva Tanguay as Temptress and Sexual Rebel

Amid the "cooch" dancers, stripping Salomes, and vaudevillized burlesquers who pleased crowds and pushed the envelope, there was one performer in particular who, perhaps more than any other, both reaped the benefits of the liberalization/objectification of the body and, at the same time, helped further pave the way for a certain kind of sexualized expression in American popular entertainments. In a sense, this performer may be seen as both the product of a system bent on selling sexualized femininity and as a challenge to existing mores pertaining to female behavior both onstage and off. Looking at this woman's life, also both onstage and off, provides a fascinating case study on sexuality and the vaudeville stage at the turn of the century. We turn, therefore, to the life and work of Eva Tanguay, who, despite her popularity, somehow yet remains an elusive personage in the historical writing on American popular culture. We shall see that there may have been reasons for this exclusion.

By most accounts, Eva Tanguay (pronounced "TANG-way") was vaudeville's biggest star and highest earner. She was "the greatest attraction and biggest moneymaker" in the world of big-time vaudeville, according to one account.[1] Vaudevillian-turned-author Joe Laurie, Jr., opined that Tanguay, more than any other performer, "represented the true spirit of vaudeville."[2] The famed performer Sophie Tucker dubbed Tanguay "the biggest attraction in vaudeville, barring none," and certainly the most famous and highly publicized. According to Tucker, Tanguay made up to $5,000 per week at the height of her career.[3]

Tanguay's birthplace was Marbleton, Quebec, Canada. An atlas published in 1922 has Marbleton as a "post-village" north/northeast of the town of Sherbrooke, Quebec. Population: 600. But the hometown of this one-time superstar, some 30 miles from the Maine border, fails to show up on some more recent maps and atlases that claim to be comprehensive, listing innumerable hamlets and villages in such far-flung locales as Kazakhstan, Chad, and Cambodia.[4]

In 1935, Tanguay, her health failing and her stage career a distant memory, opened a costume shop at 6027 Hollywood Boulevard in Los Angeles. But the store, whose main attraction consisted in many of the outlandish and innovative costumes Tanguay herself had designed and worn onstage, no longer exists.[5] In fact, a survey of the block reveals that not only is Tanguay's shop, in any iteration, extinct, but the very address—6027 Hollywood Boulevard—is not extant either, the lot having since been rezoned to accommodate several small businesses and offices.

It is as if the life of Eva Tanguay, who defined the most popular form of mass entertainment in her day, has been erased from the artifacts of cultural memory. Her hometown is obscure, and the site of her shop is nowhere to be found, suggesting the notion, if not the actual fact, of erasure. This notion, erasure, serves as a meaningful term for understanding the life, work, and influence of Eva Tanguay. As we will see, Tanguay was both a product of her era, and yet one who defied mores and traditions, especially in regard to emergent notions of womanhood and women's sexuality. Perhaps because of her historical specificity, and her simultaneous resistance to conventional categorization, she has been somehow forgotten.[6]

Writings about Tanguay, despite her erstwhile popularity, are hard to come by. Though she long spoke of authoring an autobiography, which she planned to call *Up and Down the Ladder*, no such work exists.[7] Nor is there a biography of the actress (as of 2003 at least), though many exist for other vaudeville stars and stage performers who were her contemporaries. In 1943 Tanguay claimed she gave source materials for a biography to writer and sometime radio personality Elza Schallert, who was married to *Los Angeles Times* drama critic Edwin Schallert. No book was ever produced, and Tanguay initiated legal proceedings for the return of her materials or a payment of $75,000. In the suit, filed in Los Angeles County Superior Court, Tanguay alleged she had surrendered to Elza Schallert materials suitable not only for a biographical book but suitable as well for "adaptation for a stage, screen or radio story." Tanguay claimed Schallert had held the materials since mid-January of that year. But Tanguay was either fabricating the incident or lacked the evidence to make her argument tenable. A peeved judge dismissed the case, "with prejudice as to all defendants," on October 14, 1943.[8]

Until the end, Eva Tanguay longed for an extended written documentation of her life and work. In the bungalow at 6207 Lexington Avenue (in Los Angeles, the street number a curious anagram of the street address of her failed costume shop) where she finally died, she plastered old "age-yellowed photos" of herself on the walls. One visitor, probably quite accurately, suggested that this collage-like display of pictures, many of which were publicity shots, permitted Tanguay to relive "the fading glory of her illustrious career."[9] In this regard, Tanguay's life might as well have informed the tale of fading starlet Norma Desmond in the film *Sunset Boulevard*, which was to be released several years later.

The closest Eva Tanguay came to seeing a book written about her was a series of articles which appeared in the Hearst papers' magazine supplement the *American Weekly*. Starting in the last week of 1946 and running for five consecutive weeks, the series, entitled "I Don't Care," after Tanguay's trademark musical number, told her life story allegedly from her own pen (though almost surely ghost-written, given Tanguay's bedridden state[10]). The series, accompanied by lavish illustrations of an

Eva Tanguay, vaudeville's biggest star. (Billy Rose Theatre Collection, The New York Public Library for the Performing Arts, Astor, Lenox, and Tilden Foundations.)

idealized Eva clad in revealing outfits, in fact revealed little about her own personal and professional history. Rather, it contained many sad, if sometimes whimsical, reminiscences about life, her career, and several of her ill-fated romances. "I have been lying on a sickbed in California for the last six years and the legs that carried me around the footlights of the world won't carry me any more. Of all the millions who paid all the millions of dollars to see me, few people come to see me any more," went the woeful tale, sounding like the preface to a self-penned eulogy—which in fact it might as well have been.[11] As if to mark her complete erasure from the zeitgeist, Eva Tanguay did not live to see the end of the serialized *American Weekly* autobiographical series in newsprint: she passed away on January 11, 1947, the cause of death either a heart attack or a stroke—or both—depending on which report one reads. Her death rated lengthy obituaries in several of the major New York and Los Angeles papers, but only brief mentions in *Time* and *Newsweek*.[12]

Ironically, though, perhaps the greatest act of biographical erasure was the production of a 1953 biopic about Tanguay entitled *The I Don't Care Girl* produced by Twentieth Century–Fox. The film not only invented numerous "facts" about Eva Tanguay's life, and indeed centered the narrative around relationships she never had, it altogether sanitized and bowdlerized a performance style that had been marked by what has been described as a "brazen and electric" sexual suggestiveness.[13] Moreover, though much of the film is supposedly set in the first decades of the twentieth century, when Tanguay rose to fame and fortune, the costumes, sets, dance numbers, and mise-en-scène fairly shout a late-1940s, jazz-inflected modernism. *The I Don't Care Girl*, which starred Mitzi Gaynor in the title role, was not even reviewed in the *New York Times* and seems to have barely limped at the box office. Anthony Slide, in *The Encyclopedia of Vaudeville*, calls the picture simply "dismal."[14] The Library of Congress retains a copy of the movie, which can be viewed by appointment, but it seems safe to assume that *The I Don't Care Girl* will never be released on video or DVD.

In order to understand why the movie erased and rewrote the actual life and particular qualities of Eva Tanguay, it is necessary first to understand how the narrative went about recounting the life of the onetime vaudeville superstar. The movie (in striking Technicolor) begins with Mitzi Gaynor, as Tanguay, performing an elaborate stage number while a theater full of spectators—mostly men—look on in a kind of oddly rapt daze. But shortly after Gaynor/Tanguay begins her stage turn, the producer of the show declares, "There's something wrong with Eva Tanguay!" and instructs a technician to bring down the curtain. The title sequence follows, and, after it, we find ourselves on the Twentieth Century–Fox lot. A lone man walks up to a security guard at the gate and tells him that he has heard they are making a picture about Tanguay's life. The loner says he knows something about the actress's life, and is duly directed to the office of George Jessel, who plays himself as the film's producer. We then cut to Jessel's office where the onetime vaudevillian-turned-Fox-producer is making clear to several of his staff screenplay doctors his dissatisfaction with the progress of the Tanguay picture. "Well, GJ, how'd you like the script?" asks one of the brown-nosing scribes. Jessel, it turns out, does not like it one bit. "It's all worthless," says Jessel. "I'll tell you why. It simply tells us that Eva Tanguay was a madcap. But what made her a madcap? What made her the terror of all theatrical managers?"

"Maybe she had an unhappy childhood. Maybe her father beat her," offers one

The life story of Eva Tanguay, perhaps vaudeville's biggest attraction, was subjected to the conservative value system of dominant-culture 1950s America in the movie *The I Don't Care Girl* (1953), starring Mitzi Gaynor as Tanguay, who is seen in the baby carriage here. (Billy Rose Theatre Collection, The New York Public Library for the Performing Arts, Astor, Lenox, and Tilden Foundations.)

of the script whizzes. "She could have been neurotic," hypothesizes the other, resorting to the ubiquitous Freudianism of the early 1950s.

"I don't want any psychoanalysis," retorts Jessel. "I want to know about Eva Tanguay the woman.... Boys, underneath those feathers and sequins and that wild mop of curls is a woman, with a brain, and a heart, and a soul."

Thus begins the filmic reconstruction of the life of vaudeville's most popular actress—a rendering arguably brainless, heartless, and soulless, at least with respect to its title subject. For rather than coming from Tanguay herself, though, the narrative is the product of men seeking to impose hegemonic order on the life story of a woman who often resisted hegemonic imperatives. What Jessel and his cohorts decide, throughout the course of the film, is that Eva Tanguay's life is best told through the eyes of the men she loved, the men whose affections she sought, and to whose wishes she continually bent.

The trouble is, however, that Tanguay's life was hardly defined by her love affairs. As we will see, constructing the life of Eva Tanguay as a concatenation of romantic entanglements would be tantamount to telling the life of B.F. Keith as little more than a series of failed business undertakings. The film, then, is a kind of early post-modern odyssey. Three men, producer George Jessel, director Lloyd Bacon, and, most important of all, Fox production chief Darryl Zanuck, both in the movie and in the real-world Hollywood entertainment machine, have artificially recounted the life of a woman via the romantic remembrances of men who never existed; the framing device by which they have done so is the production of a movie about the life they are struggling to recount. In so doing, they rob that biography of authenticity, imposing instead their own cinematic, narrative, and cultural sensibilities on the subject matter. One might be inclined to exonerate *The I Don't Care Girl* on the basis of some postmodern interrogation of authenticity and authorship. However, the very "dismal" nature of the final product suggests more accurately that this would be giving the film more than its due.

Though former vaudevillian George Jessel clearly had a major hand in the creation of *The I Don't Care Girl*, as did director Lloyd Bacon (who directed over a hundred studio-era films including *42nd Street* [1933] and *Knute Rockne, All American* [1948]), it was Darryl Zanuck who made the deepest imprint on the picture. In fact, no Zanuck-era Fox film was ever very far from Zanuck's dictatorial purview. Films made under Darryl Zanuck's watch inevitably "bore his authority" as their defining feature, according to a recent Zanuck biographer. The producer's notions of taste, propriety, and entertainment value were all squarely and extraordinarily inscribed, even given his executive position, on the Fox pictures created under his stewardship. After all, he was known as "Cinemogul Zanuck."[15] Indeed, though Darryl Zanuck himself never appears in *The I Don't Care Girl*, his presence nonetheless looms palpably just offscreen—a kind of deus ex machina figure who never quite descends in all his glory, but certainly seems at any moment as though he could. At one point, Jessel instructs his secretary that he is not to be bothered—unless "Zanuck wants me." In fact, some of Jessel's actual dialogue, particularly the monologue where he instructs his writers to fashion a script delivering "Eva Tanguay the woman," was taken directly from a production memo by Zanuck addressed to Jessel.[16]

Though he oversaw the production of movies in many genres, Darryl Zaunck was perhaps best known for his biographical films or biopics, a genre some have credited him with having "virtually invented." Zanuck, conservative and patriotic, was in many ways the perfect symbol and author of cultural ideas of his age. His biopics were, more often than not, "sanitized, edited" versions of a famous individual's life. This was especially so in the case of Eva Tanguay, whose scant need for a husband and untrammeled sexual allure made her a kind of cultural rebel in her own day, and thus a conundrum within 1950s American dominant cultural values. Add to this the fact that Zanuck often struggled when dealing with female biopic subjects, and one can better understand why *The I Don't Care Girl* is the inoffensive (from a certain moral, though not cinematic, standpoint) and ineffectual product that it is. In so many ways—from the extended, jazzy dance numbers (dance in Zanuck's films, it has been argued, was often an emblematic "substitute for sex") to the costumes that seem more at home in post–World War II America than its pre–World War I counterpart—the film tells us less about the life of a vaudeville temptress from the turn of the century and much more about the values of wealthy, white, male, American film executives circa 1950. In the creation of visual materials, such as films, paintings, or advertisements, critic John Berger may have put it best: "The past is never there waiting to be discovered, to be recognized for exactly what it is. History always constitutes the relation between a present and its past."[17] In depicting Eva Tanguay's life on film, Darryl Zanuck engaged in the consummate act of historical erasure.

Nor is Eva Tanguay easily to be found in the works of scholars and historians. Not only is there no book-length study of Tanguay, but there was, as of the time this book was being researched, not even a graduate student's dissertation devoted entirely to her. In fact, only one doctoral dissertation even in part seems to have dealt with the life of Eva Tanguay. "An Investigation of the Life Styles and Performance of Three Singer-Comediennes of American Vaudeville: Eva Tanguay, Nora Bayes, and Sophie Tucker," which earned Jane R. Westerfield her Doctor of Arts degree at Ball State University, Muncie, Indiana, in 1987, devotes one chapter—some fifty pages—to Tanguay's life and accomplishments. The chapter is a fairly straightforward work of traditional theater history, recounting Tanguay's early stage career, rise to stardom, fall from grace, and incidents from her private life that seem especially relevant. Westerfield counts "her outlandish publicity stunts, her strange, unusual costumes, her choice of repertoire when she had her own vaudeville act and her outrageous attitude toward life" as among the many reasons for Tanguay's success.[18]

Westerfield concludes that Tanguay's onstage antics and offstage lifestyle were "remarkably parallel in nature." Both were "erratic, eccentric and often irresponsible."[19] This summation provides Westerfield's work with an organizing logic and may be seen as a kind of gestalt statement, for the author wants us to read Eva Tanguay's stage career as an extension of her private life—or vice-versa. In this regard, the dissertation seems to agree with some of the other scant accounts of Eva Tanguay's life and stage career. Westerfield also suggests that Tanguay was a visible symbol of "a cultural revolution taking place in American life." Tanguay, in Westerfield's estimation, "gave voice and gesture to the restlessness and discontent of her era."[20] Taking Westerfield's notions about Eva Tanguay and placing them more fully in their proper and fully-developed social and historical context, however, will even more effectively elucidate the actress's work, personality, and overall significance in American popular culture. In a sense, to better understand Eva Tanguay, on the stage and off, one must engage not only in theater history, per se, but a bit of social history as well.

The Westerfield dissertation may be most useful where it addresses the matter of Tanguay's sexual suggestiveness onstage. This aspect of the performer's life, more than perhaps any other, rises to the surface of what biographical descriptions there are. Tanguay, we are told, "almost single handedly jolted the maudlin, eye-dabbing public of the early 1900's with the 'vigor of unashamed sex.'"[21] We are to understand that through her revealing costumes, suggestive lyrics, and sensual gyrations on stage, the performer posed a threat to polite society and the managers who ran the theaters where she made her living. She is said to have caused "chagrin among her employers," notably B.F. Keith.[22] As we have seen, B.F. Keith, E.F. Albee, and the other big vaudeville magnates were canny, shrewd men who together crafted the beginnings of mass entertainment in the United States. Though they may occasionally have tried to temper Tanguay's performances, they hardly wanted to tamper with a formula that worked so well. It was Tanguay, after all, who drew a record 12,000 fans to the 44th Street Music Hall in 1913 and who enjoyed the longest uninterrupted run in the New York City vaudeville circuits—some 14 months—from 1908 to 1909. As early as 1907, even before her career peaked, the *New York Dramatic Mirror* recognized Tanguay as a "magnet" able to attract crowds like none other.[23] To portray Eva Tanguay as constantly at odds with the repressed and repressing Albee and Keith is to miss what may actually have been going on.

Other vaudeville historians who discuss Tanguay also fix upon her sexuality, and try to argue that her ribaldry and license on the stage were carried out in open defiance of strict censorship codes. One well known chronicle of the vaudeville stage has Tanguay as an "electrified hoyden, a temperamental terror to the managers," who was able to break the rules as she did only because in the end she proved "a riotous joy to her audiences." Her act was termed "assault and battery," and she supposedly "got more sex into her shouted numbers than could be found in a crib street in a mining town," all under the "very nose" of E.F. Albee.[24] Tanguay may have used sex as a drawing card, but she was hardly trying to outwit E.F. Albee, a man who built an entertainment empire by advertising cleanliness and wholesomeness—and then, quite often and deliberately, delivered otherwise. Others see Tanguay as having prospered for having capitalized on "the new aggressiveness of the American female" in the wake up cultural upheaval and the "gradual relaxation of strict conventional attitudes toward sex."[25] To some, then, Eva Tanguay was a bellwether rather than simply an anomaly.

When she died, even the newspapers remembered Tanguay chiefly for her sexual daring on stage. The *New York Times* wrote:

> She did much to bring vaudeville out of its decorous front. She sang songs which were daring for the time, such as "I Want Someone to Go Wild with Me" and "It's All Been Done Before But Not the Way I Do It"… One of her most profitable acts was in "Salome" in 1908 and she once said that her costume consisted of "two pearls." Censors complained loudly, while the act rolled up a record gross at the box office.[26]

Similarly, the *Los Angeles Times* eulogized, "Sometimes her lyrics and costumes drew the wrath of local Puritans, but the customers lined up for blocks."[27]

Eva Tanguay clearly took a chance in putting forth sexuality as her main drawing card. Although, as we have seen, she was far from the only woman in vaudeville to do so, we must not underestimate the degree of criticism which a woman who dared to seem impure or lacking in virtue—especially in so public and mercantile a venue as the vaudeville stage—opened herself up to. "To a woman the most sacred thing is her virtue," argued the *Arena* in 1895, just before Tanguay took to the vaudeville boards, "[virtue is] the seal of her purity, the crown of her womanhood." It was only love—by which the author means a certain kind of socially sanctified heterosexual love—which might legitimately permit a woman to "lay aside the virgin sanctity of her person." [28] About the same time, *Scribner's Magazine*, complaining of a widespread "lack of womanliness in American women," argued that in order to be womanly, a female had to be "a good mother, the devoted wife, the gentle sister, the quiet guardian of the hearth-fire."[29] Clearly, Eva Tanguay chose to ignore such cultural strictures, and sought instead to extend and redefine what might be acceptable in regard to virtue, purity, and female behavior. She rode in posse with other female vaudevillians who pushed the limits of respectability, and, in a sense, worked in concert with the Keiths and Albees to deliver a product that would titillate, amuse, and arouse spectators desirous of a mass entertainment that was at once evocative of certain elements of the unseemly past, and yet hinted at a future in which consumerism and sex appeal would commingle intimately.

Discussions of Eva Tanguay's sexual expression on stage seem inextricably to link such efforts to an equally strong expression of her unique personality. It is as if onlookers and writers could not separate her rebellious eroticism from her uniqueness and unforgeable personality. "It is virtually impossible to overestimate Tanguay's personality.... Precisely when the vaudeville public was listening to such treacle as 'You'll Be Sorry Just Too Late,' Tanguay was screaming 'I Want Some One to Go Wild with Me'; 'It's All Been Done Before but Not the Way I Do It'; and 'Go as Far as You Like.'" In short, Tanguay's success onstage "had been due to the exploitation of her personality" combined with sometimes racy songs and always suggestive dance movements. It is as if, in Tanguay's case, the two were inseparable.[30]

Eva Tanguay seems to have realized early on that her lack of conventional stage talents—singing, dancing, etc.—would compel her to develop a different sort of appeal, one that would distinguish her from her peers and help her gain a foothold in the competitive world of vaudeville. "I couldn't dance and I couldn't sing," she once admitted. Her first appearance on Broadway was in a musical comedy in which she played "Coloma, the Hoo-doo, a bare-footed Fiji Islander with a flimsy voile slit skirt," a tempting number suggestive of Odiva and other would-be vaudevillian exotics whose exoticness was inextricable from a certain kind of colonial sexual allure. Tanguay claims that at the time of that appearance, there was "but one thought" on her mind. Namely, "to move so fast and whirl so madly that no one would be able to see my bare legs." Thus, in her account, were sown the seeds of her signature cyclonic choreography.[31]

Tanguay seems to be arguing that she developed a wild and energetic performance style to cover up for her sexual allure. But it is clear that she soon realized the success to be had by a fortuitous combination of the two. It may be hard to put one's finger on the exact source of Tanguay's success—there is, after all, so little documentation of her performance style. But she did possess "boundless energy" and "sang suggestive songs in an inimitable fashion," according to Anthony Slide in *The Encyclopedia of Vaudeville*.[32] And according to Jane Westerfield, in her dissertation on vaudeville actresses, Eva Tanguay "seemed to careen from one corner of the set to the other, wriggling her hips, waggling her breasts, kicking her legs wildly, and shaking her derriere." Her dance numbers are said to have approached "the reenactment of erotic fantasies in front of her audience."[33] Tanguay, then, may have raised eyebrows, but she did so with the implicit authorization of patriarchal powers seeking to develop a new kind of sexualized entertainment product—one based on the female body.

It was not long before the press picked up on Tanguay's unique and inimitable style. "Miss Tanguay's chief claim to recognition is a superabundance of energetic vitality that finds vent in a series of movements in which every muscle in her body is brought into full play," wrote the *New York Dramatic Mirror* in 1904.[34] Three years later, she was deemed a "little human dynamo." To many onlookers at the time, she was "indescribable," noteworthy above all else for her "energy, vitality and ginger," her "altogether charming and effervescent manner," which would make even those theater patrons with "sluggish blood in their veins feel compelled to sit up and take notice."[35] Again, those who saw Eva Tanguay onstage, and observed her effect on the crowd, could not but see as parts of a greater whole the performer's unique personality, romping energy, and sex appeal ("ginger"). For Tanguay, the female body was a site of experimentation and histrionic caprice, one which could rise above conventional cultural standards and yet appeal to an increasing mass market for commoditized female sexual showmanship. Her "semidelirious dances," which would be, as the *Mirror* correctly observed, "valueless in other hands," soon earned her the nickname "the Cyclonic One."[36]

Tanguay, "she of the dimpled smile and the nimble feet and the extremely active body,"[37] almost suggested a kind of mental derangement or pathology—an almost Freudian-termed hysteria—to certain observers. In 1910, *Variety* mused that "no sane person" could put together the kind of act, and make it such a hit, that Eva Tanguay had.[38] Accordingly, Tanguay became known as a "wild" performer, one who was untamed and untamable, one who lived outside of society's norms and mores. With what would seem to be a clever and calculated awareness of this identity, Tanguay made a motion picture in 1916 called *The Wild Girl*, in which she not only exhibited her gyrational dancing and revealing costumes, but played an itinerant gypsy girl as well, one who lived in the wild and was in touch with nature.

The Wild Girl was produced by Selznick Pictures, but was financed by the Eva Tanguay Film Corporation, an entity the actress herself shrewdly created to capitalize on her stage success. The Tanguay Film Corporation had made a "self-promoting feature" in mid-1916 called *Energetic Eva*,[39] but no prints of this earlier film exist according to librarians at the Museum of Modern Art Film Study Center (the question was put them in 1999). The ridiculous plot of *The Wild Girl*, directed by Howard Estabrook, begins with a dying stranger abandoning a baby girl in a "gypsy camp" with a note explaining that when the child turns eighteen, she is to "inherit a Virginia estate." The chief of the gypsies, perhaps wanting somehow to more fully capitalize on this infant-cum-investment, instructs "Sabia," the tribal matron, to "dress and rear her as a boy." Years pass. The gypsy band, unlike so many other supposed Romany tribes before it, makes its way to Virginia. It is at this point that the abandoned one's true gender, which had for so long eluded the members of the tribe, is detected. Vosho, son of the tribal chief, demands to marry "Firefly," as he/she has come to be called. But much like Eva Tanguay herself, Firefly will not abide a non-mutually determined marriage. She flees the gypsy camp and "meets up with Donald McDonald, a local newspaper editor." But unlike Vosho, McDonald does not pick up on the fact that Firefly is a woman, and hires her to run errands for him. Not surprisingly, she falls in love with the McDonald. Eventually, Vosho is vanquished, Donald discovers Firefly's true identity, and he and Firefly are joined in love.[40]

Predictably, Tanguay sought to transport the wild abandon of her vaudeville shows to the moving picture screen. "In this, her first production, she displays to advantage all those qualities which have made her name *the by-word for entertainment* with audiences the world over," read the copy of an advertisement for *The Wild Girl* in *Moving Picture World*, a film industry trade paper of the day.[41] According to the same publication, Tanguay spared no expense in creating the sets and costumes for *The Wild Girl*, just as she had for stage shows.[42]

This promotional shot of Eva Tanguay capitalizes on, and in fact exaggerates, her shapely form and seductive posture. (Billy Rose Theatre Collection, The New York Public Library for the Performing Arts, Astor, Lenox, and Tilden Foundations.)

In crafting a stage and screen persona that focused on an irreproducible, blatantly sexual, and highly individualized body, Eva Tanguay appealed to certain progressive-minded social reformers of the day. "Woman's body ... is increasingly looked upon as her personal property," remarked the *Atlantic Monthly* in 1912. More than any other material entity, it was this self-determined "home for their souls" which

A promotional still from *The Wild Girl*, a 1916 movie starring Eva Tanguay. (Courtesy of The Academy of Motion Picture Arts and Sciences.)

women now sought. So long as that home rested "on someone else's feelings and caprices it is no home for the soul: it is only a tavern."[43] Perhaps more than any other performer of her day, Tanguay represented a growing desire to control and freely express her body and its sexual potentials. Some at the time, such as the writer for the *Atlantic*, were willing to forgive the degree of wildness and tempestuousness that often accompanied such efforts, recognizing that it did not necessarily make sense to speak of the "the 'unquiet women' to-day," but rather of "the unquiet world."[44] Eva Tanguay both shaped and reflected that "unquiet world" in her stage offerings. If ever a vaudevillian recognized and capitalized on "unquiet," it was she.

Others were less forgiving of women who chose to put forth an "unquiet" or wild body and personage, and tended to see such efforts as ripping at the very fabric of society. In 1891, the publication the *Nineteenth Century* identified a new type of woman in American society. The title of the piece, "The Wild Women as Social Insurgents," speaks volumes. Author Lynn Linton described this new phenomenon as "that loud and dictatorial person, insurgent and something more, who suffers no one's opinion to influence her mind, no venerable law hallowed by time nor custom consecrated by experience, to control her actions. Mistress of herself, the Wild Woman as social insurgent preaches the 'lesson of liberty' broadened into lawlessness and license."[45] The emergent "Wild Woman" united "personal independence" with "power over men," tossing self-restraint and conformity out the window. The "one word she cannot spell is Fitness." Thus, what ultimately made the "Wild Woman" so very "wild"—that is, unsubmissive—was her failure to accept the propriety and decorum of what was presumed to be her naturally submissive role. In seeking to equate herself with men in terms of power and desire, the "Wild Woman" in fact engaged in "obliterating the finer traits of civilization," threatening society's very essence.[46]

But women like Tanguay, according to the *Nineteenth Century*'s Linton, were of an especially pernicious breed: actresses and dancers. For the very "restlessness" that characterized the "Wild Woman" drove her "afield in search of strange pleasures and novel occupations," the more novel and divergent from mainstream social acceptability the better. "Nothing daunts this modern Io," Linton felt, she "appears on the public stage and executes dances which one would not like one's daughters to see, still less perform. She herself knows no shame in showing her skill—and her legs."[47] It was impossible, in this editorialist's eyes, for a woman to be somehow both fundamentally female—that is, modest—and also succeed as a performer. The two goals were simply irreconcilable. Indeed, even if enacting a kind of choreographed sensual abandon, the woman onstage nonetheless surrendered "her beauty when at these violent exercises."[48] For Eva Tanguay, such impossible double-binds would not do. Rather, her unique success was often based on a flaunting of those very hypocrisies and tensions in which she and other women found themselves constricted.

For observers of Lynn Linton's stripe, women were to be graceful and decorous, even onstage. In the article "What Men Like in Women," written for *Cosmopolitan* in 1901 (and uncannily similar to some articles in that same magazine many decades later), Rafford Pike argued that there was "one thing which appeals to every man of taste and imagination, and that is grace." Accordingly, if there were one trait above all else that men could not abide in women, it was awkwardness, perhaps because men were themselves so fundamentally awkward; in his view, grace therefore profoundly signified *la différence*.[49] Eva Tanguay was many things onstage, but graceful was hardly one of them. Rather, she was, according to *The Encyclopedia of Vaudeville*, variously "outrageous or repellent, with bosoms bursting out of bras and thighs rippling with fat."[50] A woman like Tanguay ran the risk of losing her feminine identity through the raucous and volatile paces through which she put her body onstage, even though it often pointed to a new kind of female sex appeal. "Whenever she elects to be something more than a gentle cow with its calves," noted a writer in *Harper's Bazar* in 1907, a woman runs the risk of becoming 'unsexed.'"[51] In many ways, then, Tanguay onstage was a challenge to certain prevailing and dominant notions of womanhood. Rather than unsexing herself, though, she offered new possibilities for the public face of female sexuality, even if such offerings were always, in the end, subtly authorized by male business powers.

Of course, for a performer like Eva Tanguay to succeed as she did, there might also have been operational, in the society and culture of the time, other strains of belief which yearned deeply for a woman's wildness and novel expressiveness. For some of those nursing such thoughts, the stage was the perfect outlet for a woman caught amid the upheaval of changing roles. *Harper's Weekly* identified the era as that of "the woman in drama." Wrote Arthur Pollock, "Nothing so well demonstrates the changing attitude of the world toward and the increasing importance attributed to her position in society as the effect she is having upon all phases of the theater." According to Pollock, "woman is now a dominating factor in all things theatrical."[52] Women like Tanguay could excel on the boards because the stage offered a locale where a woman's body and personal attributes might be displayed to greatest profit—in contradistinction to more abstract forms of creativity, such as writing, painting, and musical composition in which a woman did not seem to put forth her corpus so strongly and directly as an artistic signifier. Because of woman's supposed nearness to "Nature," and her ability to shape "humanity as if she were its earth, and mother," the editor of *Harper's Monthly* editorialized in 1910, one should expect women to excel in the "purely personal arts—singing and dancing," even though it was conceded that in nature, the male animal is commonly the more vocal or the singer, per se. Woman could capitalize on her "physical charm" by staying away from the more cerebral forms of artistic abstraction, those relying heavily on symbolic form and language. Rather, according to what might be termed the "personal arts" point of view, women should embrace and put forth their bodies as a means of exploiting their natural gifts and penchants.[53] A woman like Eva Tanguay, who sang for a living, though in some sense defying the natural model, could be nonetheless condoned by certain onlookers.

Actresses could be lauded for their mimetic capacities as well, since they were thought to be much closer to the inner well of human emotion. Attempting to explain why, in its view, there were so many more famous actresses than actors in the history of the stage (a point highly debatable, of course, but left intact here for the purposes of the present investigation), the *Arena* magazine in 1901 ascribed it to a natural female "emotional explosiveness." But the *Arena* was sympathetic with women. This "explosiveness"—and attendant success on the stage—was due largely to the "same repression of sex and social compunction that puts women by their very natures in the position of actors." Therefore, according to this argument, great actresses "in a way express their own natures."[54] Thus, good acting skills could be the happy by-product of social repression.

French actor, writer, and theorist Constant Coquelin, writing for *Harper's Bazar* in 1901, felt women made good actresses because they combined a man's sense of humor with an intrinsic emotionality. "The sense of humor is universal," wrote the Frenchman, "It knows neither time nor country nor sex," citing the famous French actress Sarah Bernhardt (who made very successful tours of vaudeville in 1910 and 1912).[55] "Her sense of the ridiculous is most keen," waxed Coquelin. It was a woman's very awareness of sorrow and tragedy—that is, what was and in many ways still is considered to be a woman's fundamentally more emotional nature—that made them better suited to the stage than men. So argued the Frenchman.[56]

Many felt that women, as a social category, made for not only the equal of men on the boards, but for better stage artists than men altogether—even as purely mimetic performers. Much like those critics who scoffed and smirked at scantily-clad males in vaudeville, *Cosmopolitan*'s Alan Dale, in 1906, was mildly repulsed by "ablebodied men pretending to be somebody else," or "worse still—cavorting around in musical comedy." Men on stage disturbed male dignity, Dale felt. In fact, seeing them on stage, he confessed that he often felt the urge to stand up and shout, "Go out into the world and do something—build things, invent things, write things, talk things, but do stop posing as blooming, silly make-believes." (Clearly, for Dale, working in the theater was not really being "out in the world"—though one wonders if he would have reserved the same scorn for B.F. Keith and E.F. Albee and their business exploits.) It was the women onstage who, endowed with "sweet, feminine sincerity," made "the play live and pulsate, the 'pretending' less evidential," for Dale. To him, acting was "innate" in women, engrafted and absurd on men. For women were experts in "simulation," men somehow incapable of it in any convincing way in the writer's estimation. These words are, to be sure, something of a back-handed compliment. For him, men are at their best when they are "out" in "the world," making, building, doing, and articulating a verbal discourse. More importantly, though, Dale attaches to woman a kind of built-in falseness, an ability to dissemble and imitate of which man is simply less capable. But Dale the editorialist redeems himself (somewhat) by offering cultural and historical reasons for woman's innate superiority at the mimetic arts. He acknowledges that woman has been "the under-dog for centuries," thus encouraging her to develop the ability to simulate and pretend.[57] Investigating along similar lines, Cora Sutton Castle, in her quasi-scientific 1913 "Statistical Study of Eminent Women," found that, throughout history, the theater had been "the stepping stone to eminence for more than eight times as many women as became noted for their religion."[58]

As actresses and performers, women, particularly Eva Tanguay, ran the risk of seeming awkward and unwomanly. Yet at the same time, they were fulfilling a cultural prejudice which viewed them as inherently *always* on stage, in one form or another, hiding some putative true self buried deep in the folds of their feminine wiles. In 1913, in *Munsey's Magazine*, Karin Michaelis posed the question, "Why Are Women Less Truthful Than Men?" Wrote Michaelis, "Does a woman really lie more than a man? Yes, unquestionably yes, if the lies are reckoned by their number." Woman's lies, according to Michaelis, were vast in number, "like weeds along the roadside."[59] According to Michaelis, while men could readily distinguish between lies and truth, women could not, and therefore lied in "many little things simply because she is a woman." Her very person was, to some extent, viewed as a lie. "She puffs out her hair with pads and artificial braids, and uses dye to conceal the fading of its color. She improves her complexion with powder and paint." Womanhood, then, in the estimation of Michaelis and others like her in the period, was itself a kind of consummate performance. To be a woman was inexorably to be false in one way or another. This extended beyond hair and dress and permeated a woman's entire attitude and bearing. "The wife, perhaps, has never told her husband a falsehood, but is not her conduct a continual lie?" observed well-known feminist Charlotte Perkins Gilman in a 1908 *Harper's Bazar* piece in which she attempted to explore the roots of women's socially-forced dissembling.[60] To be a woman was perforce to be mutable, variable, and never settled in one's own person—or at least such was a prevailing view in the dominant culture.

Women lied too in their sexual liaisons, said some, and in this arena committed perhaps their greatest transgressions against truth. "To the American woman, flirtation is as innocent a sport as tennis, dancing, or skating," wrote Karen Michaelis of *Munsey's*. And while other leisure pursuits were more or less salutary, flirting was "a mendacious game," one again based on ruse and deception. It was wrong, in her view, "to give to men, with glances, smiles, and a thousand coquettish tricks, promises that she does not intend to keep," making no mention of course that men may seek and solicit such behavior. No matter. By flirting as she did, American women were the falsest females in the world.[61]

Rafford Pike, writing in *Cosmopolitan*, argued similarly that frankness was simply not in woman's nature, especially where sexual flirtation was concerned. "Coquetry," in his view, was the very opposite of sincerity, frankness, conviction, and other admirable traits based on a supposed veracity. By practicing such "indifference" to virtue, according to Pike, women's "very bones are turned to water and when their hearts are melting like wax before the flame of their desire." And the editor of *Harper's Monthly* put forth similar sentiments when he argued that the "modern feminization of culture" was resulting in the strengthening of the "plastic side of our nature"—that which could be molded, transformed, and remade at will to meet the needs of any situation. To Susanne Wilcox of the *Independent*, "subtlety and subterfuge" constituted the "pre-eminently female characteristics in the animal as well as human world."[62]

For his part, George Bernard Shaw, no stranger to either female psychology or actresses, felt simply that women lied easily due to an inherent weakness of their psyche. "She has no conscience," the Irish playwright told *Cosmopolitan* magazine in 1907, though he was suggesting a kind of conscience linked more to social and self betterment than to frivolous pleasures.[63] The editor of *Scribner's Magazine* put it bluntly in 1901 when he wrote, "[I]t is the business of woman rather *not* to be original."[64] Thus women were seen as naturally fit for creative endeavors which seemed to rely on dissimulation rather than originality, masking rather than revelation. In some people's eyes, the stage was thus a natural, (more) socially sanctioned outlet for creative women like Eva Tanguay.

Yet there was a price to be paid for actresses and performers like Tanguay who chose the boards as a means of artistic expression. Given the commonly held beliefs about women, many viewed Tanguay and other performers like her as capable *only* of falseness, of acting, of dissimulation. For a woman to engage in artistic creation did not mean that she would create an original reflection of truthful nature but rather that she would simply summon up her own innate powers of falsity and put them on display. Whereas men could claim originality in artistic creation, women, by virtue of their nature, could never hope to do so. Speculating about the creative process in women, author Winifred Kirkland, writing for the *Atlantic Monthly* in 1916, stated that she could in no way "see that woman's brain is the equal of man's in originality, in concentration, or in power of sustained effort." For Kirkland, women lacked true powers of creation and originality because they were always creating from a highly personal place within. For a woman to create, argued Kirkland, she had merely to give face to her already dissimulating self; her creative intellect was inseparable from her body, emotions, and soul. If men fit the dualistic Cartesian mind-body paradigm nicely, women did not, the female brain being "so hard to separate … from the rest of the woman." Men, composed of "plainly discernible pieces," could distinguish personal experience from individual creation. But a woman functioned as a more unified whole, the personal indistinguishable from the intellectual. For a woman to craft intellectual and artistic products with the same aplomb as a man, her best bet would be to "copy a man's mental methods"—and Kirkland herself admitted to doing this; her brain, like most women's, she surmised, was "a vague and volatile mass, shot through with fancies, whimsies, with flashes of intuitive and illuminative wisdom," and thus not easily put to the purpose of true artistic or intellectual creation.[65]

Tanguay was in a tough spot. On the one hand, she would have risked alienating her crowds and employers if she claimed utter and uncompromising originality as an artist (not to mention being taken seriously in such a lofty claim). On the other hand, in the ultra-competitive world of mass entertainment—a world hewn with the profit motive by men like E.F. Albee and B.F. Keith—she had to define herself as somehow unique and different, if only or largely from her fellow actresses. The solution, as we have begun to see, involved the creation of an energetic, sexually charged stage persona which many assumed mimicked her private life, though this was in fact rarely the case. She took the risk of seeming awkward and volatile in creating an appealing, if slightly forbidden, embodiment of staged amusement.

If Eva Tanguay was to suffer from attempting to present originality in a profession which naturally led others to assume simulation and falsity, she turned such prejudices to her advantage by putting forth a close relative of originality—namely, individuality. "People may differ as to the amount of stage talent possessed by this rather erratic young woman," wrote the *New York Clipper* in 1913, "but there is no gainsaying the fact that the stage has not a performer just like her." Another observer of Tanguay's felt the actress, above all else, emblazoned "the 'I' stamp" on all her stage doings, in part by divulging to the crowd what appeared to be a hefty measure of "personal information."[66]

For a woman in Tanguay's day to put forth her individuality—and, moreover, in Tanguay's case, to capitalize on it—was a tricky matter. A man writing for the *Westminster Review* in 1902 opined that the facet of the nascent woman's movement responsible for "the most general perturbation and resentment in the average man" was women's newfound and constant (in his view) "individuality in purpose and action," a self-guiding cultivation of her "innate genius according to her own promptings and in her own manner." Every woman felt keenly the "need of self-expression," according to a female editorialist of the day, no matter that such self-expression might be "careless" or "reckless." In the *Atlantic Monthly* in 1910, Margaret Deland, exploring the changing landscape of feminine identity and goals, regarded a newfound drive for "individualism" as among the most important factors animating that change.[67] Individualism increasingly became a trait with which women were associated, if not downright accused of, in turn-of-the-century America. For Eva Tanguay, individualism was inextricably linked with an erotic of performance and bearing, though an erotic that fit well into the apparatus of the vaudeville industry.

Such a drive toward individualism, and individuality, as exemplified by Eva Tanguay, however, could lead to that most unfeminine of traits in the Victorian world, selfishness. Indeed, some at the time considered the struggle against selfishness to be the central battle of a woman's life, one that had to be kept at daily, vigilantly, like "the struggle against dirt and disorder," not so much to vanquish the enemy as to keep it ever at bay. "Just as I must bathe and brush and comb and polish this tiresome body of mine every day, so must I work away at curbing my selfishness, at polishing my manners, at trying to deserve that it shall be said of me, 'she is a lady,'" wrote Maud

Howe in *Harper's Bazar* in 1909."[68] For Howe, being unselfish was as important as grooming and keeping up the appearance of personal cleanliness and beauty that was the natural burden of womanhood. To be unselfish, and thus unindividualistic, a woman had to undertake a regimen aimed not only at psychological control but all aspects of being and bearing, from informal elocution enhancement to understanding the proper level, tone, pitch, and timbre of a truly ladylike voice. "Never call to your children or your servants," admonished Howe, who thought any hint of imperiousness (aside from having servants, it would seem) decidedly unfeminine. "If they are in another part of the house, either ring for them or go find them."[69] It is hard to imagine a woman whose stage persona adhered less to such recommendations than Eva Tanguay. Loud, "cyclonic," awkward, and unabashedly individualistic, Tanguay embodied an emerging possibility of woman—one that was both at odds with certain aspects of hegemonic culture and yet one that also clearly posed a deep fascination for the growing throngs of mass-entertainment seekers in turn-of-the-century America.

As an actress, as a woman, as one who projected sexual allure onstage, and as an individualist, Eva Tanguay stood astride the cusp of cultural upheaval. She could be criticized or admired, but not ignored. In some ways, she exemplified the "new woman" emerging shortly after the turn of the century. The "new woman," according to James Henle of *Harper's Weekly*, might especially be found in the performing arts, counted among the females who were "let loose upon the world as bankers' daughters, teachers, stenographers, and actresses."[70]

Eva Tanguay's journey to the stage began at an early age, especially given her immediate background. She was born on August 1, 1878, in the small village of Marbleton, Quebec. Her mother was French-Canadian, while her father, Dr. Gustave Tanguay, was a Paris physician who "heard the call of the wild." When Eva was seven, the Tanguay family moved to Holyoke, Massachusetts; Dr. Tanguay died soon afterwards.[71]

According to most biographical accounts, around 1886, with the Tanguay family near utter destitution, Eva was spotted on the street by the owner of a local theatrical touring company and was hired to fill a number of child roles, including that of Little Lord Fauntleroy.[72] Tanguay remained with the Redding Stanton Repertoire Company for several years, and graduated to soubrette roles in what would seem to be stock, nineteenth-century melodramas. In these parts, recounted Tanguay, "I dashed in night after night to save the heroine from being sawed in two by the vile villain."[73]

Tanguay's first New York appearance was in a show called *The Engineer*, produced by Bertram and Willard at the People's Theatre on the Bowery. After that job, she got a shot at a musical comedy at the Imperial Music Hall on Broadway—the one where she decided to dance too fast for the audience to notice her bare legs—though she fails to mention the name or date in her putatively self-written piece in the *American Weekly*.[74]

By 1901, Eva Tanguay was given a role in a major musical comedy production on Broadway, *My Lady*, at the Victoria theater. The show, with book by R. A. Barnet, and music by H. L. Heartz, E. W. Corliss, Robert Morse, and D. K. Stevens, was described as "a three-act extravaganza travestying *The Three Musketeers*," according to the *New York Dramatic Mirror*. The show had originated in Boston at the Tremont Theatre on 5 February 1900 under the name *Mindi and the Musketeers*. It moved to the Columbia Theatre, Boston, several weeks later, and debuted at the Victoria in New York under the name *My Lady* on 11 February 1901, before "a very large audience."[75]

Though Tanguay claimed initially to have hit upon the idea of dancing as fast as she could to hide her scanty attire before her stint in *My Lady*, her experience in the *Musketeers* spoof must have made a much deeper and lasting impression on her. For it was in this show that she was exposed to the drawing power of feminine beauty and sexual allure, dressed up in exotic costumes, and put on display before an eager audience. "If *My Lady* is a go in New York it will be due chiefly to its dazzling display of feminine beauty," wrote the *New York Dramatic Mirror*. *My Lady*'s "plenitude of pulchritude" and "extensive array of stunning costumes" succeeded, according to the *Mirror*, in transforming the stage at the Victoria into nothing short of "a garden of loveliness." Though the *Mirror* found the score "light, tuneful, spirited," it had less kind things to say about the plot, which the paper regarded as "a tiresome series of ancient jests, stupid lines and unfunny 'business.'" And the lines *were* stupid. At one point, one of the musketeers is sobbing into a handkerchief, from which small bits of lead are shaking loose. "Look, he weeps bullets!" cries another character. "No, they are musket-tears!" rejoins the weeper. "And this is 1901," grimaced the *New York Times*. At least one critic, though, singled out Eva Tanguay as among those deserving special "mention."[76] Little wonder that *My Lady* has been more or less forgotten in the annals of theater history.

Tanguay's next stint on Broadway came in a musical called *The Office Boy*, written by Ludwig Englander, which also debuted at the Victoria Theatre, in November 1903. The *New York Times* described *The Office Boy* as little more than a "vehicle" for comic performer Frank Daniels, an assemblage of ripe "opportunities for the comedian." With a convoluted, farcical plot involving the law office of "Ketcham & Cheatham," a botched robbery attempt, and several romantic intrigues, the *Times* determined that *The Office Boy* was "likely to please those who want to laugh and grow fat."[77]

Though largely a showcase for Daniels's comedic talents, however, *The Office Boy* provided Eva Tanguay with another opportunity to shine onstage. She was found to be "as lively as ever," despite the fact that her choreography "does not at any time suggest the poetry of motion." The future Cyclonic One, it seems, was developing dance steps that had "a quality of abandon that many people like just as much" as the more tame and artful variety.[78] Thus Tanguay, as early as 1903, was refining her distinctive style of energetic, if ungraceful, dancing and stage movement which would serve her so well on the vaudeville stage in the near future.

About this time, Tanguay appeared in another musical which would lead to perhaps the most important developments in her career. The musical was called *The Chaperones*, with music by Isidore Witmark and book and lyrics by Frederic Ranken. Set in Paris and Alexandria, Egypt, in the first and second acts, respectively, the "rudimentary plot has something to do with a dashing adventuress named Aramanthe Dedincourt (Miss Trixie Friganza), who furnishes chaperones, or guides, in the form of pretty girls, to strangers in Paris at so much 'per,'" according to a description in *Theatre* magazine.[79]

As with her other musical comedy efforts, Tanguay stood out, despite being relegated to a small part. According to the *Theatre*, Tanguay played "a madcap girl detective named 'Phrosia' who's after a stolen seal." But Tanguay garnered special attention for herself in her rendering of a song called "My Sambo." In fact, it became clear to many watchers that *The Chaperones* was little more than a chance for various loosely-connected singers, dancers, and comedians to strut their respective stuff—not at all unlike a vaudeville program, and common for musical comedies of the day, which rarely boasted anything like the cohesive "book" that was to become evident in musical theater later on in the century. As such, it was a golden opportunity for the particular talents of Eva Tanguay, and she did not squander it. One critic wrote of his delight at "that catchy coon song, 'My Sambo,' which Miss Tanguay sings and dances with amazing *entrain*...." The "coon song" genre was popular at the turn of the century; "My Sambo" in particular contained the lyrics, "I got a beau, I love him so. He's my sweet 'lasses Sam. I love him like rasper' jam. I never cared for a man but Sambo!"[80] As with other coon songs, and minstrel show elements, the mimicking of supposedly authentic African-American cultural nuances permitted white performers a degree of rawness and license not permitted in their own racial persona.[81] Eva Tanguay almost certainly made full use of such an opportunity to let loose, wail with emotion, and further develop the "wild" persona that would become her stock-in-trade.

With Tanguay's rendering of "My Sambo" gaining popularity, the "madcap" comedienne was given a chance to star in a musical in 1904 called *The Blonde in Black*. Due to the success of the song, though, the title was changed to *My Sambo Girl* for its 1904 debut. *My Sambo Girl* was crucial to Tanguay's career, not only because it provided her with a chance to demonstrate her formidable talents in a larger role, but also because it featured Tanguay singing a number called "I Don't Care," which was to become her inseparable trademark—even when she wished to shake it off—for the rest of her life. Written by Jean Lennox, who the *New York Telegraph* called a "poetess" and the *New York Star* described as "a handsome young woman with a happy knack for saying smart things in smart verse,"[82] and Harry Sutton, the song "I Don't Care" was a kind of explosion of gaiety and nonchalance, perfect for the emerging talents of Eva Tanguay. It went:

> I don't care, I don't care
> What they may think of me.
> I'm happy-go-lucky, men say I'm plucky
> So jolly and care-free.
> I don't care, I don't care
> If I do get the mean and stony stare,
> If I'm never successful, it won't be distressful,
> 'Cos I don't care.[83]

Something about the song caught the public imagination. Its lightheartedness no doubt appealed to urban amusement-goers, and the energy and tinge of eroticism Tanguay brought to its rendering must have added additional appeal. Perhaps predictably, she later came to loathe the song that was her entrée to vaudeville, national fame, and considerable wealth. By 1913, she was ranting that "that wretched song" was at the root of all her problems. "Everybody thinks I'm crazy or impossible to get along with. The most terrible stories are told about me. And why? Because that wretched song 'I Don't Care,' has pursued me night and day from the first time I sang it." She had no friends, she alleged, because of "I Don't Care," and no respect either. She could not remember "how many hundred times" that song had caused her to weep.[84] Tanguay was of course exaggerating for histrionic effect (she was, after all, an actress), but although it is unlikely she lost her friends due to a song, it is possible that she felt severely hemmed in by the tyrannical success of "I Don't Care." The song hung around her neck like a golden shackle, one that led her into a world of wealth and notoriety, yet also held her fast, unable to move on.

As she turned her musical comedy career into a vaudeville career, about 1905, she began adding other songs to her repertoire. These numbers contained the vitality and zest of "I Don't Care," and yet added a noticeable dollop of sexuality. Such songs as "I Want Someone to Go Wild with Me," and "It's All Been Done Before But Not the Way I Do It," according to the *New York Times*, "did much to bring vaudeville out of its decorous front." She added to her sex appeal by creating a fabulously successful Salome act—astride the others that were then glutting the vaudeville stage—in 1908. As Salome, it was said that her costume "consisted of two pearls."[85] Even amid all the racy, flesh-betraying, attention-grabbing Salomes plying the boards at the time, Eva Tanguay rose above the pack. She filled houses to every inch of standing room capacity.[86] In Salome, Eva Tanguay may have found the perfect way to combine her frenetic choreography, sultry and untrammeled personality, and libidinal flare into a format already vastly popular with the growing throngs of urban mass entertainment seekers.

The Salome act drew heavy sighs from anti-vice crusaders, but went on to ring up a "record gross," according to the *Times*. The following year, Tanguay appeared, to great positive attention, in Florenz Ziegfeld's *Follies of 1909*. Tanguay's leading spot in the Follies had originally been meant for Sophie Tucker, whom Tanguay beat out for the role. Ziegfeld then had his associates rewrite the part "especially for" Tanguay.[87]

As she drew increasing attention for her brazen lyrics and energetic style, she also began to make a name for herself as a wearer of outrageous, and typically alluring, costumes, which, claimed the comedienne, she had always designed herself. Sometimes, her outfits were merely vehicles designed to accentuate her already Rubensesque form, her "shapely" figure often appearing solely in "tights." The tights get-up was so form-revealing that it led to a police intervention later in 1913. When Tanguay appeared in her signature tights at Morrison's Theatre in July a plainclothes policeman named McVey approached the comedienne with the intention of arresting her for violation of Article 2,152 of the Penal Code, "which suggests that artists who appear in Sunday night sacred concerts at the variety theaters shall wear only clothes of the sort which can be worn in the streets," according to one account. For her part, Tanguay was incensed. Her costumes—or lack thereof—were a key part of her act and constituted no small part of her drawing power, and therefore her income. "Don't touch me! Don't you dare come near me! How dare you! Go right away from here!" yelped Tanguay at the hapless constable. The police prevailed, but the actress was let go on $500 bail.[88]

On other occasions, Tanguay would add an exotic flair to her form-fitting or revealing costumes, such as a "harem skirt that was a dream in white and purple silk" according to the *New York Clipper*. But most of the time, the costume, no matter how fancy or bejeweled, served one main purpose: the display of the body of Eva Tanguay in all its sensual, becurved glory. "Her bodices fit even tighter with more form revelation than ever before, impossible though it may seem," wrote *Variety* in 1914, just as Tanguay's career was beginning to drop off. Like other vaudeville actresses of her day, Eva Tanguay heightened the sexual allure of her costuming by conducting changes onstage. In 1930, the Depression in its onset, and her figure long past its ideal, Eva Tanguay concocted a dress made entirely of one dollar bills. As accompaniment, she sang a song called "Money" while a "negro jazz band" kept the rhythm.[89]

In utilizing unusual, decorative, and always revealing costumes, Eva Tanguay was taking a tack that many other female vaudeville performers also took. She was making the female body both a site of sexual, spectatorial allure, and also a site of conspicuous consumption. In effect, her costumes conflated the notion of consumption with that of sexuality—a tactic not unfamiliar in latter-day twentieth century market culture. But Tanguay was also exemplifying a common belief of her day, specifically, that in order for a female to fully be a woman—to perform her gender, in a sense—she had to be clad in the ostentations of "glitter" and "ornament." "One of the most powerful stimulations to either sex is glitter," wrote Prof. W. I. Thomas of the University of Chicago in an article on woman's "adventitious character" in the *American Journal of Sociology* in 1906. "It is true," continued the professor, "that the wooing connotation of ornament was originally its most important one, and that it was characteristic of man in particular; but woman has generalized it as an interest, and as a means of self-realization." Women utilized ornament and attention-grabbing finery not only to attract men but to outdo other women. In fact, held Prof. Thomas, so central had the acquisition of these features become in the character of woman, she now saw their assumption not merely as a means to an end, but a very existential end in and of itself.[90] Yet one detects more than mere quasi-scientific analysis—common to the social sciences of the day. One also smells a disapproval of woman's use of ornament, even as the author acknowledges its necessity. "Ornament," according to this sociologist, is meant both to lure men and beat out other women in the process. Women like Tanguay were in a sense caught between the need to fully realize their feminine identity via alluring ornament and a society that found such efforts slightly suspect. In many ways, Eva Tanguay managed that conflict to her best advantage.

Others were more overtly critical of women who relied too heavily on costume or dress to gain attention. One Mrs. Rhodes Campbell, writing for the *Arena* magazine in 1898, complained of seeing too often on the street and in other public milieus a "schoolgirl overdressed and in the worst possible taste." What made for such an offense to common sensibility? "A jaunty velvet cape, hat with nodding plumes and flowers, and at an angle which challenges our wonder and admiration as to its 'coherence of parts,'" according to the peeved Mrs. Rhodes. Not only were the constituent elements each in their own way breaches of decorum, so too was their seemingly scattershot assemblage. But more than mere aesthetics, it was the attitude conveyed by such choices of personal style and self-ornamentation that most irritated the author. The "evident consciousness" of the wearer's prettiness, the fact that she carried herself "with the self-possession and cool assertiveness of a woman of the world," were far more troubling. To Rhodes, womanly decorum was marked by "simplicity and naturalness" in the presentation of self—even though certainly she had in mind the baroque and variegated ensembles of Victorian-style fashion. Yet women increasingly insisted on experimenting with clothes that reflected and reaffirmed, in her view, their growing awareness of some kind of erotic power.[91]

Even the noted protofeminist Charlotte Perkins Gilman felt women should exhibit modesty, especially in the realm of dress and personal adornment. For Gilman, writing in the *Independent* in 1905, modesty and self control were "a mark of wisdom, of ability to recognize facts ... a root virtue." Modesty led one to enjoy clearer

In addition to being a sensual temptress, Eva Tanguay was the queen of the outrageous on the vaudeville stage. She claimed that she designed all of her own costumes, which would include this chandelier-like headdress. (Billy Rose Theatre Collection, The New York Library for the Performing Arts, Astor, Lenox, and Tilden Foundations.)

perceptions, better judgment, and a fundamental appreciation of justice. According to Gilman, the "most familiar" form of self control was "maiden modesty," and a woman ought to aim at "sex-modesty" which, above all else, involved "an instinct of concealment," and a "tendency to withdraw." In fact, Gilman saw modesty as a mark of evolutionary development. As women became "more developed humanly," in her view, they would recognize, and grow distasteful of, "the glaring immodesty of continual advertisement of sex."[92] On the one hand, Gilman seems to have been hoping that women would eventually come to rely less and less on sexual expressiveness, particularly in the area of bodily adornment. On the other hand, though, she leaves little room for a woman such as Eva Tanguay who deployed sartorial immodesty to her own material benefit. Rare were the observers of the day who noticed that women were held to different standards from men, or that such standards might not have a basis in natural law at all. "[T]he standard of judgment which condemns the woman and pardons the man is solely a social standard," argued J. Bellangee in the *Arena* in 1895.[93] Such sentiments, though, were few and far between.

In flaunting both the material ornament of her costumes and, at the same time, using those costumes as a means of advertising her sexualized form, Eva Tanguay played a key part in the socio-sexual upheavals of the early 1900s. She helped show many women that a certain degree of flash and glamour in dress could make a woman both attractive and individualized. Perhaps more importantly, she helped show many men a new model of consumable female sex appeal, there on display, if elegantly wrapped. Such dual appeal was surely important to the men who made considerable sums of money promoting Eva Tanguay and others like her.

At the same time that Eva Tanguay was making a name for herself as vaudeville's curiously clad (or unclad) vixen, she was also acquiring a well-publicized reputation for combativeness, insubordination, and unpredictable—at times even violent—behavior. In 1909, Tanguay's famed fury made an exemplary show of itself. That same year she had a run-in with Willa Holt Wakefield, who *Variety* described as "a pianologist, noted this season as being one of the best and cheapest acts playing the United Booking Offices circuit."[94]

In March of that year, Wakefield was in the middle of a multi-week run at Hammerstein's Theatre in New York. Wakefield had been suffering some form of nervous prostration and she brought her personal physician to the theater with her. However, when she attempted to enter the stage door, despite being dressed and ready to appear onstage and despite having played a matinee at the theater that very day, she was barred from doing so. Presently, she encountered her manager, Louis Newman, wandering about the street, also barred from Hammerstein's. Wakefield managed to sneak into the theater, change into her civilian attire, and retreat back out of the venue, confused, anxious, and angry. When questioned about the matter, theater owner Willie Hammerstein tried to make it seem as if Wakefield had voluntarily debarred herself from performing, saying he had given the popular performer the option of going on right before or right after Eva Tanguay. "She declined to do either, and I closed her," said Hammerstein, who added a crucial addendum: "Last week I asked Miss Wakefield, in deference to my headliner for this week (Eva Tanguay), to withdraw all her billing and advertising matter. She did so. Miss Tanguay had no knowledge whatsoever of this."[95]

But the truth seems to have been otherwise. This was 1909. Eva Tanguay was at the height of her popularity, having recently finished her house-packing Salome turn and her appearance in Ziegfeld's *Follies*. No vaudeville owner could afford to alienate Eva Tanguay, the most popular star in vaudeville, no matter how unreasonable her demands (which in this case appear to have been a desire not only to be heavily promoted but to have Ms. Wakefield's—a potential rival's—promotional materials removed). Tanguay was beginning to play hardball. She was learning to use her influence and popularity to her best advantage, even if that meant the arbitrary and capricious exercise of power. For her part, Wakefield tried to mend fences with Tanguay, Hammerstein, and the United Booking organization, claiming she would have occupied "any spot on the program had I been given sufficient notice," and would have happily appeared before Eva Tanguay, after her, or "after the moving pictures rather than disappoint some of my friends who I knew were in the audience."[96] But she told a different story to others who were willing to listen. She was said to blame "all her troubles on Eva Tanguay," according to the *New York Times*. Tanguay, it seems, had indeed objected to having Willa Holt Wakefield appear on the same bill, no doubt sensing a potentially keen competitor. Upon learning that she had been blackballed by Tanguay, Wakefield threatened to quite the Keith-run United Booking Office for Keith rival William Morris. No one seemed to care, and Willa Holt Wakefield "left the theater in high dudgeon." [97] In the battle of the divas, Eva Tanguay had fought and won. Not only was she establishing a name for herself as potentially explosive, she was, more significantly, learning to look out for her own rights and commercial and artistic prerogatives. In a time when women were commonly expected to be selfless and servile, Eva Tanguay was striking out new territory for female behavioral codes within the dominant culture.

As it turned out, Tanguay's mêlée with Willa Holt Wakefield was to be one of the more peaceable of her career. Five months after the Wakefield incident, Eva Tanguay was arrested in Louisville for allegedly attacking one Clarence Hess, "a youthful stage employee," with a hatpin; Hess eventually filed suit against Tanguay for $1,999.90 in damages. The facts of the incident are sketchy, but it seems that when Tanguay was playing McCauley's theater in Louisville, stagehand Hess failed to get out of the way fast enough as the "cyclonic" actress darted from stage to dressing room. Tanguay, whom, it should be noted, was not rushing to get *on*stage, somehow managed to knock the hapless stagehand down a flight of stairs and stab him, if lightly, with the hatpin, at which point other members of the technical crew began to have at the performer. Outnumbered by an ornery backstage staff probably exasperated with her temper tantrums, Tanguay found herself protected only by the theater's prop master George Rough, "her champion." When the police arrived, Tanguay produced a wad of cash and told the arresting officer, "Take it all and let me go, for it is now my dinner time."[98] The Hess incident may seem comical in historical retrospect, but it suggests that Tanguay, who had grown accustomed to defining the limits and capabilities of her body on stage, was perhaps beginning to do the same offstage as well. In the end, after a three-hour trial, Tanguay was ordered to pay a mere forty dollars for the infliction of what Hess claimed were "three punctures in the abdomen."[99] In another incident, which also found Tanguay wielding a sharp instrument, the actress cut a stage curtain "to shreds" at a vaudeville theater in Evansville, Indiana, after the house manager fined her for missing a matinee.[100] There is no evidence that she ever returned to that theater again.

For a woman to be combative, self-interested, and even physically violent in Tanguay's day was no mean feat. It meant transgressing accepted codes of femininity and creating a new model of public womanhood. Still, Tanguay must have provided a kind of off-beat hope for nascent feminists. Though *Harper's Bazar* argued that the "birth of a son is a happy event [and] that of a daughter, a trial," the proto-feminist magazine nonetheless concluded, in an article called "The Destiny of Woman," that "[i]n a word, woman should have the courage and pride of her sex."[101] Rather than viewing Eva Tanguay as a reckless hysterical, as certain of her contemporaries might no doubt have done, or as simply a "madcap," we might instead see the comedienne as an early example of what would later in the century become something of a cultural cliché: the so-called liberated woman. Liberated financially (at least until the Depression left her virtually penniless) and professionally, Eva Tanguay sought to liberate her person bodily as well, even if it meant wounding the occasional stagehand.

Tanguay also charted an unusual course in her personal involvement with men. Though she was married three times, the love and partnership of men never seemed important to her, each marriage falling apart in short order. Perhaps in part because she did not have to rely on a man for financial security, Eva Tanguay was able to function as a kind of social rebel in the days long before many women realized that companionate marriage was a choice—one which could be ignored or adhered to—rather than, strictly speaking, a fated necessity.

Each time she married, Tanguay chose men in show business. Her first marriage, to dancer John Ford, lasted three years. But it was a union her heart was not in, and fell apart nearly as soon as it began, even though the divorce took a little over three years to come through on paper, in 1917. "Three days after my marriage to John Ford I was beginning to figure a way out of it," wrote Tanguay.[102]

Tanguay had met Ford while playing a theater in Ann Arbor, Michigan. Ford was one of the performers in her backup troupe, and she remembered him as "very dapper with his cane and his spats, a happy-go-lucky fellow." They had become friendly, but solely on a professional level. One afternoon, as Tanguay approached the theater to get ready for that day's performance, she spotted Ford "standing at the corner, swinging his cane, quite the dude." According to the actress, Ford had "a twinkle in his eye," whereupon he told her that there was a justice of the peace office across the street and allowed as how the two of them ought to pop into it and get married. She thought he was joking. "Then Johnny started in about how lonely he was and how much he loved me. I laughed again and ran for the theater. Marriage was the last thing on my mind. Johnny followed me to the dressing room and went on pleading," Tanguay later recalled. Having staved off his protestations all afternoon and through much of show, Tanguay found herself staring at him later that day as he trod the boards. "The boy was clever. He was good-looking. I found myself beginning to wonder," she later said. Still, she hoped he would let the marriage proposal pass. Johnny Ford did not relent. Later that evening, after the show, he pounded her with more evidence of his supposed love and affection for her, and clearly Tanguay, for her part, began to wonder if having someone care for her in such a way might not be just the thing that was missing from her otherwise unpredictable life. Somehow, Ford got Eva Tanguay into that justice of the peace office and the two were wed. They returned to the theater for the show that night, Ford immersed in nuptial bliss, Tangauy not. "Back in my dressing room before the night show I began to cry," she recalled. "Why had I done such an impulsive thing? Here I was a successful headliner. I had received proposals from dozens of men, wealthy men, able to give me everything money could buy. I had turned all of them down. I had plenty of money. I could do as I pleased." Now she was married, and to a less successful actor at that. She wondered that night, as the crowd cheered Ford on the stage, why they didn't chant, "Poor Eva! Poor Eva!" From the very start of her capricious nuptials with Ford, Eva Tanguay realized that her economic security and sexual desirability were her own to control, and that marriage was something she did not need to opt for. This made her somewhat unique among women in her day. Nonetheless, the 33-year-old actress was joined in wedlock to John Ford, one year her junior, with three members of the troupe acting as witnesses, on November 24, 1913.[103]

As should be apparent, the union was doomed from the outset. Tanguay was not truly in love with Johnny Ford and, based on an overview of her entire romantic life, it seems likely she never wanted to tie herself down to one man. By 1915, Tanguay had separated from Ford; the two were formally divorced two years later. In his countersuit against Tanguay, Ford accused his wife of carrying on "intimacies with many men."[104]

It is indeed likely that Ford was right, that Eva Tanguay carried on with other men—perhaps many—even in marriage. She was a woman who flaunted her sexual self on the stage, and it appears she made no effort to curtail her sexuality or sexual appetites off of it. Perhaps the most infamous episode of Tanguay's trysting occurred in 1907. Martha Zittell, wife of *New York Mail* drama critic C. Florian Zittell (later Tanguay's manager), suspected her husband was carrying on a liaison with the Cyclonic One. Mrs. Zittell hired two private detectives to investigate the matter. The gumshoes dressed themselves as bellhops in order to gain entry to Tanguay's hotel room, whereupon they discovered Florian and Eva in carnal embrace. The *Cleveland News* wrote that the sleuths-cum-bellhops "found [Mr.] Zittell in pajamas and Miss Tanguay even more scantily clad than she has ever appeared in any of her stage productions."[105] It is almost as if such behavior were expected of Tanguay.

But the affair and its attendant publicity did not lead to a black cloud of scandal hanging over Tanguay and her career. Nearly the opposite, in fact. Less than a year later, a record number of people—some 25,000—packed the Brighton Beach Music Hall to see the comedienne during her week-long engagement. She also filled Keith & Proctor's Fifth Avenue with a record 1,783 audience members the same month. It is likely that Eva Tanguay avoided scandal because she never tried to create an image of virtuousness for herself, eschewing what some historians have identified as the dominant ideal of "feminine purity" common to Victorian, and even post-Victorian, America. She was a woman who looked to the future, rather than the past, for her paradigm. Accordingly, audiences, who were beginning to read the image of popular performers through their offstage personas, grew fascinated rather than disgusted.[106]

Though her marriage to Johnny Ford was less than a model relationship, it was by far the best of the three marriages to which Eva Tanguay was party. Sometime in the late 1910s or early 1920s, she reportedly married a fellow vaudevillian named Roscoe Ails. There is little information on this union, its very existence mentioned only in Tanguay's obituary in *Variety* and the *New York Times* (and it seems probable that the *Times* merely copied *Variety*).[107] Since Tanguay fails to mention it in the *American Weekly* serial, it is possible there was never such a marriage at all.

In July 1926 Eva Tanguay wed for the third and final time, to a pianist named Alexander Booke. Just a few months later Tanguay sought an annulment, claiming that, among other things, Booke had married her under an alias and had "deceived her in other ways" as well. The actress charged that Booke had gone by the names Allen Parado (or Parada, depending on which account one reads) and Chandas Ksiaziewicz.[108] As with her marriage to Ford, Tanguay appears once again to have made a poor and hasty decision. But then, it does not seem that choosing a proper husband was ever very high in Eva Tanguay's personal priorities. "My marriage to Parada, like the first one, turned out to be a mistake, as I learned all too soon.... In two months I got a divorce and went on my way again—alone."[109] Tanguay put more attention and greater focus into the creation of her costumes and the fine print in her contracts than into her nuptial undertakings.

Of all of Eva Tanguay's romantic and quasi-romantic entanglements, one more than any other seems to have had a genuinely profound effect upon the actress, and may have trained her early on not to rely on men for either emotional or financial security. Sometime early in her vaudeville career, Tanguay, playing New York, went to her dressing room to find flowers and a card waiting for her. "Dear Miss Tanguay," read the card, "This is my first visit to New York City. I was fortunate enough to see your performance. I am only a wanderer but at present fascinated to the extreme and desire your presence at dinner." The Wanderer claimed he had "no motive only to sit with you." He asked her presence at 6:30 that evening at the Astor Hotel. Tanguay agreed to meet the Wanderer and seems to have fallen for him almost from the start, describing him many years later as "my Prince Charming ... tall, a six-footer, with fine hair, beautiful teeth, elegantly groomed."[110]

Though Tanguay sought some kind of romantic relationship with the Wanderer (she never revealed his name in print) it did not come to pass. Still, the two grew close over the next few months and the Cyclonic One kept her hopes alive. By anticipating and filling her needs, the wandering gentleman made himself "indispensable" to Eva Tanguay. "His technique was perfect," allowed the cyclonic vaudevillian. And although the Wanderer still demonstrated little or no romantic affection for Tanguay, he showed her enough attention to earn a place as her de facto manager, eventually going "on the payroll."[111]

In time, though Eva Tanguay and the Wanderer were still not romantically linked, their friendship began to take on the hallmarks of what in contemporary psychological discourse might be referred to as an "abusive relationship." Once, when Tanguay struck up a conversation with a fellow actor in a bar on a cruise ship, the Wanderer became "livid with rage" and shouted at the comedienne, "Understand this ... you are not to talk to anyone else. You belong to me." Shortly after this unpleasantness, their relationship began to unravel, as Tanguay realized what kind of a man she had attached herself to. The Wanderer, it turned out, was using Tanguay's money to ferry another woman from city to city with him as he traveled. "I was footing the bill," Tanguay later wrote. The Wanderer seems to have stolen cash and some $40,000 worth of diamonds from her.[112] The subtext one may glean from this tale is that her involvement with the Wanderer, despite its technically platonic status, forewarned her about attachments to men. The men she did choose to marry were financially and, in terms of power and popularity, her inferiors. In any case, she never seems to have considered staying with any of them for very long.

On the stage, Tanguay challenged and mocked at marriage as well. In 1908, she sang a song called "That Wouldn't Make a Hit with Me." She belted out the lyrics:

> When you marry some old guy
> Who hasn't the decency to die,
> Or you marry some old pill
> Who can neither cure nor kill,
> That wouldn't make a hit with me.

Though sung with a perceived "charming naiveté,"[113] Tanguay was shedding a new light on marriage—a humorous, cynical take that had been so often the province of male comics in vaudeville at the time. Some nostalgic onlookers tried to argue that even when "mauled and pawed over" in the "ditties of vaudeville," a certain "dignity clings" to the ideas of motherhood and marriage nonetheless.[114] But Tanguay's raw words proffered no such dignity; instead, they forced audience members to distance themselves, if comically, from the central institution of bourgeois culture, legal wedlock.

In treating marriage lightly, both in her personal life and in her vaudeville act, Eva Tanguay was pressing one of the social hot buttons of the day. There were those who saw marriage as an endangered species—endangered largely by women like Tanguay, who seemed selfish and slightly reckless. In the words of one social critic of the era, the times had, for the archetype of "angel wife and mother, substituted for spiritual love the frankly erotic instinct," bringing about a "half-humorous barbarism" that was in the processing of smashing the domestic world that had come before. Anyone who spoke of "modesty or delicacy or tenderness or spirituality or purity, would provoke a smile at once, and would be set down as a grandmotherly prig." The rules had changed, in the eyes of this critic, and could be boiled down to this succinctly sententious truism: "Woman is now the hunter, man is her game."[115] Few individuals embodied the "frankly erotic instinct" and eschewed "modesty or delicacy" more completely than Eva Tanguay. She was indeed the hunter in her married relationships, though the prey turned out to be less than prize possessions.

Some began to notice that not only were women's needs and desires changing in regard to marriage, but many were choosing to go through life altogether unwed—as, in effect, Tanguay had decided to do. An article in *Popular Science Monthly*, on "The Celibate Women of To-Day," attributed what it saw as a growing phenomenon to woman's increasingly selfish wants and needs. Because women, in the author's estimation, had come to see themselves as "individuals," rather than as simply "the sex," they sought personal fulfillment, where once they might have accepted a mate whose "race, religion and social position," coupled with her mandate to marry, would otherwise have led to a connubial union. These days, with interests in culture, politics, travel, and "a hundred other directions," the new woman was harder pressed to find her match in a companionate marriage. The notion of finding a mate who could be one's equal, one's friend, one's match, suggested vexing problems for those seeking to couple at the time—very much as it still may, according to certain twenty-first century advice-givers and pundits. "Such a complex individuality does not easily find its complement," noted *Popular Science Monthly*. Put another way, in living a life more fully defined outside of the home, individualist women of the day were having a harder time building the home relationship at all. In addition, noted the article, getting married might mean giving up a salary, or settling for a man who was not of "superior intelligence."[116]

Others saw women like Tanguay as specifically unmarriageable due to their heated pursuit of professional and artistic goals. "The born artist puts her passionate appreciation of the elemental instincts into tangible form, and often by doing so gets rid of them from her daily life," wrote Juliet Wilbor Tompkins in *Cosmopolitan* in 1907. In Tompkins's estimation, a woman had simply just so much psychic "fuel" to expend in her life. Should she choose to burn it on creative pursuits, it would be in low reserve, or completely used up, when it came to romantic matters. It was either to be "a burnt offering to love and maternity," or what drove "the productive processes of her art."[117] But not both. In this thermochemical calculus of allegedly conflicting desires, a woman like Eva Tanguay, in devoting so much energy and effort to her art, had clearly to forgo any meaningful wife/mother relationships for want of "fuel." Moreover, according to writers like Juliet Wilbor Tompkins, women who made the choices that Eva Tanguay made would eventually discover that they had erred. In fact, Tompkins suggests that part of what permitted the creative female's "zest in freedom" was her subtle, simultaneous recognition that the door to marriage was still ajar. However, the day she woke up and realized that "the door has blown shut," and that the period of "joy ignorance" had ended, with her feminine allure fading and no man at the ready, the artistic single woman would no doubt come to regret that she "rode her career as a charger" rather than seeking to become a wife and mother.[118] Thus, the illusion of choice was simply that, an illusion, and one that would surely eventuate in unhappiness. Famed psychologist Havelock Ellis saw the individual of remarkable talent or "genius" as perforce unmarriageable. "Such ability," he wrote in an *Atlantic Monthly* article, "involved a radically different temperament, for it means seeing the world from a different angle from other people and feeling it with a different sensibility." The artistic genius, according to Ellis, was "necessarily solitary."[119]

Some viewed the modern woman, caught between the proprietary marriages of yesterday and the choice-driven, companionate marriages of today, as doomed to failure in wedlock. The modern woman, argued Rafford Pike (who, the reader may recall, had argued a year earlier against womanly awkwardness) hated "the social order as it is," leading her in her "disappointment and disgust" to "cry out loudly against marriage" and other social customs which she might feel she had no part in constructing. Accordingly, Pike argued, they were neither happy nor unhappy being married. Rather, they had "failed most wretchedly, yet they are not aware of it."[120] Eva Tanguay may have been like many other women of her day in being acutely aware of the shortcomings of the married state. However, her celebrity, wealth, and itinerant life-style afforded her an opportunity that most married women did not have, the opportunity to live alone and play at a palette of lovers.

Even women who chose marriage early and firmly as the way to expend their "fuel" came under fire from certain social critics and observers of the day. One writer, Mrs. Amelia E. Barr, writing for the *North American Review*, went so far as to suggest that many women married simply to engage in abundant, if safe, flirtation with other men. According to Barr, even more than the technological advances of industry, technology, and politics, the most astonishing thing about the present historical moment was the rise of women with their own unique opinions, careers, aesthetic sensibilities, behavior patterns, conceptions of gender, and "perhaps more astonishing than all, the women who make marriage the cloak for much profitable postnuptial flirtation." With flirtation the main thing on most brides' minds, Barr saw the virtuous marriage as a thing of the past. Flirtation, in her view, had to lead to, and was itself a form of, disloyalty.[121] For Barr and others like her, many modern women were conducting a kind of guerilla warfare. Safely in the social cloak of marriage, the modern bride wanted nothing more than to seek quasi-sexual thrills in flirting with strange men. The new bride was defining her sexuality by the way that dozens, perhaps hundreds, of men reacted to her flirtations. For Eva Tanguay, such activity was carried out largely onstage, rather than in some private, supra-nuptial sphere.

If Eva Tanguay ultimately resisted marriage, it may also have been due to a deep desire to resist motherhood, perforce the complement of wifehood at the turn of the century. Not only did Tanguay perhaps feel that her lifestyle rendered her ill-suited to motherhood, but it is likely that others would have felt this way as well. Increasingly, there were calls to discourage pregnant women, or those hoping to become pregnant, from working.[122] Such a prescription was not possible for Eva Tanguay, who performed until her body began to fail (which it did, as it turns out, when she was still quite young).

To some women—perhaps many—Eva Tanguay must have also been an icon of hope, a living symbol of a woman who had freed herself from the traditional cultural bonds of matrimony and motherhood, choosing instead a life of glamour, wealth, and freely-chosen sexual liaisons. Her persona onstage and off must have seemed exciting to those American women who felt trapped in their marriages and ensnared by the cultural demands of motherhood. "Deep in my soul was a bitter resentment toward God for having made me a woman," wrote an anonymous diarist in the *Ladies' Home Journal*. As she felt herself bound in by the exigencies of matrimony and motherhood, and looked at teenage girls playing together outside her window, the diarist identified "an awful sinking of the heart, and [I] knew distinctly, without equivocation, that I wanted to be out in front there with those happy, light-hearted youngsters." She felt as Tanguay did the night of her hasty wedding to John Ford. Yet unlike the vaudeville star, this ordinary woman could not simply drop her family responsibilities, and seek the comfort of other men, for her "baby cried and cried."[123]

In her own way, Eva Tanguay, especially onstage, seemed forever to give off the air of a light-hearted youngster. Though inside she was often wracked with feelings of depression and worry, her outer façade must have seemed to many a tantalizing alternative to conventional life. In rejecting the traditional role of woman as wife and mother, Tanguay was thus seen as rejecting the responsibilities of adulthood. Some at the time believed this fitting. In the view of the *Nation*'s Margaret Ladd Franklin, writing in 1913, the female mind seemed "hardly to get beyond the stage of adolescence."[124] Eva Tanguay thus not only embodied but in fact celebrated the inherently adolescent nature of woman, both onstage and off. "She likes and dislikes by flashes—with the acute sensibilities of a child," observed the *New York Dramatic Mirror* of Eva Tanguay in 1915,[125] just one of many organs of discourse that further accused Tanguay of an inherent immaturity.

Even as she indulged in fleeting or failed romantic attachments, Tanguay's popularity continued to grow. In 1908, just before the smashing popularity of her Salome turn, Eva Tanguay was voted the second most popular act in vaudeville, drawing 6,083 votes in a poll taken among patrons of Percy Williams's Colonial Theatre—not far behind winner Irene Franklin (with 7,414 votes), but way ahead of third place contestant Alice Lloyd, who garnered only 2,948 votes. By 1911, Tanguay had become the most popular act in vaudeville, however. That year, impresario Percy Williams awarded a diamond medal to Tanguay in recognition of her status as "the greatest box office attraction" at his theater, beating out not just women, like Valeska Suratt, but a number of men, including Nat Goodwin.[126]

Perhaps the greatest measure of Eva Tanguay's success, though, was the number of Tanguay imitators—performers who made their living simply aping or burlesquing Eva Tanguay's act—that began springing up around 1909–10. Bessie Browning, who began making a name for herself as a Tanguay copy, was recognized as one of the stronger entries in this unusual category. "Tanguay is so often imitated," noted the *New York Clipper* (indicating the size of the Tanguay copy wave), "and usually so badly done, that it is a relief to see a good imitation of the 'whirlwind' every once in a while."[127] The *New York Dramatic Mirror*, though, considered Billie Seaton "Eva Tanguay's 'best little imitator,'" and lauded Seaton for "the merits of her costumes (or lack of them)," or put another way, what the *Mirror* described as "the startling gownless-ness of her costume" and her "risqué" musical numbers.[128] In order to copy Tanguay—ultimately, an impossible task—one had to reveal one's body and tint one's song lyrics noticeably toward the blue. William J. Gane, manager of a theater that employed Seaton, felt that paying the Tanguay imitator to appear made simple economic sense. He could not afford the genuine article, so he signed Billie Seaton, who he considered "a great mimic," and, with the money he saved, even bought her an array of Tanguay-like costumes. The audiences showed up enthusiastically.[129]

Men too got in on the Tanguay facsimile wave. In July 1910 the *New York Dramatic Mirror* reported on Harry Breen, at Keith & Proctor's Fifth Avenue, "who calls himself the male Eva Tanguay." If there were money to be made in looking or sounding like Tanguay, men as well as women wanted in on it. Several years later, Gaby Deslys created an act based on Tanguay's trademark tune, "I Don't Care."[130]

For her part, Eva Tanguay did not always see the flattery in copy acts. In fact, she viewed them as legally infringing on her economic livelihood, an understandable fear given the mass-market competitiveness of the vaudeville business and many stars' interchangeability (though this was less of a threat to Eva Tanguay, the ultimate individualist). "Authors of books are protected; why not an originator of his or her line of work?" opined Tanguay. "Night and day, I plan and worry and pay out most of what I earn only to have it stolen by *imitators*." She understood that she was being imitated because she, like others who had been copied, constituted the best material on the stage. Still, it was, in her opinion, more or les futile to try to copy her, as her performances depended on her mood, whim, and mental state at the time of their execution. "I could not imitate myself, for I do not know my points, and always working naturally, I leave all to my condition." Tangauy estimated that each of her songs cost her between $50 and $100 to develop and rehearse, and that each fabulous, revealing, outrageous costume required hours and hours of planning and serious "brain work."[131] Though her words are tinged with hyperbole and the absurd, they nonetheless reveal a keen sensitivity to the emerging mass-market economics of entertainment. Few vaudeville performers established their bodies as being as unique and individuated as Tanguay did; yet, at the same time, few were so consistently copied.

For this reason, among others, Eva Tanguay took out lavish advertisements in the theatrical trade papers of the day, from time to time, to reassert her individuality, unique drawing power, and unrivaled success. "Eva Tanguay in justice to herself, offers the following" read the headline of a banner advertisement in *Variety* in 1915.

In the ad, Tanguay pointed out that she had been called "The Girl Who Made Vaudeville Famous," and boasted a number of other monikers, including, "The Genius of Mirth and Song"; "America's Champion Comedienne"; "The Girl Who the Whole World Loves"; "Vaudeville's Greatest"; and "The One Best Bet." The ad further protested:

> **Eva Tanguay** is the only vaudeville attraction who ever remained in New York City for three years, playing vaudeville all of that time, without leaving this city for an engagement...
>
> **Eva Tanguay** can claim that her clothes, from gowns to shoes, slippers, gloves and tights, are distinctive and replaced more often than has been done by any other woman who ever appeared upon the stage...
>
> **Eva Tanguay** has drawn more people into vaudeville theaters who were never in them before, and if they remained patrons of vaudeville thereafter, that was a benefit contributed by Eva Tanguay...[132]

Her hubris may be forgiven if one recognizes that Eva Tanguay was merely a product in a competitive, consumer marketplace, and understands that she was fully aware of this reality. Looked at in this light, one can almost view her advertisements as promotions of the brand "Eva Tanguay," a unique body in a mass market that relied on some measure of predictability.

There is, of course, little evidence that Eva Tanguay ever suffered any kind of economic setback at the hands of imitators. As her career grew, so did her personal fortune. At the height of her career she spared herself no expense, luxury, or personal comfort. She lived in a 13-room apartment near the corner of 116th Street and Morningside Drive in New York City. Red velour drapes covered the walls in one room; another featured a 14-foot-long tiger skin rug; her bedroom sported lavender drapes, gilt furniture, and a small fountain whose flowing water was lit with blue and amber lights. "The furnishings were the last word in elegance," she remarked. Following her marriage to John Ford, Tanguay bought a $40,000 home in Sea Gate, Brooklyn (on the western tip of the same peninsula as Coney Island and Manhattan Beach) and got not one but two cars. When she tired of one of her autos, "and that was often," she simply gave it away. It never occurred to her to sell it. Eva Tanguay also bought a boat. In her heyday, Tanguay was famous for carrying "nothing smaller than $1,000 bills" which she would peel off almost unthinkingly to calm a stir she had caused or reward some especially loyal cohort.[133]

Such behavior may seem endearing or eccentric in retrospect, but in her day it was potentially transgressive. In criticizing "the wild woman as social insurgent," the *Nineteenth Century*'s social theorist Lynn Linton derided females like Tanguay, for the wild woman had "no scruples about money" and was "notorious for never having small change."[134] In turn-of-the-century America, women were expected to be frugal and economical, to pay careful attention to what things cost and how to get the best deal, especially when purchasing items for the home. A woman's real concern, wrote Ida Tarbell, in the *American Magazine* in 1912, ought to be retail prices. "If she does her work intelligently she knows the why of every fluctuation of price in standards," Tarbell argued. The woman engaging in commerce as a consumer ought to become well apprised of quality and quantity in her purchases as well.[135] Few women of Tanguay's day paid so little attention to the minutiae of price fluctuations as did Eva Tanguay. Her concern was with living large, spending lavishly, and picking up the pieces later. One newspaper reported that Tanguay had "owned and lost" no less than 14 houses.[136]

For all her wealth—and life narratives like Tanguay's seem often to end this way—Eva Tangauy settled into near-poverty in her September years. Observers estimated that she lost the bulk of her $2 million personal fortune in the stock market crash of 1929. In early 1930—having resettled to Los Angeles by this time—Tanguay was forced to sell her $45,000 Toluca Lake home and some $50,000 worth of furniture, bric-a-brac, and objets d'art. Auctioneers Netzel & Netzel handled the sale of items, including several of her silk costumes, that once bejeweled her spacious ten-room abode. Another report valued Tanguay's possessions at closer to $100,000. In the end, she died with a mere $500 in "personal effects" to her name and no will.[137]

Shortly after her economic losses of 1929, and no doubt feeling the need for additional income, Tanguay planned a stage comeback, a "one woman show with a band." Convalescing from one of her many illnesses at her modest new home in a small Los Angeles apartment complex, Tanguay declared that a "New York capitalist" had agreed to back her. "As soon as I have recovered, I am going to New York to do a 'one-woman show.' I'll use the best songs in my repertoire, and, believe me, I'll try to 'panic 'em,' just to show how grateful I am that I'm alive and well!"[138]

But Tanguay was far from "well." The body that had carried her around the stage in many a cyclonic frenzy, the body that she had claimed so potently as her own, was beginning to fail. "Age overtook her with the rapidity of a sword thrust," wrote the *Los Angeles Examiner*.[139] Vaudeville and the era of performers like Eva Tanguay were ailing as well, the prognosis poor. In fact, the deterioration of Tanguay's physical and mental self seems to have handily symbolized the decay of the era that gave her success and wealth.

Her physical troubles began in the early 1920s, as her stage career—and vaudeville itself—was also slipping into an irreversibly weakened state. In December 1924 Tanguay had to cancel several engagements in Providence due to the grip, marking the first time in her career that she had been forced to call off an engagement due to illness. But it would not be the last. Of course, it would be increasingly unnecessary for Tanguay to blame her failing career on her failing heath, for vaudeville was already past its heyday, as Tanguay was past hers. She convalesced at the Hotel Embassy in New York, but appears never to have fully shaken her malady. The following year, she developed a throat abscess which diminished her ability to sing.[140]

In 1930, Tanguay fell "very ill" following a seizure at the El Fey Club, at which she was appearing, in New York City. Though she recovered temporarily, she again took sick, this time more deeply and intractably. A number of blood transfusions seemed to bring her back to the brink of recovery, but this bromide was short-lived, as Tanguay slipped to the edge of death. At this point, most of the people close to Tanguay figured she was going to die and began sending "flowers to the little bungalow where she lies near death." According to Tanguay's sister, the Cyclonic One was suffering from Bright's disease (a kidney disorder), rheumatism, and a heart condition. With little or no money to pay for her treatment, a number of theater magnates and stars, including impresario Sid Grauman, took care of Tanguay's medical expenses.[141]

Tanguay had also been battling failing eyesight for a number of years. This, perhaps more than any other single physical ill, spelled the end of her career. "My eyes grew dimmer," lamented Tanaguay. Cataracts left her hovering on the brink of blindness. She eventually had to have a red bulb placed in the center of the stage in order to orient herself on those occasions when she did still perform. But her sight was too far gone. During a show in Baltimore, Tanguay toppled off the stage and fell smack into a bass drum in the orchestra pit. The descent into blindness continued and by 1933 doctors were considering surgical removal of at least one of her eyes. Miraculously, though, her ocular faculties began to improve the following year and she regained some of her vision. Perhaps because visual appeal—and a live performer's simple need to see—were so central to her stage act with its tornado-like choreography and outrageous costumes, Tanguay's eye ailments seem to have struck the deepest emotional chord of any of her bodily malfunctions. In the mid-1930s, she indicated that when she made enough money, she would "endow a hospital to treat the sightless eyes of children." This, of course, was pure fancy, as Tanguay had barely the funds to see to her own medical care, much less endow a hospital. In fact, Sophie Tucker had paid for Tanguay's eye operations.[142]

Though Tanguay claimed she could now see "perfectly,"[143] her overall bodily condition continued to deteriorate, and by 1938 she was again being written off as near death. Her physician, Dr. Wendell Starr, called Tanguay's case "hopeless." For her part, Tanguay seemed resigned to death, perhaps because she knew a comeback was impossible and had no immediate family for which to live. "My life has been a full one," she whispered to a friend, amidst blood transfusions and intravenous injections. "It's all right. The end has to come to every one some time."[144]

Still, Eva Tanguay held on, somehow, for eight more years. By late 1946, however, she was truly at death's door. She was bedridden, again nearly blind, and unable to walk or lift objects due to advanced arthritis. "Everything is shadowy now," she confided to a rare visitor. On January 11, 1947, shadow turned to full-fledged darkness and Eva Tanguay passed on, despite some twenty-six blood transfusions. Dr. Starr attributed her death to a combination heart attack and brain hemorrhage. Some 500 people showed up at Tanguay's funeral, including several of Tanguay's peers from vaudeville (though many had themselves passed on), such as Trixie Friganza. "Eva Tanguay's Funeral Draws Stage Star 'S.R.O.'" read a headline in the *Los Angeles Examiner*.[145]

For all her physical ills, though, Eva Tanguay seems to have been equally troubled psychologically throughout her life. In late 1908, following the success of her Salome act, Tanguay reportedly suffered a nervous breakdown. It was not to be her first. In the early 1930s, Tanguay repaired to the famous Hot Springs, Arkansas, spa having again suffered an emotional collapse, in addition to the other health problems burdening her.[146]

Though on stage Tanguay played the part of the madcap, bellowing "I Don't Care" to the back of the house, she sometimes confided that she felt quite differently on the inside. "I am supposed to be a heedless, foolish, joyous, capricious minx, girl or woman, girl or minx, just as you like, with no more heart than a stone, no more feeling than an electric sign and no more serious than a moth.... Fiction—all fiction.... I never go a day without a good cry," she told a journalist in 1919. Similarly, she once admitted that although she remembered having had a carefree childhood, she was, as an adult, "not the happiest of mortals ... not quite happy in my mind." She was often described as moody and mercurial. "She likes, dislikes, by flashes—with the acute sensibilities of a child," noted one observer.[147] It is as if Tanguay's trademark childishness, which served her so well in public life, had its genesis in some dysfunction of the mind. That, at any rate, is what we are led to believe.

The necessity of appearing as whimsical and carefree offstage as on must have taken its toll on Eva Tanguay. She had continually to sell herself as a product associated with whimsy and lightheartedness; at the same time, she was a woman with problems and ills that were all too real. The pressure to keep up appearances must only have added to any depression, anxiety, or other psychological or biochemical frailties to which she may have been naturally disposed.

For all that, we might still look upon Eva Tanguay as a remarkable figure, one who personified certain social and sexual struggles of her day, and broke new ground on both these fronts. As a performer, she had no peer. She helped make vaudeville the massively popular, mass-market phenomenon that it was. She profited from the sexual liberalization of the female body authorized by the vaudeville magnates and effected by the performers described herein. She grew out of, and responded to, her particular moment in history. She rode the wave of, and yet helped define, the beginnings of mass entertainment in American culture. Accordingly, when the amusement with which she was so closely identified began to fade from the American scene, so too must she. In the intervening years, her existence was not only overlooked but even in part erased by the records of culture. This chapter has been a modest attempt to reconstruct her story in its social context; other attempts are surely needed.

five

"The Signal of Distress"
Film and the Fall of Vaudeville

For all its fanfare and popularity, for all the high salaries paid to stars like Eva Tanguay and Annette Kellerman, and for all the luxuriously appointed theaters erected by Keith, Proctor, and their peers, the vaudeville era did not survive as long as it might have. Vaudeville emerged from the concert saloon, burlesque hall, and dime museums of the 1880s, drawing on preexisting forms of variety entertainment which, it could be argued, date back as far as Greco-Roman antiquity—in spirit anyway. By the 1890s, though, it had taken on a shape all its own and coalesced into a corporate-controlled, centrally managed, standardized form of mass entertainment—among the first species of mass entertainment in the modern, consumerist United States.

By 1898, vaudeville was achieving mass-entertainment status in part by drawing its crowds from across class lines in the urban locale. The "upper circle of New York society," wrote the *New York Dramatic Mirror* in early 1898, were going to vaudeville "with a vengeance." As the century turned, vaudeville gained steam, attracting larger crowds to an increasing number of theaters. Ticket sales and attendance reached a new high in 1902, a level of interest not seen "since the commencement of the vaudeville craze," in the words of the *Mirror*, which by 1904 deemed the theatergoing public "vaudeville mad."[1]

Nothing seemed to stop the growth of vaudeville. The oligarchic handful of corporate interests that controlled the hugely popular form of amusement saw no end to the extension of their franchise. Wherever there was a city—or a town that acted like a city—there was the potential to build a profitable vaudeville theater. Once one player landed in a territory, others followed. No town would be "left uncovered by the vaudeville magnates," wrote an observer in 1906, suggesting that the United States was soon to become "thoroughly vaudevillized." And it wasn't just New York or other warhorse East Coast cities that threatened to become so. Cincinnati, Ohio, for example, was every bit as "vaudeville mad" as her sister urban milieus.[2]

Yet the rage did not last. By 1914, the urban public was beginning to draw away from the entertainment to which it had once flocked. In that year, Keith's New York houses finished in the red, losing between $100,000 and $150,000, according to *Variety*. To fight the trend, the vaudeville lords did what they knew best: they attempted to put acts that were ever novel on the boards. A routine called "Hanged," which simulated an execution, was staged in May 1914. Critics, many of whom had cheerfully smirked at the nudity and suggestiveness vaudeville offered, found nothing redeeming in "Hanged," deeming it "sordid and morbid ... gruesome ... repellant."[3] Vaudeville may have begun to seem decadent rather than simply indecorous, pandering rather than simply titillating—to some close observers, anyway.

The downward spiral continued. It was as if vaudeville had risen quickly to prominence, shone brightly, and then begun to burn through its store of fuel. Perhaps it is impossible to expect longevity of a form of entertainment that relied so centrally on novelty, on so many live bodies, and, nonetheless, on such generic standardization. But the fact is that the vaudeville magnates had found a formula that had served them well, at least for a while. Now, however, that formula was beginning to turn on its creators. "Vaudeville *is not what it used to be*," observed one theater journalist in 1914. Some vaudeville houses still packed in the crowds, but others were "flying the signal of distress." Managers and executives at the UBO and its competitors found themselves "hard-pressed to find attractions and harder pressed for audiences." A journalist suggested that some vaudeville houses might find temporary respite by booking even higher-class stars and bigger names. But, he suggested, in order to survive, many would have to turn to programs consisting entirely of motion pictures, rather than just featuring a half-dozen or so shorts as a "chaser" at the end of the bill.[4]

Though vaudeville in the United States would continue in some form or another for two more decades, with numerous attempts, usually by old, out-of-work vaudevillians, to bring back the glory days of the form,[5] the vaudeville era, in a real sense, was gone by 1918. The writer above saw the writing on the wall: Motion pictures would cleanly and profitably fill the void in the urban entertainment market left by vaudeville. Indeed, the emerging movie interests would jump in and fill it before such a void ever fully came to be. Vaudeville, which had provided the first mass venue for the commercial projection of motion pictures,[6] now saw itself defeated by the seed it had planted.

As has been suggested, the burgeoning motion picture business came under much heavier and more consistent fire from reformers and moral authorities than vaudeville did. There are, as has also been indicated, several likely reasons for this. One is that, while vaudeville may have been perceived as a form of entertainment controlled by right-intentioned Anglo-American Christian men (which it largely was), the movies were more readily seen as the province of outsiders: immigrants, Europeans, Jews, men with little formal education who came from low backgrounds and disreputable lines of business.[7] As late as the 1930s, some social observers still considered the film moguls, even those who had risen to fame and wealth, as low-born outsiders. Writing about film industry pioneer William Fox in 1930, *Fortune* magazine characterized the Twentieth Century–Fox namesake not as having worked his way up from the "bottom," but rather as having emerged from the socioeconomic "subcellar." Such a provenance—more Ellis Island than Horatio Alger—argued the influential business magazine, could not but leave an individual burdened by a crippling inferiority complex, bereft of virtue. In the wake of the 1929 stock market crash, Fox, struggling to retain control of his empire, lost out to those whom *Fortune* considered to be Fox's "highborn associates," the denizens of venerable old Wall Street firms. It was not the blue-blood Wall Streeters who were to blame, nor the spiraling economy, nor the politicians. Rather, it was William Fox's "ancient and half-obliterated distrust," his culturally determined paranoia, that ultimately destroyed the movie magnate, like a Greek tragic hero overcome by hubris.[8] Only in this case, *Fortune* saw nothing heroic about William Fox, Hungarian-born and sired by a "shiftless and irresponsible" immigrant father.[9]

It is worth noting that the vaudeville chiefs of the 1900s and 1910s never much turned to Wall Street for money in the way that the early film moguls did from the 1920s onward. Some vaudeville magnates, like B.F. Keith and E. F. Albee, secured some financing from the church. But most seem to have funded their operations with their own income. Had Keith or Proctor approached Wall Street, they would almost certainly have had an easier time obtaining backing—and respect—from their "highborn" brethren.

Nor did the early film entrepreneurs attempt to market their wares as safe or sanitized, at least not in the same way as did the vaudeville magnates, who built theater environments that seemed cleansed and controlled. In contrast to Keith theaters, which mimicked high-class refinement, early "nickelodeon" theaters were typically little more than converted store fronts, dark and perhaps dingy. Certainly they posed a threat of fire. "Many of us probably know moving pictures as a clattering, rackety performance, carried on in semi-darkness," wrote William Inglis in *Harper's Weekly* magazine in 1910.[10]

So while vaudeville theaters were built to fit into the growing commercial cityscape, meshing with and enhancing trophy properties like department stores and existing legitimate theater spaces, the nickelodeon theaters of the early twentieth century were viewed by many as a plague-like encroachment. One anti-film crusader in New York City determined that the "evil" of motion pictures lay in "the conditions in which so many [movies] are given—the dark room, filled with adults and children, absolutely without supervision, affording no protection against the evil-minded and depraved men who frequent such places and sit beside the innocent boys and girls without a question or suspicion until irreparable harm is done." His solution: turn on the lights while the moving picture was playing—no matter that it might make it harder to see the picture. Such illumination would render "any immoral or undesirable conduct" impossible.[11] It would probably have had the effect of driving patrons out of the movie house altogether, thus indeed putting an end to the ills therein.

Thus, the vaudeville magnates created spaces that were seen as safe and, because they mimicked high-culture splendor, further seen as salutary additions to the urban clime. Not so the early movie venues. The nickelodeons that began springing up in American cities after about 1905 did so quickly, like an invasion, and almost without warning. Mostly, they were converted storefronts and their dark, stuffy innards catered, at least initially, to working-class immigrants.[12]

If movies suffered a degree of moral censure that vaudeville did not, despite the fact that the latter contained its share of potentially objectionable material, it may also have been simply due to the remarkable popularity of the moving picture. In fact, that popularity grew so fast, it seems to have more than counteracted whatever discursive, marketing, and cultural shortcomings under which the movie business suffered in comparison to vaudeville with its rhetoric of purity. By 1910, some 26 million Americans were going to the movies at nickelodeon theaters every week; in New York City alone, the weekly figures amounted to between 1.2 million and 1.6 million.[13] As popular as vaudeville was, it was never quite as explosively popular as this; in part, the need for live bodies onstage, though treated as a kind of mass-entertainment commodity, limited vaudeville. Motion pictures, on the other hand, could be cranked out and copied by the hundreds. Surely vaudeville had laid the groundwork for a mass national entertainment like this. But such plans were more fully realized with the movies. Their very popularity made them push the hot buttons of crusaders and reformers in a way that vaudeville never could. The early moral objections to vaudeville and the legitimate stage, which were based in part on fears of a free-market determination of moral acceptability, came to full fruition with the rise of cinema. "Morality," observed George Bernard Shaw at the time, "in fact, is only popularity."[14] Movies, more than vaudeville, threatened to wrest the power of moral determination from cultural authorities and place it squarely within the realm of the free market—that is, in the hands of the putatively ill-informed, under-educated, pleasure-seeking masses.

In addition, motion pictures threatened to cement the massive, national scope of entertainment more firmly than vaudeville, which could at times be tailored to meet the needs of a specific locale. That is, while the vaudeville chiefs conceived of the possibility of a nationwide market (and, therefore, the possibility of a translocal notion of consumerist mass entertainment culture), the film chiefs actualized it more completely by providing a product that was created in an industrial setting and finalized before it was ever seen by a movie-going public. Eva Tanguay's act in Memphis was very close to Eva Tanguay's act in Minneapolis. But at least the *possibility* of local variation existed. Crowds were trained to keep their feedback to a minimum (other than polite applause), furthering diminishing the odds that a vaudeville performer would toss in something special. But it was understood that the possibility was there. When film came along, however, it was quite certain that what was seen in Memphis was *exactly* like what was seen in Minneapolis. And New York. And Los Angeles. And so forth.

This poses some interesting possibilities for future consideration. As entertainment has become increasingly a mass-scale, corporate controlled affair—now it is largely in the hands of a handful of huge multinational organizations—there continue to be objections of one sort or another to the content of popular amusements and its supposed deleterious effects. But those in charge have not by and large responded with claims of wholesomeness and purity. Those were the era-specific tactics of businessmen at the dawn of the modern mass-market era in the late nineteenth and early twentieth centuries; mimicking those efforts would be no more appropriate than trying to recreate vaudeville itself in the current moment. In part, this is so because the mass-entertainment businessmen who followed in the footsteps of the B.F. Keiths and the E.F. Albees have sold to a public more accepting of mass commerce as a conceit. Thus, they have tended to respond with constitutional claims of freedom of speech and expression. In other words, they have attempted to add a political element to the discourse whereas the vaudeville chiefs remained more decidedly commercial in their efforts. Put another way, the modern-day heirs of the mass-amusement paradigm instigated by the vaudeville chiefs have appealed to notions of individual rights of consumption and self-regulation rather than relying on the construction of a patriarchal force empowered to keep things clean and healthy for the masses.

In its own way, vaudeville was also more fully a public entertainment at a time when urban Americans were seeking out new and pleasing ways to spend their leisure dollars. They did so in the company of fellow urbanites in locales that placed them together en masse and in close proximity. Thus, vaudeville was much more a mass experience than are the movies today, many of whose consumers will watch them in the privacy of their own homes on DVD or cable. "The newest, most technologically advanced amusement sites are our living rooms," observes an historian of American leisure time.[15]

The end of vaudeville heralded the beginning of the end of urban public amusements more generally.[16] The American public had been given an entertainment product—vaudeville—that had much in common with its antecedent forms, the licentious burlesque hall and the ribald variety theater; at the same time, its anxieties over mass spectatorship had been quelled by promises of purity, wholesomeness, and sterility. In a sense, the battle for the hearts, minds, and wallets of amusement-seeking Americans had been won. Now it was up to the urban populace to retreat to the suburbs, to the comfort of private living rooms and the glow of the television. Here, to be sure, people could be sold representations of sexualized performance on such a massive scale that even E.F. Albee would be impressed.

Chapter Notes

Introduction

1. In: Charles Stein, ed., *American Vaudeville as Seen by Its Contemporaries* (New York: Knopf, 1984), 60–67.
2. Israel Zangwill, "The Future of Vaudeville in America," *Cosmopolitan*, April 1905, 641.
3. "Note and Comment," *New York Dramatic Mirror*, 11 December 1909, 19.
4. After the fall of vaudeville by the late 1920s, the Keith vaudeville theaters were transformed into movie houses along with onetime rival the Orpheum circuit; both were absorbed into a new national movie chain largely in the control of RCA, the Radio Corporation of America. RCA's newly hewn movie studio and theater chain took the name R-K-O: Radio-Keith-Orpheum.
5. M. Alison Kibler, *Rank Ladies: Gender and Cultural Hierarchy in American Vaudeville* (Chapel Hill and London: University of North Carolina Press, 1999), 15.
6. John Dimeglio, *Vaudeville U.S.A.* (Bowling Green, Ohio: Bowling Green State University Popular Press, 1973), 48.
7. Dimeglio, 49.
8. Stein, ed., 23.
9. Dimeglio, 49–50. Some Keith theaters also featured booster seats, marking them, allegedly, as places it would be safe for a wife and mother to bring her children. See: Kibler, 32.
10. Douglas Gilbert, *American Vaudeville: Its Life and Times* (New York: Dover Publications, 1940).
11. Robert W. Snyder, *The Voice of the City: Vaudeville and Popular Culture in New York* (New York and Oxford: Oxford University Press, 1989), 30.
12. *New York Dramatic Mirror*, 25 December 1897, 18.
13. *New York Dramatic Mirror*, 29 January 1898, 18.
14. *New York Dramatic Mirror*, 25 June 1898, 16.
15. Dimeglio, 16–17.
16. Marian Spitzer, "Morals in the Two-a-Day," in Stein, ed., 325–26; Charles Samuels and Louise Samuels, *Once Upon a Stage: The Merry World of Vaudeville* (New York: Dodd, Mead & Company, 1974), 40.
17. Samuels and Samuels, 40.
18. Kibler, 9, 206, 209.
19. Abe Laufe, *The Wicked Stage: A History of Theater Censorship and Harassment in the United States* (New York: Frederick Ungar Publishing Co., 1978), 22.
20. Joe Laurie Jr., *Vaudeville: From the Honky-Tonks to the Palace* (New York: Henry Holt and Company, 1953), 40.
21. Rush, "Plastic Posing," *Variety*, 19 June 1909, 12.
22. Dimeglio, 196.
23. Harvey Alexander Higgins Jr., "The Origin of Vaudeville," *New York Dramatic Mirror*, 13 May 1919, 720.
24. Robert W. Snyder, "Vaudeville and the Transformation of Popular Culture," in William R. Taylor, ed., *Inventing Times Square: Commerce and Culture at the Crossroads of the World* (New York: Russell Sage Foundation, 1991), 133.
25. Kibler, 27.
26. This is not meant to suggest that a "mass" entertainment locale was one in which all people were equally welcome. Indeed, African-Americans were often debarred or discouraged from entry into big-time vaudeville theaters; at best, they were typically relegated to a humiliating position in a specially demarcated gallery or balcony area.

For more on this see: Kibler, and David Nasaw, *Going Out: The Rise and Fall of Public Amusements* (New York: Basic Books, 1993).

27. Susan Strasser, *Satisfaction Guaranteed: The Making of the American Mass Market* (Toronto: Random House of Canada, 1989), 15–16.

28. Charles McGovern, "Consumption and Citizenship in the United States, 1900– 1940," in Susan Strasser, Charles McGovern, and Mathías Judt, eds., *Getting and Spending: European and American Consumer Societies in the Twentieth Century* (Washington, D.C.: Cambridge University Press, 1998), 42–47.

29. Gary Cross, *Time and Money: The Making of Consumer Culture* (London and New York: Routledge, 1993), 5.

30. Kibler, 10.

31. Philip Morris newspaper ad, 1911.

32. Cracker Jack newspaper ad, 1907.

33. Plexo newspaper ad, 1909.

34. T. J. Jackson Lears, "From Salvation to Self-Realization: Advertising and Therapeutic Roots of Consumer Culture," in Richard Wightman Fox and T. J. Jackson Lears, eds., *The Culture of Consumption: Critical Essays in American History, 1880–1980* (New York: Pantheon Books, 1983), 21.

35. Michael Schudson, *Advertising, the Uneasy Persuasion* (New York: Harper Collins, 1984), 166.

36. Stuart Ewen, *Captains of Consciousness: Advertising and the Social Roots of Consumer Culture* (New York: McGraw-Hill Book Co., 1976), 19.

37. The era that saw the growth of vaudeville also saw the emergence of the American popular music industry, usually referred to as "Tin Pan Alley," and in particular associated with publication of the song "After the Ball" by Charles K. Harris in 1892. The Tin Pan Alley entrepreneurs began to treat music (sheet music, that is) as a mass commodity for leisure-time consumption, aided by their own unique innovations in marketing, promotion, and advertising. Still, for all of Tin Pan Alley's success, it is not clear that the budding musical publishing industry in any way beat vaudeville to the punch in constructing a mass audience and consumption base. Several historians of Tin Pan Alley have pointed out that it was in fact a fairly ill-organized and informally confederated cadre of businessmen who almost inadvertently launched the sheet music frenzy. Furthermore, it has been argued that the real frenzy did not begin until the ragtime craze of the 1910s following the release of the Alley's most famous hit, Irving Berlin's "Alexander's Ragtime Band," and thus well after the rise of big-time vaudeville. Perhaps the most important observation might be that Tin Pan Alley, like other larger-scale commercial undertakings of the era, grew in part as an attaché of vaudeville. Indeed, famed Alley songwriter and publisher Harry Von Tilzer recognized the better-organized and further-reaching vaudeville chains as the very places he needed to use in order to field and market his sheet music to the mass-consuming audience. See: Philip Furia, "Irving Berlin: Troubadour of Tin Pan Alley," in William R. Taylor, ed., *Inventing Times Square: Commerce and Culture at the Turn of the Century* (New York: Russell Sage Foundation, 1991), 191–92; Nicholas E. Tawa, *The Way to Tin Pan Alley: American Popular Song, 1866–1910* (New York: Schirmer Books, 1990), 32–52; Kenneth Aaron Kanter, *The Jews on Tin Pan Alley: The Jewish Contribution to American Popular Music, 1830–1940* (New York: Ktav Publishing House, 1982), 18–30, 43; Isaac Goldberg, *Tin Pan Alley: A Chronicle of American Popular Music* (New York: Ungar Publishing Co., Inc., 1961), 111; and David A. Jasen, *Tin Pan Alley: The Composers, the Songs, the Performers, and Their Times* (New York: Donald I. Fine, 1988), 2, 67, 112, 192.

38. Lears (1983), 3.

39. *New York Dramatic Mirror*, 14 May 1898, 16.

40. Marybeth Hamilton, *When I'm Bad, I'm Better: Mae West, Sex, and American Entertainment* (New York: Harper Collins, 1995), 36.

41. Laurie, 286–87.

42. Kibler, as we have seen, convincingly asserts that vaudeville succeeded in constructing a mass audience in large measure because it was able to incorporate the high with the low, the refined with the base, the cerebral with the decidedly bodily (8).

43. Gilbert, 10.

44. Gunther Barth, *City People: The Rise of Modern City Culture in Nineteenth-Century America* (New York and Oxford: Oxford University Press, 1980), 193–96.

45. Samuels and Samuels, 16.

46. Gilbert, 113–14.

47. Stein, xiii, 11. See also: Albert F. McLean Jr., *American Vaudeville as Ritual* (Frankfort: University of Kentucky Press, 1965), 3–5, 31.

48. Snyder (1989), 28–32. Still, it would appear that audiences could not always be counted on to behave as managers would wish. In 1899, a shortened version of the play *Thérèse* went on at Proctor's vaudeville theater in New York. A critic for the *New York Dramatic Mirror* remarked, "the large audience laughed very impolitely at the most serious scene of the play, so it would seem that the time is not yet ripe for the production of one-act tragedies in vaudeville." 27 May 1899, 18.

49. Gilbert, 205.

50. Barth argues that "vaudeville" comes from popular songs on the French variety stage whose origins lay in folk music of the Vire Valley in France, or Vau de Vire. Snyder holds that "vaudeville" comes from the French "voix de ville," the "voice of the city." (Barth, XX; Snyder XX.)

51. Robert C. Allen, *Horrible Prettiness: Burlesque and American Culture* (Chapel Hill and London: University of North Carolina Press, 1991), 179, 182.

52. Leigh Woods, "Sarah Bernhardt and the Refining of American Vaudeville," *Theatre Research International* 18 (Spring 1993): 16.

53. Rush, "New Acts Next Week," *Variety*, 31 July 1909, 12. "The Vampire Dance," *New York Dramatic Mirror*, 7 August 1909, 19. *Variety*, 7 August 1909, 17.

54. Sime, "New Acts Next Week," *Variety*, 10 December 1915, 16.

55. Rush, "New Acts Next Week," *Variety*, 29 January 1910, 17.

56. Sime, "Hammerstein's," *Variety*, 10 January 1913, 23.

57. Dimeglio, 48.

58. "'Clean Burlesque' Mandatory: American Circuit," *Variety*, 12 November 1915, 3.

59. "'Clean Up In New York First' Says Out of Town Manager," *Variety*, 24 December 1910, 8.

60. Dimeglio, 49, 195.

61. Laurie, 10. Henry Jenkins, *What Made Pistachio Nuts?: Early Sound Comedy and the Vaudeville Aesthetic* (New York: Columbia University Press, 1992), 61.

62. See Kibler (13–14) for a nuanced and highly readable take on the role of women on the vaudeville stage, in its seats, and in its promotional campaigns.

63. Anna Marble, "Women in Variety," *Variety*, 22 December 1906, 14.

64. Cited in: Snyder (1989), 105.

65. Nasaw, 27.

66. Gilbert, 120. Also: Tony Pastor, "Tony Pastor Recounts the Origin of American 'Vaudeville,'" *Variety*, 15 December 1906, 17. "A Pictorial Souvenir of the Proctor Entertainments," 1902. From a clipping file in the New York Public Library for the Performing Arts Theatre Collection.

67. "During a certain act, in which a young woman sang suggestive songs, at one of our music halls last week, a man in the audience, who had brought his wife to the theater, compelled her to leave with him ... [but] [t]he wife refused to go...." *New York Dramatic Mirror*, 13 August 1910, 17.

68. *New York Dramatic Mirror*, 8 March, 1902, 18; 15 March 1902, 18.

69. Snyder (1989), 33.

70. It has been argued that vaudeville theaters and the silent cinema in fact afforded women a place to enjoy the unclad male figure, as the rowdy, masculine boxing arena was clearly off-limits. See: Miriam Hansen, *Babel & Babylon: Spectatorship in American Silent Film* (Cambridge, Mass. and London: Harvard University Press, 1991), 1.

71. Kibler, 51–53.

72. *New York Clipper*, 22 May 1897, 190; 12 June 1897, 238; 21 August 1897, 404; 28 August 1897, 429.

73. *New York Dramatic Mirror*, 18 December 1897, 18; 12 February 1898, 18.

74. Robert Wiebe, *The Search for Order: 1877–1920* (New York: Hill and Wang, 1987), 12, 21, 48, 56–8.

75. Boris Emmet and John E. Jeuck, *Catalogues and Counters: A History of Sears, Roebuck and Company* (Chicago: University of Chicago Press, 1950), 15, 36, 117.

76. Snyder (1989), 37, 43.

77. Joseph M. Schenk, "Inside Vaudeville," *Variety*, 20 December 1912, 33.

78. See: Tino Balio, "Stars in Business: The Founding of United Artists," in Tino Balio, ed., *The American Film Industry* (Madison: University of Wisconsin Press, 1985), 153–72.

79. Gilbert, 198.

80. Dimeglio, 196.

81. Snyder (1989), 141.

82. The obvious example here is RCA's 1928 purchase of what remained of the Keith-Albee and Orpheum vaudeville theater chains, alluded to in an earlier note. See: Tino Balio, "Struggles for Control, 1908–1930," in Balio, ed. (1985), 130; and Allen (1977).

83. Jenkins, 78–79.

84. Of course, since about the 1950s, ambitious businessmen have in some measure been trying to un-nationalize markets, in a sense—that is, to appeal to narrower and narrower demographic slices in an effort to sell more goods and services. The present Internet age seems to suggest the greatest possibility of narrow-marketing, as individual consumers reveal more about themselves with each purchase they make.

85. Strasser, 16.

86. "The Vaudeville Stage," *New York Dramatic Mirror*, 29 June 1895, 12.

87. For example, Dimeglio notes that at the time of its peak popularity, ca. 1900, there were some 2,000 vaudeville theaters in the U.S. and Canada (Dimeglio, 11). By sharp contrast, by 1910 there were over 10,000 theaters in the United States alone devoted largely or entirely to the exhibition of motion pictures. (See: Russell Merritt, "Nickelodeon Theaters, 1905–1914: Building an Audience for the Movies," in Balio, ed. 86.

88. See: Erenberg, 233–59.

89. Quoted in: Nasaw, 249.

90. The first multiplexes began to emerge in shopping malls in the 1960s. The first "fourplex" opened in Kansas City in 1966, the first "sixplex" in Omaha, Nebraska, in 1969, and the first "eightplex" in Atlanta in 1974. They proliferated from there in the 1970s, 1980s, and 1990s. See: Douglas Gomery, *Shared Pleasures: A History of Movie Presentation in the United States* (Madison, Wisconsin: University of Wisconsin Press, 1992), 97.

91. Nasaw, 241–249. These comments should not be construed to mean that African-American theatrical forms did not take root in the big cities, where "white flight" (to dust off a well-known sociological trope) was beginning to occur. Indeed, black vaudeville flourished during the 1910s and 1920s. For an excellent descriptive history see: Mel Watkins, *On the Real Side: Laughing, Lying, and Signifying— The Underground Tradition of African-American Humor That Transformed American Culture, from Slavery to the Civil War* (New York: Simon & Schuster, 1994), especially Chap. 9: "The

Theatre Owners Booking Association and the Apollo Theatre ... *changing the joke and slipping the yoke.*"

92. Robert Allen's *Horrible Prettiness* contains perhaps the best extended argument of the differences between the two forms.

93. Laurence Senelick, *Cabaret Performance, Volume I: Europe, 1890–1920: Songs, Sketches, Monologues, Memoirs* (New York: Performing Arts Journal Publications, 1989), 8.

One— "*Dressed in the Form of Art*"

1. In 1907, New York's Mayor McClellan ordered so-called "nickelodeon" movie houses shut down, following outcry from religious leaders; they were reopened by Gaynor, who would shortly become mayor.

2. See: Robert C. Allen, "The Movies in Vaudeville: Historical Context of the Movies as Popular Entertainment," in Balio, ed., 57–82.

3. There are many versions of this argument. For a good one see: Gregory Black, *Hollywood Censored: Morality Codes, Catholics, and the Movies* (Cambridge: Cambridge University Press, 1994), 33.

4. Gilbert, 201.

5. "Cardinal Lauds Mrs. B.F. Keith," *Boston Herald*, 20 January 1927. No page number available. From a clipping file at the New York Public Library for the Performing Arts Theatre Collection.

6. Laurie, 343.

7. Strasser, 14.

8. Francis Couvares, "Hollywood, Main Street, and the Church: Trying to Censor the Movies Before the Production Code," in Francis Couvares, ed., *Movie Censorship and American Culture* (Washington and London: Smithsonian Institution Press, 1996), 130.

9. Laufe, 21; Lewis Erenberg, *Steppin' Out: New York Night Life and the Transformation of American Culture, 1890–1930* (Westport, Connecticut, and London: Greenwood Press, 1981), 14.

10. Laufe, 18.

11. Jack McCullough, *Living Pictures on the New York Stage* (Ann Arbor, Michigan: UMI Research Press, 1981), 46, 81–84, 98.

12. Laufe, 18–19, 24–25.

13. Francis Couvares, "Introduction," in Couvares, ed., 2.

14. "Mlle. De Leon Censured," *New York Dramatic Mirror*, 17 July 1909, 18.

15. *New York Dramatic Mirror*, 27 July 1901, 16.

16. Dimeglio, 146.

17. Erenberg, 63.

18. "Theatrical Censorship," *New York Times*, 12 June 1907, 8:3.

19. "Catholics Denounce Stage Immorality," *New York Times*, 11 February 1909, 16:3.

20. "For a Play Censorship," *New York Times*, 24 February 1909, 9:4; "Wants Theatrical Censors," *New York Times*, 19 October 1909, 6:2.

21. "Play Censors in Plainfield," *New York Times*, 9 February 1909, 1:2; "Theatre Censors Organize," *New York Times*, 16 February 1909, 1:5.

22. "Foresees a Stage Censor," *New York Times*, 10 February 1909, 1:2.

23. "Farley Begins War on Infamy of Stage," *New York Times*, 19 December 1912, 9:1.

24. Ibid. One concerned citizen even felt that theatrical posters should be censored. "The immoral plays do not do all the harm," wrote a New York resident in the *Times*, "There are still posters advertising the worst of them. Some of these representing the latest dances must have done damage to our children." "Offensive Posters," *New York Times*, 11 February 1909, 6:5.

25. "Farley Begins War on Infamy of Stage," 9:1–2.

26. "Ethical Band Plans Drama Inquisition," *New York Times*, 21 February 1912, 20:1.

27. "'Clean Up in New York First' Says Out of Town Manager," *Variety*, 24 December 1910, 8.

28. Alan Dale, "Dramatic Censors and Some New Plays," *Cosmopolitan*, June 1909, 74–75.

29. "Suggestive Songs," *New York Clipper*, 9 November 1912, 8.

30. *New York Dramatic Mirror*, 3 June 1899, 10.

31. Ibid.

32. *New York Dramatic Mirror*, 6 January 1900, 18.

33. *New York Dramatic Mirror*, 24 November 1900, 18; 11 February 1905, 18.

34. *New York Dramatic Mirror*, 15 December 1906, 16; 9 February 1907, 17.

35. "Supreme Court Decides Sunday Shows Illegal," *Variety*, 7 December 1907, 2.

36. *New York Dramatic Mirror*, 23 February 1907, 17.

37. *New York Dramatic Mirror*, 16 March 1907, 18.

38. *New York Dramatic Mirror*, 28 September 1907, 16; 12 October 1907, 15; 19 October 1907, 16.

39. "War on Sunday Vaudeville," *New York Times*, 1 December 1908, 9:2; "Sunday Vaudeville Crusade on December 13," *New York Times*, 3 December 1908, 9:3.

40. *Variety*, 25 April 1908, 6.

41. "Diluted Vaudeville To-Day's Show Menu," *New York Times*, 27 December 1908, 1:1+.

42. Ibid.

43. "Police Permit Only Tame Vaudeville," *New York Times*, 28 December 1908, 1:7.

44. "Commends the Mayor," *New York Times*, 28 December 1908, 3.

45. *New York Dramatic Mirror*, 9 January 1909, 17.

46. "Mayor Makes War on Sunday Vaudeville," *New York Times*, 29 December 1908, 3:1; 'The Stillwell Bill," *New York Clipper*, 15 February 1913, 16D.

47. *New York Dramatic Mirror*, 5 June 1909, 11; 12 February 1910, 21.

48. Nicola Beisel, *Imperiled Innocents: Anthony*

Comstock and Family Reproduction in Victorian America (Princeton: Princeton University Press, 1997), 3, 71.

49. "Who's Bernard Shaw? Asks Mr. Comstock," *New York Times*, 28 September 1905, 9:1.

50. Beisel, 44.

51. Snyder (1989), 12.

52. Herbert George Wells, "Mankind in the Making," *Cosmopolitan*, June 1903, 224–28.

53. "Free Libraries Bar Bernard Shaw's Books," *New York Times*, 21 September 1905, 9:6.

54. "George Bernard Shaw," *New York Times*, 21 September 1905, 8:3. The libraries in Brooklyn did, however, place Mark Twain's *Huckleberry Finn* and *Tom Sawyer* on the "restricted" list the following year. "Never Too Ill for a Story," *New York Times*, 27 March 1906, 9:5.

55. "Alger's Boy Books Barred," *New York Times*, 8 August 1907, 1:6. For more on Horatio Alger's virtues see Alan Trachtenberg's Introduction to the Signet Classic edition of *Ragged Rick Or, Street Life in New York with the Boot-blacks* (New York: Penguin, 1990), v–xx.

56. "Change Texas Text Books," *New York Times*, 8 August 1908, 2:2.

57. "Movement Started for a Clean Press," *New York Times*, 14 December 1908, 9:1.

58. Laurie, 390–91.

59. "May Stop Anarchist Paper," *New York Times*, 16 March 1908, 1:4.

60. James Mock and Cedric Larson, *Words That Won the War: The Story of the Committee on Public Information, 1917–1919* (Princeton: Princeton University Press, 1939), 19.

61. "Suppression," *Nation* 68, 25 May 1899, 388.

62. "American Managers on Censorship," *New York Times*, 12 September 1909, v, 7.

63. "Problem of Stage Censorship," *New York Times*, 20 June 1909, v, 7.

64. "Censoring the Stage at Home and Abroad," *New York Times*, 21 February 1909, v, 4.

65. "A Mayor's Morality," *New York Times*, 8 June 1909, 6:3.

66. "Theatrical Morality," *New York Times*, 13 February 1909, 8:3.

67. "Blame the Public for Immoral Plays," *New York Times*, 12 February 1909, 13:3.

68. "Walter Defends 'The Easiest Way,'" *New York Times*, 15 February 1909, 7:1–2.

69. "Discussing the Social Evil," *Nation*, 5 October 1911, 308–09.

70. Mark, "Eugene O'Rourke and Co.," *Variety*, 20 April 1912, 15.

71. "A Glance at Acts New to the Metropolis," *New York Clipper*, 11 June 1910, 433. This production of *The Derelict* was perhaps a shortened iteration of a play called *L'Épave* (*The Derelict*), by Guggenheim and Le Faure, which appeared in Paris in 1903. The *New York Times* described it as "a costume play dealing with a wreck of the 'Grande Armée' who, after Waterloo, had been left for dead on the field of battle. Recovering consciousness, though not reason, he passes four years as a human derelict. Then, sane once more, he plunges into intrigue and conspiracy against King Louis XVIII." A series of duels, betrayals, and revelations follow. The *Times* reviewer found it "somewhat undecided in action and not convincing." (*New York Times*, 1 November 1903, III, 25:2.)

72. "Filth on the Stage," *Nation*, 11 September 1913, 246.

73. "Syndicate Books 'The Moulin Rouge,'" *New York Times*, 17 February 1909, 9:1.

74. Couvares, "Introduction," 3.

75. Antonio Marro, "Influence of the Puberal Development on the Moral Character of Children of Both Sexes," *American Journal of Sociology* 5 (September, 1899): 195–98.

76. Herbert George Wells, "Mankind in the Making," *Cosmopolitan*, May 1903, 79.

77. John Lowry Simpson, "Continence vs. Contraception," *New Republic*, 31 July 1915, 335.

78. Erenberg, 7.

79. "Sex in Fiction," *Nation*, 16 December 1915, 716.

80. Edward W. Chamberlain, "In the Midst of Wolves," *Arena*, November 1894, 835.

81. Arthur Schuckai, "Nudity and Idiocy," *Harper's Weekly*, 30 January 1915, 116.

82. *New York Clipper*, 25 May 1912, 14.

83. Will H. Low and Kenyon Cox, "The Nude in Art," *Scribner's Magazine*, December 1892, 741–49.

84. "The Nude in Pictures," *New York Clipper*, 15 December 1915, 29.

85. Ellen Key, "Woman in a New World," *Harper's Weekly*, 24 January 1914, 7–9; 31 January 1914, 9–11.

86. Lary May, *Screening Out the Past* (New York: Oxford University Press, 1980), 44.

87. Erenberg, 14, 132–45.

88. Celia Haddon, *The Sensuous Lie* (New York: Stein and Day, 1983), 26, 35.

89. Thomas Laqueur, "Sexual Desire and the Market Economy During the Industrial Revolution," in Donna Stanton, ed., *Discourses of Sexuality: From Aristotle to AIDS* (Ann Arbor: University of Michigan Press, 1992), 186.

Two— "Clean, Great, and National"

1. For more on the standardized, formulaic quality of vaudeville see: Frederick Snyder, "Theater in a Package–the Origins of Mass Entertainment," (Ph.D. diss., Yale University, 1970).

2. *New York Dramatic Mirror*, 26 January 1901, 16.

3. "B.F. Keith: The Man Who Dared and Won," *New York Star*, 24 October 1903, no page number given, from a clipping file in the New York Public Library for the Performing Arts.

4. Laurie, 340.

5. "Vaudeville Founded by Keith Thirty Years Ago This Week," *Philadelphia Telegraph*, 1 December 1913, no page number given, from a clipping file in the New York Public Library for the Performing Arts. Also, "B.F. Keith Dead," *New York Clipper*, 4 April 1914, 1.
6. "B.F. Keith: The Man Who Dared and Won."
7. Allen (1991), 180.
8. Laurie, 342 ; "B.F. Keith Dead."
9. Nasaw, 20.
10. Anthony Slide, *The Encyclopedia of Vaudeville* (Westport, Connecticut and London: Greenwood Press, 1994), 278.
11. "B.F. Keith Dead."
12. Allen (1991), 181.
13. In: Dimeglio, 25.
14. "Albee on Vaudeville in 1912–13," *New York Clipper*, 5 October 1912, 10.
15. Nasaw, 24.
16. Allen (1991), 182; "B.F. Keith Dead"; Nasaw, 20.
17. Nasaw, 20.
18. *New York Dramatic Mirror*, 8 December 1906, 16.
19. Brochure for B.F. Keith's New Theatre Boston. From a clipping file in the New York Public Library for the Performing Arts.
20. Photo caption accompanying: E.F. Albee, "The Future of Show Business," *Billboard*, 19 December 1914, 38.
21. "E.F. Albee, Co-Founder of Vaudeville," *New York Times*, 23 March 1930, ix, 4:6. According to Odell, *No Thoroughfare* played in New York at the Broadway Theatre, opening September 28, 1868, "the French version of a story by Charles Dickens and Wilkie Collins" which had been produced in Paris under the title *L'Abîme*, a "tense melodrama." See: George C. D. Odell, *Annals of the New York Stage, VIII, 1865–1870* (New York: AMS Press, 1937), 446–47.
22. "E.F. Albee, Co-Founder of Vaudeville."
23. Samuels and Samuels, 38.
24. "E.F. Albee, Co-Founder of Vaudeville."
25. Nasaw, 20.
26. "A Brilliant Career Ended," *New York Dramatic News*, 4 April 1914, no page number given, from a clipping file in the New York Public Library for the Performing Arts.
27. Snyder (1989), 30.
28. "B.F. Keith: the Man Who Dared and Won."
29. Allen (1991), 185.
30. Brochure for Keith's New Theatre Boston.
31. Ibid.
32. E.F. Albee, "Some Interesting Details," *New York Dramatic Mirror*, from 1906. No date or page number given.
33. In: Anthony Slide, *Selected Vaudeville Criticism* (Metuchen & London: Scarecrow Press, 1988), 206.
34. *New York Dramatic Mirror*, 26 January 1901, 16.
35. E.F. Albee, "Twenty Years of Vaudeville," *Theatre Magazine*, May 1920, 408.
36. *New York Dramatic Mirror*, 25 August 1900, 8.
37. *New York Dramatic Mirror*, 20 February 1904, 18.
38. See for example: Harvey Alexander Higgins, "The Reconstruction of Vaudeville," *National Magazine*, May 1919, 173.
39. B.F. Keith, "What Pleases in Vaudeville," *Criterion*, September 1900, 24.
40. "Keith's Seventeenth Anniversary," *New York Dramatic Mirror*, 26 January 1901, 16.
41. *New York Dramatic Mirror*, 23 February 1901, 18.
42. *New York Dramatic Mirror*, 22 June 1901, 16.
43. Kibler points out that many women in the vaudeville audience too enjoyed hearing marriage decried and lampooned (48).
44. "Cardinal Lauds Mrs. B.F. Keith," *Boston Herald*, 20 January 1927, no page number given, from a clipping file in the New York Public Library for the Performing Arts.
45. Laurie, 339.
46. "Cardinal Lauds Mrs. B.F. Keith."
47. *New York Dramatic Mirror*, 16 January 1904, 18.
48. *New York Dramatic Mirror*, 16 May 1908, 17.
49. Snyder (1991), 133.
50. Harvey Alexander Higgins Jr., "The Origin of Vaudeville," *New York Dramatic Mirror*, 13 May 1919, 720; *New York Dramatic Mirror*, 13 June 1906, 2.
51. McLean, 16–17.
52. E.F. Albee, "Keith Vaudeville," *New York Clipper*, 15 February 1913, viii.
53. "Albee on Vaudeville in 1912–13."
54. Joseph M. Schenk, "Inside Vaudeville," *Variety*, 20 December 1912, 33.
55. Snyder (1991), 137.
56. Snyder (1991), 137–38. And see: Robert Allen, "Contra the Chaser Theory," *Wide Angle* 3/1 (1979), 4–11.
57. *New York Clipper*, 24 February 1906, 11; *New York Dramatic Mirror*, 5 May 1906, 17; *New York Dramatic Mirror*, 2 June 1906, 17; *Variety*, 23 June 1906, 2; *New York Clipper*, 23 February 1907, 30; *New York Dramatic Mirror*, 2 March 1907, 19.
58. "Williams Goes with Keith," *Variety*, 16 February 1907, 2.
59. *New York Clipper*, 2 February 1907, 1328; *New York Clipper*, 13 April 1907, 227.
60. Snyder (1991), 141.
61. *New York Clipper*, 18 May 1907, 16–17.
62. *New York Clipper*, 1 June 1912, 9.
63. *Variety*, 7 March 1913, 3.
64. See: *New York Clipper*, 8 May 1909, 319.
65. Snyder (1991), 139 ; "Against the Irresponsible," *New York Dramatic Mirror*, 26 December 1908, 17.

66. Snyder (1989), 38.
67. "White Rats of America," *New York Clipper*, 4 August 1900, 516. For a very thorough explication of the White Rats and their moral rhetoric, see Kibler, 171–208.
68. *New York Clipper*, 2 February 1901, 1100.
69. "Vaudeville and Minstrel," *New York Clipper*, 2 March 1901, 7.
70. Snyder (1989), 40.
71. *New York Clipper*, 8 July 1911, 3.
72. "Attorney General Asked to Dissolve the U.B.O.," *Variety*, 11 October 1912, 1.
73. William E. Sage, "Albee Talks on Vaudeville," *Cleveland Leader*, 24 December 1912, no page number given, from a clipping file in the New York Public Library for the Performing Arts.
74. *New York Clipper*, 24 January 1914, 1.
75. "From the Drama Mailbag," *New York Times*, 24 November 1940, ix, 2:5.
76. "F. F. Proctor Dead; Dean of Vaudeville," *New York Times*, 5 September 1929, 29; Laurie, 365–69; *New York Star*, 21 November 1908, no page number given, from a clipping file in the New York Public Library for the Performing Arts.
77. Laurie, 370.
78. Barth, 204.
79. *A Pictorial Souvenir of the Proctor Entertainments*, 1902, from a clipping file in the New York Public Library for the Performing Arts.
80. Laurie, 370.
81. *New York Dramatic Mirror*, 6 August 1904, 15.
82. *New York Dramatic Mirror*, 1 January 1898, 16.
83. See: "Keith & Proctor to Dissolve," *New York Clipper*, 5 August 1911, 1.
84. "How Martin Beck Became Vaudeville's Chief Mogul," *Variety*, 11 December 1909, 27; "Martin Beck Dies; Theatre Veteran," *New York Times*, 17 November 1940, 49:1; "From the Drama Mailbag;" Laurie, 360.
85. *New York Dramatic Mirror*, 23 July 1910, 17.
86. "Martin Beck Clearly Defines His Attitude," *New York Star*, 18 September 1909, no page number given, from a clipping file in the New York Public Library for the Performing Arts.
87. "United Booking Offices Cleans Up All 'Big Time,'" *Variety*, 4 May 1912, 5; *Variety*, 26 May 1906, 5.
88. "Martin Beck Dies; Theatre Veteran."
89. Ibid.
90. Laurie, 481–98.
91. Snyder (1989), 43.
92. Marian Spitzer in Stein ed., 231.
93. In: *Variety*, 10 April 1909, 10.
94. Snyder (1989), 141.
95. Hamilton, 35–36; Jenkins, 78.
96. "'Watch Your Lyric' Slogan Emanates from the U.B.O," *Variety*, 10 December 1915, 5.
97. "Williams Sells Theatres," *New York Clipper*, 4 May 1912, 10.
98. *Variety*, 27 April 1907, 4.
99. *Variety*, 4 May 1907, 13.
100. *Variety*, 7 September 1907, 2.
101. *Variety*, 26 October 1907, 2; 6 November 1907, 2; *New York Dramatic Mirror*, 16 November 1907, 14.
102. "Another Big Keith Deal," *New York Clipper*, 6 September 1913, 1.
103. "Vaudeville of the Year," *Variety*, 10 December 1910, 20.
104. *New York Clipper*, 3 July 1909, 536.
105. "A Brilliant Career Ended," *New York Dramatic News*, 4 April 1914, no page number given, from a clipping file in the New York Public Library for the Performing Arts.
106. "Vaudeville's Clearing House," *New York Clipper*, 29 November 1913, 1.
107. Gimlet, "Imaginary Interview No. 2," *Standard and Vanity Fair*, 13 January 1912, 12.
108. Snyder (1989), 37.
109. "Evolution of Cheap Vaudeville," *Variety*, 14 December 1907, 10; *New York Clipper*, 7 August 1909, 653; *New York Clipper*, 19 August 1905, 655.
110. "Pallbearers for Albee," *New York Times*, 14 March 1930, 21:1
111. Alfred Chandler, "The Beginnings of 'Big Business' in American Industry" and "Development, Diversification, and Decentralization," in Thomas K. McCaw, ed., *The Essential Alfred Chandler: Essays Toward a Historical Theory of Big Business* (Boston: Harvard Business School Press, 1988), 73, 227.
112. Chester W. Wright, *Economic History of the United States* (New York: McGraw-Hill Book Co., 1949), 496.
113. Thomas C. Cochran, *Two Hundred Years of American Business* (New York: Basic Books, 1977), 51. Also see: Wright, 478–498.
114. Though the battle between the Charles Frohman-led theatrical "Syndicate" and the Shuberts suggests that leaders in the field of "legitimate" theatre were also beginning to think nationally, there were some significant differences from vaudeville. The Shuberts, who won the "war," gained a *monopoly* rather than true free-market dominance; moreover, they did not do so until *after* 1907. See: Peter A. Davis's essay in William R. Taylor, ed., *Inventing Times Square* (1991), 147–57.
115. Cochran, 117–120; Strasser, 222.
116. By the mid-1890s there were some 20,000 regularly published newspapers and magazines in the United States. Wright, 497.
117. Schudson, 159.
118. Richard Tedlow, *New and Improved:The Story of Mass Marketing in America* (Boston: Harvard Business School Press, 1996), xxi-xxii.
119. Cochran, 124; Alfred D. Chandler, "The Rise of Big Business," in Harry N. Schreiber, ed., *United States Economic History: Selected Readings* (New York: Knopf, 1964), 345–46; for an able, if brief, account of the rise of branding and Nabisco's "Uneeda" line see: Bryan Burrough and John Helyar, *Barbarians at the Gate: The Fall of RJR Nabisco* (New York: Harper Perennial, 1991), 29–30.

120. "What Greater Vaudeville Promises This Winter," *New York Times*, 1 September 1907, part VI, 2:1. European, or at least European-*seeming*, acts provided big-time vaudeville with both an exotic edge and a dollop of high-cultural cachet. Where actual Europeans could not be found, American simulators filled in. (Harrison Graves, *Chase's Herald: Devoted to Polite Vaudeville*, 26 January 1903, 1; Hartley Davis, "In Vaudeville," *Everybody's Magazine*, August 1905, 240.)

121. Alfred Chandler, "The Rise of Big Business," in Schreiber, ed., 358.

122. Lawrence Glickman, *A Living Wage: American Workers and the Making of Consumer Society* (Ithaca and London: Cornell University Press, 1997), 125.

123. Stuart Ewen, *All Consuming Images: The Politics of Style in Contemporary Culture* (Basic Books, 1988), 41.

124. Wiebe, 48.

125. Wright, 607.

126. Steven Diner, *A Very Different Age: Americans of the Progressive Era* (New York: Hill and Wang, 1998), 4.

127. Strasser, 7.

128. Roland Marchand, *Advertising the American Dream: Making Way for Modernity, 1920–1940* (Berkeley and Los Angeles: University of California Press, 1985), xxi, 9, 12.

129. T.J. Jackson Lears, *Fables of Abundance: A Cultural History of Advertising in America* (New York: Basic Books, 1994), 171.

130. Emmet and Jeuck, 15–16.

131. Emmet and Jeuck, 43.

132. Tedlow, 271.

133. Tedlow, 272.

134. Emmet and Jeuck, 31, 36, 43, 93–94, 150, 172.

135. Strasser, 213.

136. Various advertisements for products; Frank Presbrey, *The History and Development of Advertising* (Garden City, NY: Doubleday, Doran & Co., 1929), 341; Strasser, 41–42.

137. Strasser, 129; Tedlow, 355.

138. Tedlow, 29, 50, 66, 70.

139. Marchand, 17.

140. Lears (1983), 4–6.

141. Lears (1983), 19.

142. Marchand, 14.

143. Lears (1994), 160.

144. Lears (1994), 173.

145. Kathryn Kish Sklar, "The Consumer's White Label Campaign of the National Consumers' League, 1898–1918," in Strasser, McGovern, Judt, eds., 17–19, 27.

146. Presbrey, 349, 402; Marchand, 22.

147. Marchand, 205, 269; Ewen (1976), 45.

148. *New York Clipper*, 8 January 1910, 1217.

149. *Variety*, 21 January 1916, 5; 4 February 1916, 5.

150. *Variety*, 26 December 1914, 36.

151. Presbrey, 302, 307.

152. Presbrey, 329, 336.

153. Stephen Fox, *The Mirror Makers: A History of American Advertising* (New York: William Morrow & Co., 1984), 14–16. Ayer conducted the "first crude marketing survey" according to James Playstead Wood in *The Story of Advertising* (New York: Ronald Press, 1958), 244, on behalf of makers of farm machinery.

154. Presbrey, 348.

155. Cochran, 125.

156. Lorin F. Deland, "At the Sign of the Dollar," *Harper's Monthly Magazine* (March 1917), 526.

157. Presbrey, 315.

158. Presbrey, 312.

159. Deland, 525.

160. John Brisben Walker, "Beauty in Advertising Illustration," *Cosmopolitan*, September 1902, 491.

161. Rudi Laermans, "Summary of Learning to Consume: Early Department Stores and the Shaping of the Modern Consumer," in Neva Goodwin, Frank Ackerman, and David Kiron, eds., *The Consumer Society* (Washington, D.C., and Covelo, California: Island Press, 1997), 139. Also see: McGovern.

162. Presbrey, 368–69, 389, 402, 426; and Wood, 289.

163. Wood, 224.

164. Wood, 238.

165. Wood, 250–51.

166. Wood, 256–57.

167. Brisben Walker, 494–97.

168. Wood, 245.

169. Wood, 335–38.

170. Presbrey, 412.

171. Stoddard Goodhue, "The Battle of the Microbes," *Cosmopolitan*, September 1913, 434–42.

172. C. D. Zimmerman, "Dust—is it Dangerous?," *Scientific American*, 18 April 1903, 299.

173. However, the more one looks at the matter of germ-born disease at the turn of the century, the more one is struck with the fact that by about the first two decades of the twentieth century infectious diseases were well on their way to being genuinely under control. For more on the rise of "germ theory," and detailed public health assessments of various infectious diseases of the era, see: J. N. Hays, *The Burden of Disease: Epidemics and Human Response in Western History* (New Brunswick, New Jersey and London: Rutgers University Press, 1998), 150; William H. McNeill, *Plagues and Peoples* (Garden City, New York: Doubleday, 1976) 267.; John Duffy, *The Sanitarians: A History of American Public Health* (Urbana and Chicago: University of Illinois Press, 1990) 414–21; U.S. Bureau of the Census, *Historical Statistics of the United States, Colonial Times to 1970, Bicentennial Edition, Part 1* (Washington, D.C., U.S. Government Printing Office 1975), 58; George Rosen, *Preventative Medicine in the United States, 1900–1975: Trends and Interpretations* (New York: Prodist, 1977), 4.

174. Elbert Hubbard, "Is It a Disgrace to Be Sick?," *Cosmopolitan*, October 1904, 742–43.

175. "Beauty as a Means of Health," *Scientific American*, 2 May 1891, 273.
176. Oscar E. Anderson Jr., *The Health of a Nation: Harvey W. Wiley and the Fight for Pure Food* (Chicago: University of Chicago Press, 1958), 190.
177. Harvey W. Wiley, *The History of a Crime Against the Food Law* (New York: Arno Press, 1976), 4. (Originally published 1929.)
178. Anderson, 2–6.
179. Anderson, 8.
180. Bernard A. Weisberger, "Doctor Wiley and His Poison Squad," *American Heritage*, February/March, 1996, 14.
181. Tattler, "Notes from the Capital: A Preacher of Purity," *Nation*, 27 July 1916, 79–80.
182. Anderson, 9–11.
183. In: Anderson, 126–27.
184. Wiley, 24.
185. Anderson, 12–27, 70.
186. Anderson, 69.
187. Anderson, 120.
188. Anderson, 72–73, 129.
189. Wiley, 57–66.
190. Both in: Wiley, 76–77.
191. Wiley, 56.
192. Anderson, 188.
193. *United States Statutes at Large*, 59th Congress, 1905–07, Vol. 34, Part I, Chap. 3915, 768–70.
194. "Harvey W. Wiley: Pioneer Consumer Activist," *Good Housekeeping*, February 1990, 146.
195. Weisberger, 14.
196. Tattler, 79 ; "Harvey W. Wiley: Pioneer Consumer Activist," 146.

Three— "Of Pleasing Face and Form"

1. Jon Stratton, *The Desirable Body: Cultural Fetishism and the Erotics of Consumption* (Manchester and New York: Manchester University Press, 1996), 25–58, 62–63.
2. Stratton, 98–9.
3. William Leach, *Land of Desire: Merchants, Power, and the Rise of a New American Culture* (New York: Pantheon Books, 1993), 58, 65–6. [Dos Passos quoted in Leach.]
4. Lears (1994), 148–49.
5. Laurie, 149.
6. Sime, "New Acts Next Week," *Variety*, 4 April 1913, 16.
7. *New York Dramatic Mirror*, 9 April 1904, 18.
8. *New York Dramatic Mirror*, 22 September 1900, 18; *New York Dramatic Mirror*, 3 December 1898, 18.
9. *New York Dramatic Mirror*, 24 August 1907, 14.
10. *Variety*, 4 April 1913, 16.
11. *New York Clipper*, 5 April 1913, 16.
12. "Good Singing, Poor Comedy," *New York Dramatic Mirror*, 31 August 1907, 14.
13. *New York Dramatic Mirror*, 26 February 1898, 16.
14. *New York Dramatic Mirror*, 28 October 1899, 18.
15. *New York Dramatic Mirror*, 28 November 1903, 21.
16. *New York Clipper*, 12 June 1897, 238.
17. *New York Dramatic Mirror*, 5 February 1910, 21.
18. *Variety*, 29 January 1910, 16.
19. *New York Dramatic Mirror*, 5 May 1900, 18.
20. *New York Dramatic Mirror*, 17 December 1898, 18.
21. *New York Clipper*, 22 May 1897, 190.
22. *New York Clipper*, 12 June 1897, 238.
23. *New York Clipper*, 3 April 1897, 76.
24. Gilbert, 363.
25. *New York Clipper*, 3 June 1911, 5.
26. *New York Dramatic Mirror*, 30 November 1907, 13.
27. Dash, "New Acts Next Week," *Variety*, 12 July 1912, 16.
28. *New York Dramatic Mirror*, 20 January 1900, 18.
29. *New York Dramatic Mirror*, 22 October 1898, 20.
30. *New York Dramatic Mirror*, 3 September 1904, 18.
31. *New York Clipper*, 30 October 1909, 961.
32. *New York Dramatic Mirror*, 7 October 1899, 18.
33. *New York Clipper*, 9 April 1898, 92; 7 May 1898, 160.
34. Kibler, 157.
35. *New York Dramatic Mirror*, 14 May 1898, 16.
36. *New York Dramatic Mirror*, 10 December 1898, 18.
37. *New York Dramatic Mirror*, 17 August 1907, 11.
38. *New York Clipper*, 24 September 1910, 797.
39. *New York Clipper*, 26 November 1910, 1021.
40. Kibler, 157.
41. *New York Dramatic Mirror*, 24 January 1903, 18.
42. *New York Dramatic Mirror*, 17 January 1903, 18.
43. *New York Dramatic Mirror*, 31 October 1903, 18.
44. Laurie, 228.
45. Robert C. Allen, "The Movies in Vaudeville: Historical Context of the Movies as Popular Entertainment," in Balio, ed., 65.
46. *New York Dramatic Mirror*, 18 October 1902, 18; 1 November 1902, 18.
47. Dash, "Fifth Avenue," *Variety*, 3 February 1912, 20.
48. Dash, "New Shows Next Week," *Variety*, 30 January 1914.
49. Laurie, 40.
50. *New York Clipper*, 11 November 1899, 768.
51. *New York Dramatic Mirror*, 21 September 1901, 18.

52. Rush, "New Acts of the Week," *Variety*, 26 February 1910, 17.

53. *New York Clipper*, 22 January 1898, 776.

54. "Mlle. Odiva's Great Act," *New York Telegraph*, 15 May 1910. No page number available. From a clipping file at the New York Public Library for the Performing Arts Theatre Collection.

55. *Variety*, 14 May 1910. No page number available. From a clipping file at the New York Public Library for the Performing Arts Theatre Collection.

56. *New York Dramatic Mirror*, 13 April 1901, 18.

57. Dash, "New Acts Next Week," *Variety*, 1 November 1912, 20.

58. From a clipping file at the New York Public Library for the Performing Arts Theatre Collection.

59. Samuels and Samuels, 40.

60. *New York Dramatic Mirror*, 5 December 1908, 17.

61. *New York Clipper*, 19 June 1908, 487.

62. Rush, "New Acts Next Week," *Variety*, 2 January 1909, 13.

63. "A Midsummer Rhapsody to Annette Kellerman," *New York Star*, 7 August 1909. No page number available. From a clipping file at the New York Public Library for the Performing Arts Theatre Collection.

64. Laurie, 34.

65. *Variety*, 28 November 1908, 12.

66. Annette Kellerman, "Miss Annette Kellerman Tells How to Dress Comfortably," *New York Journal*, 19 January 1909. No page number available. From a clipping file at the New York Public Library for the Performing Arts Theatre Collection.

67. Zoe Beckley, "Don't Wear Any Clothes, Annette's Sincere Advice," *New York Mail*, 18 December 1916. No page number available. From a clipping file at the New York Public Library for the Performing Arts Theatre Collection.

68. Ewen (1976), 180.

69. Patricia King Hanson, ed., *American Film Institute Catalog of Motion Pictures Produced in the United States, Feature Films, 1911–1920* (Berkeley, Los Angeles, London: University of California Press, 1988), 656.

70. Percy Hammond, "Annette Kellerman in Pretty Pictures," *Chicago Tribune*, 19 May 1914; "Annette Kellerman Film Sets Record at B.F. Keith's," *Cincinnati Times Star*, 24 August 1914. No page numbers available. From a clipping file at the New York Public Library for the Performing Arts Theatre Collection.

71. "Annette's Form Wakes Malden," *Morning Telegraph*, 14 February 1915. No page number available. From a clipping file at the New York Public Library for the Performing Arts Theatre Collection.

72. "Annette Posters Shock Hizzoner," 14 January 1915. No other information available. No page number available. From a clipping file at the New York Public Library for the Performing Arts Theatre Collection.

73. "Daughter of the Gods a Great Opportunity," *New York Dramatic News*, June 1917, 23; "How the Newest Film Spectacle, 'A Daughter of the Gods,' Was Made," *New York World*, 22 October 1916. No page number available. From a clipping file at the New York Public Library for the Performing Arts Theatre Collection; Hanson, ed., 193–94.

74. Stephen Bush, "'A Daughter of the Gods,'" *Moving Picture World*, 4 November 1916. No page number available. From a clipping file at the New York Public Library for the Performing Arts Theatre Collection.

75. "Kellerman Form Causes Woman to Beat Husband," *Toledo Blade*, 10 January 1917. No page number available. From a clipping file at the New York Public Library for the Performing Arts Theatre Collection.

76. Hanson, ed., 749.

77. Dash, "New Acts Next Week," *Variety*, 3 April 1909, 16.

78. Laurie, 34.

79. The documentary movie *The Original Mermaid: The Amazing Story of Annette Kellerman*, originally made for Australian television (produced by Ian Collie and written and directed by Michael Cordell; a Hilton Cordell Production; 52 mins.), provides a rich and interesting overview of Kellerman's life and work, with special attention to her deep connection to the water as a swimmer and performer. The author of the present work is featured briefly in the documentary.

80. *Variety*, 9 June 1906, 6.

81. *Variety*, 14 July 1906, 10.

82. "Players and Playhouses," *Los Angeles Times*, 17 July 1907. No page number available. From a clipping file at the New York Public Library for the Performing Arts Theatre Collection.

83. "Lula Salbini," *Cincinnati Commercial*, 8 October 1906. No page number available. From a clipping file at the New York Public Library for the Performing Arts Theatre Collection.

84. Laurie, 31.

85. "Great Lafayette's Protégé Appears at the Miles in Startling Bathing Suit," *Detroit Free Press*, 18 September 1913. No page number available. From a clipping file at the New York Public Library for the Performing Arts Theatre Collection.

86. Alice Rohe, "Be Good; Bathe Three Times a Day," *New York World*, 15 June 1906. No page number available. From a clipping file at the New York Public Library for the Performing Arts Theatre Collection.

87. "Selbini's Fair Critics Took to the Woods," *Pittsburgh Leader*, 23 September 1906. No page number available. From a clipping file at the New York Public Library for the Performing Arts Theatre Collection.

88. "The Great Lalla Selbini," *New York Telegraph*, 22 May 1913. No page number available. From a clipping file at the New York Public Library for the Performing Arts Theatre Collection.

89. Rohe.
90. McCullough, 12–16, 37.
91. *New York Clipper*, 12 November 1898, 642.
92. *New York Dramatic Mirror*, 26 November 1898, 18.
93. Walt, "New Acts Next Week," *Variety*, 11 December 1909, 16.
94. *New York Clipper*, 25 May 1912, 14; 28 September 1912, 7; 13 April 1913, 7.
95. *New York Dramatic Mirror*, 26 October 1907, 14; 26 September 1903, 18. Actress Adah Isaacs Menken had made a career of posing, seemingly nude, as Mazeppa during the 1860s. See: Don Wilmeth, Tice Miller, eds., *Cambridge Guide to American Theatre* (Cambridge: Cambridge University Press, 1993), 310–11. See also: Wolf Mankowitz, *Mazeppa: The Lives, Loves, and Legends of Adah Isaacs Menken* (London: Blond & Briggs, 1982).
96. See: *New York Clipper*, 30 March 1901, 115.
97. *New York Dramatic Mirror*, 26 December 1908, 17.
98. *New York Dramatic Mirror*, 23 February 1901, 18.
99. Sime, "New Acts Next Week," *Variety*, 12 November 1910, 5.
100. *New York Dramatic Mirror*, 9 November 1907, 13; 22 December 1900, 64.
101. "The Nude in Pictures," *New York Clipper*, 25 December 1915, 29.
102. Jolo, "New Acts Next Week," *Variety*, 24 April 1914, 14.
103. Sime, "New Acts Next Week," *Variety*, 19 May 1910, 16; 17 February 1912, 16.
104. *Variety*, 10 January 1913, 23.
105. "Beauty Poses in a Sketch," *New York Dramatic Mirror*, 21 November 1908, 17.
106. Laurie, 37.
107. "They Have 'An Affair of Honor' Now at Koster & Bial's," *New York Times*, 27 December 1898, 7:2.
108. *New York Dramatic Mirror*, 7 January 1899, 18; 21 January 1899, 18; *New York Clipper*, 31 December 1898, 740. Gilbert, 190.
109. Dash, "New Acts Next Week," *Variety*, 17 September 1910, 14.
110. Sime, "New Acts Next Week," *Variety*, 7 May 1915, 12.
111. Mary Rita Fleischer, "Collaborative Projects of Symbolist Playwrights and Early Modern Dancers" (Ph.D. diss., City University of New York, 1998), 15.
112. Fleischer, 17.
113. "New Vaudeville Acts," *New York Clipper*, 6 December 1913, 19.
114. Sime, "New Acts Next Week," *Variety*, 31 October 1914, 18.
115. *New York Dramatic Mirror*, 24 September 1904, 18.
116. Sime, "New Acts Next Week," *Variety*, 3 December 1910, 14.
117. Wynn, "New Acts Next Week," *Variety*, 2 July 1910, 14; *New York Clipper*, 9 July 1910, 529.
118. *Variety*, 25 May 1907, 10.
119. *New York Dramatic Mirror*, 4 February 1899, 18.
120. *New York Dramatic Mirror*, 21 August 1909, 23.
121. Sime, "New Acts Next Week," *Variety*, 21 November 1914, 18.
122. "La Milo," *Detroit News*, 20 November 1906. No page number available. From a clipping file at the New York Public Library for the Performing Arts Theatre Collection.
123. "Stage Venus Wears No Tights," *New York Telegraph*, 6 May 1906. No page number available. From a clipping file at the New York Public Library for the Performing Arts Theatre Collection. "Lady Godiva is to Ride Here Again," *New York American*, 9 November 1914. No page number available. From a clipping file at the New York Public Library for the Performing Arts Theatre Collection.
124. "Gauze and Grouch Ride With Godiva," *Chicago Tribune*, 8 August 1907. No page number available. From a clipping file at the New York Public Library for the Performing Arts Theatre Collection.
125. "La Milo, the Perfect Woman," *New York Star*, 25 November 1914. No page number available. From a clipping file at the New York Public Library for the Performing Arts Theatre Collection.
126. "About La Milo's Beauty," *Cincinnati Commercial Tribune*, 17 February 1915. No page number available. From a clipping file at the New York Public Library for the Performing Arts Theatre Collection.
127. Vance Thompson, "Women Who Pose," *Cosmopolitan*, December 1901, 180, 185.
128. John Southworth, *The English Medieval Minstrel* (Suffolk: Boydell & Brewer, 1989), 6–7.
129. Felix Cherniavsky, *The Salome Dancer: The Life and Times of Maud Allan* (London: McClelland & Stewart, 1991.), 142.
130. Richard Bizot, "The Turn-of-the-Century Salome Era: High- and Pop-Culture Variations on the Dance of the Seven Veils," *Choreography and Dance* 2 (1992), 76.
131. Anthony Slide, *The Encyclopedia of Vaudeville* (Westport, CT: Greenwood Press, 1994), 449.
132. *Variety*, 8 August 1908, 15.
133. "All About 'Salome,'" *Variety*, 1 August 1908, 7.
134. Bizot, 78.
135. In: Sime, "New Acts Next Week," *Variety*, 1 August 1908, 14.
136. *Variety*, 2 February 1907, 10.
137. *New York Clipper*, 29 August 1908, 701.
138. "All About 'Salome.'"
139. Laurie, 204. There were few outlets for African-American performers in mainstream white vaudeville. There was, however, a vibrant black vaudeville circuit which nurtured some of the country's finest talent (even though, like the circuits described in this work, it was controlled

by a white businessman, F. A. Barrasso). For further reading see chapters 3, 4, and 9.

140. *New York Clipper*, 10 August 1912, 14. "All About 'Salome,'" *Variety*, 1 August 1908, 7. Walker was also famous for teaching "white elite society how to do the cakewalk," according to David Krasner in his book on African-American theatre. See: David Krasner, *Resistance, Parody, and Double Consciousness in African American Theatre, 1895–1910* (New York: St. Martin's Press, 1997), 76, 83, 92.

141. *New York Clipper*, 12 September 1908, 763.

142. *New York Dramatic Mirror*, 26 September 1908, 17.

143. *New York Clipper*, 15 August 1908, 653.

144. Reprinted in: *Variety*, 3 October 1908, 2.

145. See: Elliot Willensky, *When Brooklyn Was the World* (New York: Harmony Books, 1986), 25, 228.

146. *Variety*, 3 October 1908, 2.

147. "Says Salome Spirit Pervades Theatre," *New York Times*, 22 February 1909, 9:5.

148. "The 'Salome' Dance Gets into Politics," *New York Times*, 24 August 1908, 2:5

149. "Conditions of the Stage," *New York Times*, 14 February 1909, part V, 8.

150. "No 'Salomes' on Orpheum Circuit," *Variety*, 12 September 1908, 1.

151. *New York Dramatic Mirror*, 26 August 1908, 17; 5 September 1908, 19; 24 October 1908, 17.

152. Fleischer, 144–48.

153. *Variety*, 9 August 1912, 20; 12 December 1908, 14. *New York Dramatic Mirror*, 1 August 1908, 14.

154. "All About 'Salome.'"

155. *New York Clipper*, 9 February 1909, 1360.

156. *New York Clipper*, 5 March 1910, 81.

157. *Variety*, 22 May 1914, 14.

158. *New York Clipper*, 27 May 1911, 5.

159. *Variety*, 17 February 1906, 6.

160. Charles Darnton, "Stageland," *Blue Book Magazine*, October 1908, 1341.

161. "La Sylphe in New Salome Dance," *New York Mirror*, 8 August 1908. No page number available. From a clipping file at the New York Public Library for the Performing Arts Theatre Collection.

162. *New York Dramatic Mirror*, 8 August 1908, 14.

163. *Variety*, 11 July 1908, 14.

164. Sam M'Kee, "La Sylphe Declares She Doesn't Wish to Be a Burlesque Queen," *New York Telegraph*, 20 July 1908. No page number available. From a clipping file at the New York Public Library for the Performing Arts Theatre Collection.

165. *New York Dramatic Mirror*, 25 July 1908, 14.

166. *Variety*, 18 July 1908, 12.

167. *Variety*, 25 July 1908, 16.

168. *New York Clipper*, 28 August 1909, 731.

169. *New York Clipper*, 31 July 1909, 629.

170. "Police at Winter Garden," *New York Times*, 27 June 1911, 9:4.

171. "Folks Film Bill Vetoed By Mayor," *New York Times*, 1 January 1913, 6:3.

172. "Police Not Shocked by Russian Dances," *New York Times*, 1 July 1911, 11:1.

173. Ibid.

174. "Want to Suppress Dance," *New York Times*, 28 June 1911, 5:1.

175. "Russian Dancers Appeal," *New York Times*, 3 July 1911, 7:3.

176. "Princess is Sensation," *Milwaukee News*, 14 August 1912; "Princess Rajah at Keith's," *Louisville Post*, 11 March 1912. No page numbers available. From a clipping file at the New York Public Library for the Performing Arts Theatre Collection.

177. *Variety*, 23 January 1909, 17.

178. *Variety*, 3 June 1909, 6.

179. Kibler, 50.

180. "Good Show at Keith's," *Toledo Blade*, 12 October 1920. No page number available. From a clipping file at the New York Public Library for the Performing Arts Theatre Collection; Sime, "New Acts of the Week," *Variety*, 17 April 1909, 16.

181. *New York Dramatic Mirror*, 30 January 1909, 10.

182. *New York Clipper*, 30 January 1909, 1245.

183. *Variety*, 9 January 1909. No page number available. From a clipping file at the New York Public Library for the Performing Arts Theatre Collection.

184. *New York Dramatic Mirror*, 27 July 1901, 14. *New York Dramatic Mirror*, 17 July 1909, 18.

185. "Charmeon [sic]" Dies; Nation's First Strip Teaser," *New York Evening Post*, 28 December 1936. No page number available. From a clipping file at the New York Public Library for the Performing Arts Theatre Collection.

186. See: *New York Dramatic Mirror*, 25 December 1897, 18; *New York Clipper*, 18 December 1897, 602; *New York Dramatic Mirror*, 29 January 1898, 18; *New York Clipper*, 26 February 1898, 860; 22 June 1901, 364; and 17 March 1900, 51.

187. *New York Dramatic Mirror*, 29 June 1901, 16.

188. *Variety*, 11 September 1909, 11.

189. *New York Clipper*, 1 January 1910, 1181.

190. Florence Heath, "Ladies How Does Your Figure Correspond with the Measurements of Charmion," *Denver Post*, 9 October 1904. No page number available. From a clipping file at the New York Public Library for the Performing Arts Theatre Collection.

191. "Charmion Herself," *Des Moines Register*, 9 December 1908. No page number available. From a clipping file at the New York Public Library for the Performing Arts Theatre Collection.

192. *Variety*, 21 November 1908, 17.

193. "Dress on the Stage," *Vogue*, 10 October 1907. No page number available. From a clipping file at the New York Public Library for the Performing Arts Theatre Collection.

194. Nellie Revell, "Alhambra Acts Are Enter-

taining," *New York Telegraph*, 9 October 1913. No page number available. From a clipping file at the New York Public Library for the Performing Arts Theatre Collection.

195. "Valeska Suratt Scores Triumph at the Palace," *New York American*, 4 November 1913. No page number available. From a clipping file at the New York Public Library for the Performing Arts Theatre Collection.

196. Alan Dale, "Valeska Suratt, 'a Riot of Clothes at Palace,'" *New York American*, 8 November 1913. No page number available. From a clipping file at the New York Public Library for the Performing Arts Theatre Collection.

197. Sime, "Valeska Suratt," *Variety*, 20 November 1909, 12.

198. "Valeska Suratt Startles New York With Playlet," *Terre Haute Tribune*, 12 December 1909. No page number available. From a clipping file at the New York Public Library for the Performing Arts Theatre Collection.

199. "Mayor Shut Valeska's Show," *Sun*, 11 May 1910. No page number available. From a clipping file at the New York Public Library for the Performing Arts Theatre Collection.

200. "Suratt Farce Coarse, Vulgar," *Philadelphia Times*, 5 April 1910. No page number available. From a clipping file at the New York Public Library for the Performing Arts Theatre Collection.

201. Valeska Suratt, "Personality—That's Me!," *Green Book Magazine*, September 1915, 420.

202. Stuart Ewen, *All Consuming Images: the Politics of Style in Contemporary Culture* (New York: Basic Books, 1988), 29.

203. *New York Clipper*, 31 October 1903, 859; "Charlotte Wiehe Pleases," *New York Times*, 22 October 1903, 9:3.

204. "Borrowing the French-Eis Idea," *New York Telegraph*, 15 August 1909. No page number available. From a clipping file at the New York Public Library for the Performing Arts Theatre Collection.

205. *New York Dramatic Mirror*, 7 August 1909, 19; *Variety*, 31 July 1909, 12; *Variety*, 7 August 1909, 17; *New York Clipper*, 23 October 1909, 941.

206. *Variety*, 17 January 1913, 19; "Three Arrested for Star Act at Hammerstein's," *New York Telegraph*, 21 February 1913; "Jury Thought Dance Proper," *New York Telegraph*, 28 March 1913; *Moving Picture World*, 4 October 1913. No page numbers available. From a clipping file at the New York Public Library for the Performing Arts Theatre Collection.

207. Sime, "New Acts Next Week," *Variety*, 10 December 1915, 16.

208. "Bert French and Miss Eis Go to Trial," *New York Review*, 22 February 1918. No page number available. From a clipping file at the New York Public Library for the Performing Arts Theatre Collection.

209. *New York Dramatic Mirror*, 27 January 1900, 18.

210. *New York Dramatic Mirror*, 8 March 1902, 18; 16 March 1902, 18.

211. *New York Dramatic Mirror*, 19 October 1901, 18. Kibler argues that Sandow was criticized by some for his "lack of manliness" (53).

212. *New York Dramatic Mirror*, 7 November 1903, 18; 27 August 1904, 16; Laurie, 122.

213. *New York Clipper*, 18 March 1899, 48.

214. *New York Dramatic Mirror*, 27 April 1901, 18.

215. *Variety*, 30 January 1915, 16; *New York Dramatic Mirror*, 30 November 1901, 18.

216. *New York Dramatic Mirror*, 22 June 1901, 16.

217. *Variety*, 31 October 1908, 16.

218. Ibid.

219. *New York Dramatic Mirror*, 25 April 1908, 17; 7 July 1900, 16; 24 September 1898, 18.

220. *New York Dramatic Mirror*, 6 July 1901, 16.

221. *New York Dramatic Mirror*, 18 February 1899, 18.

222. *New York Dramatic Mirror*, 24 December 1898, 18.

223. Snyder (1989), 153; Laurie, 421–22.

224. *New York Clipper*, 28 June 1913, 17.

225. *New York Clipper*, 27 June 1914, 6.

226. *Variety*, 11 October 1912, 20; *New York Dramatic Mirror*, 18 December 1897, 18; 12 February 1898, 18.

227. *New York Clipper*, 8 April 1911, 5; 28 May 1910, 389.

228. *New York Dramatic Mirror*, 13 February 1902, 20.

229. *New York Dramatic Mirror*, 14 November 1903, 20; 9 December 1899, 18.

230. *New York Dramatic Mirror*, 1 August 1903, 16.

231. *Variety*, 18 June 1915, 13; *New York Dramatic Mirror*, 4 November 1899, 18; *Variety*, 1 May 1914, 3.

232. *New York Dramatic Mirror*, 14 November 1908, 17; *Variety*, 13 September 1912, 8; "Vaudeville to Spare Suffragists," *New York Times*, 6 August 1913, 7:3.

Four— "Wild Woman"

1. Eva Tanguay, "I Don't Care," *American Weekly*, 29 December 1946, 12.

2. Laurie, 58.

3. Sophie Tucker, *Some of These Days: The Autobiography of Sophie Tucker* (© 1945, Sophie Tucker), 80.

4. See, for example, the *DK World Atlas* (DK Publishing, Inc., 1997) and even the *Reader's Digest Atlas of Canada* (Montréal: The Reader's Digest Association, Ltd., 1995).

5. "Eva Tanguay Opens Store," *Los Angeles Examiner*, 10 March 1935. No page number available. From a clipping file in the Southern California Regional History Office, University of South-

ern California; "Eva Tanguay Opens a Shop," *New York Times*, 10 March 1935, ii, 8:3.

6. Kibler book features a photo of Eva Tanguay on its cover, but the book mentions its cover subject only sparingly in its pages. This is not a criticism of *Rank Ladies*, but rather a suggestion of the disappointment those interested in Tanguay face when turning to sources for information about her life. The present work, too, will surely fall short, to some, in certain regards.

7. "Eva Tanguay Dies in Hollywood, 68," *New York Times*, 12 January 1947, 59:1.

8. Los Angeles Superior Court, case 488459, 30 September 1943, and 14 October 1943. Filed by Louis Labarere, attorney for plaintiff.

9. Joseph Santley Jr., "300 at Funeral of Eva Tanguay," *Los Angeles Examiner*, 15 January 1947. No page number available. From a clipping file in the Southern California Regional History Office, University of Southern California.

10. In Tanguay's obituary, the *New York Times* described the late actress as "a lonely but courageous invalid for most of the last two decades." When the occasional friend or well-wisher would stop by her small cottage, she would murmur, through the door, "Don't come in. Eva Tanguay is not here." "Eva Tanguay Dies in Hollywood, 68."

11. Tanguay, 12.

12. "Eva Tanguay, of 'I Don't Care' Fame, Dies at 68," and "Death Takes Eva Tanguay," *Los Angeles Examiner*, 12 January 1947. No page number available. From a clipping file in the Southern California Regional History Office, University of Southern California; "Eva Tanguay Dies in Hollywood, 68"; "Death Takes Eva Tanguay"; "Eva Tanguay, of 'I Don't Care' Fame, Dies at 68"; *Newsweek*, 20 January 1947, 52; *Time*, 20 January 1947, 81.

13. McLean, 23.

14. Slide, 490.

15. George Custen, *Twentieth Century's Fox: Darryl F. Zanuck and the Culture of Hollywood* (New York: Basic Books, 1997), 1, 3.

16. George Custen, *Bio/Pics: How Hollywood Constructed Public History* (New Brunswick, New Jersey: Rutgers University Press, 1992), 173.

17. John Berger, *Ways of Seeing* (London: British Broadcasting Corporation and Penguin Books, 1972), 11.

18. Jane R. Westerfield, "An Investigation of the Life Styles and Performance of Three Singer-Comediennes of American Vaudeville: Eva Tanguay, Nora Bayes, and Sophie Tucker," (D.A. diss., Ball State University, 1987), 15.

19. Westerfield, 51.

20. Westerfield, 55.

21. Westerfield, 22, 31.

22. Westerfield, 25–7.

23. *Variety*, 12 December 1913, 18; *New York Clipper*, 20 February 1909, 39; *New York Dramatic Mirror*, 22 June 1907, 16.

24. Gilbert, 327.

25. McLean, 23.

26. "Eva Tanguay Dies in Hollywood, 68." (Note: the *New York Times*' wording here seems to have been directly lifted from the Associated Press Biographical Service, No. 2977, issued 15 August 1942, though such is not indicated in the *Times* piece.)

27. "Eva Tanguay, of 'I Don't Care' Fame, Dies at 68."

28. J. Bellangee, "Sexual Purity and the Double Standard," *Arena*, February 1895, 372.

29. Aline Gorren, "Womanliness as a Profession," *Scribner's Magazine*, May 1894, 612.

30. Gilbert, 328–29.

31. Tanguay, 29 December 1946, 12.

32. Slide, 488.

33. Westerfield, 28.

34. *New York Dramatic Mirror*, 19 March 1904, 18.

35. *New York Dramatic Mirror*, 11 May 1907, 17; *New York Dramatic Mirror*, 20 April 1907, 17.

36. *Variety*, 8 December 1906, 2; *New York Dramatic Mirror*, 4 May 1907, 16; Slide, 488.

37. *New York Dramatic Mirror*, 6 July 1907, 14.

38. *Variety*, 24 September 1910, 14.

39. Patricia King Hanson, ed., *American Film Institute Catalog of Motion Pictures Produced in the United States, Feature Films, 1911–1920* (Berkeley, Los Angeles, London: University of California Press, 1988), 1037.

40. Hanson, ed., 1038.

41. *Moving Picture World*, 1 September 1917, 1335.

42. *Moving Picture World*, 22 September 1917, 1872.

43. Earl Barnes, "The Economic Independence of Women," *Atlantic Monthly*, August 1912, 262–63.

44. Barnes, 265.

45. Lynn Linton, "The Wild Woman as Social Insurgent," *Nineteenth Century*, October 1891, 596.

46. Linton, 596–97.

47. Linton, 600.

48. Linton, 598.

49. Rafford Pike, "What Men Like in Women," *Cosmopolitan*, October 1901, 610.

50. Slide, 488.

51. Marie Corelli, "Man's War Against Woman," *Harper's Bazar*, May 1907, 426.

52. Arthur Pollock, "The Woman in the Theatre," *Harper's Weekly*, 4 September 1915, 237.

53. "Editor's Study," *Harper's Monthly*, February 1910, 478.

54. "The Artistic Impulse in Man and Woman," *Arena*, October 1900, 419.

55. See: Leigh Woods, "Sarah Bernhardt and the Refining of American Vaudeville," *Theatre Research International* 18 (Spring 1993), 16; "Bernhardt Arrives Younger Than Ever," *New York Times*, 2 December 1912, 11:1; "Chicago Cheers Bernhardt," *New York Times*, 3 December 1912, 2:6; and "Bernhardt and Vaudeville," *New York Times*, 23 September 1910, 12:6.

56. Constant Coquelin, "Have Women a Sense

of Humor?", *Harper's Bazar*, 12 January 1901, 67–8.

57. Alan Dale, "Why Women Are Greater Actors Than Men," *Cosmopolitan*, September 1906, 517–18.

58. Cora Sutton Castle, "A Statistical Study of Eminent Women," *Popular Science Monthly*, June 1913, 601.

59. Karin Michaelis, "Why Are Women Less Truthful Than Men," *Munsey's Magazine*, May 1913, 185.

60. Charlotte Perkins Gilman, "Woman, the Enigma," *Harper's Bazar*, December 1908, 1194.

61. Michaelis, "Why Are Women Less Truthful Than Men?", *Munsey's Magazine*, June 1913, 345.

62. Pike, 613; "Editor's Study," *Harper's Monthly*, May 1910, 640; Susanne Wilcox, "The Unrest of Modern Woman," *Independent*, 8 July 1909, 62. For an able investigation of the relationship between vaudeville and the "feminization" of culture, see the introductory chapter to Kibler.

63. "Bernard Shaw on American Women," *Cosmopolitan*, Sept 1907, 560.

64. "The Point of View," *Scribner's Magazine*, April 1901, 507.

65. Winifred Kirkland, "The Woman Who Writes," *Atlantic Monthly*, July 1916, 48.

66. *New York Clipper*, 11 January 1913, 7; *Variety*, 27 May 1911, 5.

67. "The Individuality of Woman: From a Masculine Point of View," *Westminster Review*, November 1902, 508; Florida Pier, "The Gentler View: The Need of Self-Expression," *Harper's Weekly*, 5 June 1909, 28; Margaret Deland, "The Change in the Feminine Ideal," *Atlantic Monthly*, March 1910, 292.

68. Maud Howe, "What is a Lady?," *Harper's Bazar*, February 1909, 179.

69. Howe, 180–81.

70. James Henle, "The New Woman," *Harper's Weekly*, 20 November 1915, 503.

71. Slide, 488; Westerfield, 5.

72. Westerfield, 5.

73. Tanguay, 29 December 1946, 12.

74. Tanguay, 29 December 1946, 12.

75. *New York Dramatic Mirror*, 23 February 1901, 16.

76. Ibid; "The Office Boy," *New York Times*, 14 February 1901, 9:3.

77. "The Office Boy."

78. Ibid.

79. "The Chaperones," *Theatre*, July 1902, 5–6.

80. Westerfield, 8; "The Chaperones," 6; Tanguay, 29 December 1946, 13.

81. For more see: Eric Lott, *Love and Theft: Blackface Minstrelsy and the American Working Class* (New York: Oxford University Press, 1993).

82. *New York Telegraph*, 14 April 1908 and *New York Star*, 3 April 1909. No page numbers or titles available. From a clipping file at the New York Public Library for the Performing Arts.

83. Tanguay, 29 December 1946, 12.

84. Karl K. Kitchen, "Undone by a Song," *Theatre*, May 1913, 143.

85. "Eva Tanguay Dies in Hollywood, 68."

86. *New York Dramatic Mirror*, 15 August 1908, 14.

87. "Eva Tanguay Dies in Hollywood, 68"; Tucker, 80; "Ziegfeld Gets Eva Tanguay," *New York Times*, 7 July 1909, 9:2.

88. Tanguay, 29 December 1946, 13; *New York Clipper*, 9 January 1909, 1179; "'I Do Care!' Cried Tanguay," *New York Times*, 5 July 1909, 1:3.

89. *New York Clipper*, 13 May 1911, 6; *Variety*, 14 November 1914, 18; "Eva Tanguay Big 'Hit' in Topline at Pantages," *Los Angeles Times*, 7 August 1928. No page number available. From a clipping file in the Southern California Regional History Office, University of Southern California; "Eva Tanguay to Appear in Dress Made of $1 Bills," *Los Angeles Examiner*, 17 October 1930. No page number available. From a clipping file in the Southern California Regional History Office, University of Southern California.

90. W. I. Thomas, "The Adventitious Character of Woman," *American Journal of Sociology* 12 (July 1906): 39.

91. Mrs. Rhodes Campbell, "The American Girl: Her Faults and Her Virtues," *Arena*, August 1898, 254–55.

92. Charlotte Perkins Gilman, "Modesty: Feminine and Other," *Independent*, 29 June 1905, 1447–50.

93. Bellangee, 370.

94. "Act Closed at Hammerstein's Without Notice 'Flops' Over," *Variety*, 13 March 1909. No page number given. From a clipping file at the New York Public Library for the Performing Arts.

95. "Act Closed at Hammerstein's Without Notice 'Flops' Over."

96. Ibid.

97. "Blames Eva Tanguay," *New York Times*, 9 March 1909, 2:5.

98. "Eva Tanguay Arrested," *New York Times*, 2 March 1910, 18:4.

99. "Eva Tanguay Fined," *New York Times*, 4 March 1910, 7:2.

100. The Associated Press Biographical Service: Sketch 2977.

101. Charles Wagner, "The Destiny of Woman," *Harper's Bazar*, June 1906, 486.

102. Eva Tanguay, "I Don't Care," *American Weekly*, 26 January 1947, 6. (Though I am giving Tanguay credit here for having authored the "I Don't Care" series in the *American Weekly*, that credit is strictly nominal. As I have stated earlier, the articles were almost certainly ghost written by someone else, though someone who had undoubtedly interviewed her in great and comprehensive depth. Still, I will continue to state that she wrote them, in the body of the text, for ease's sake in a section largely devoted to a highly personal narrative.)

103. Tanguay, "I Don't Care," *American Weekly*,

19 January 1947, 7; "Eva Tanguay Marries," *New York Times*, 25 November 1913, 3:7.
104. "Eva Tanguay Alone Now," *New York Times*, 14 May 1915, 11:6; "Eva Tanguay Divorces J. W. Ford," *New York Times*, 20 December 1917, 9:2; Gilbert, 330.
105. "Eva Tanguay is Named by Wife as Corespondent," *Cleveland News*, 29 September 1907. No page number given. From a clipping file at the New York Public Library for the Performing Arts.
106. "Eva Tanguay Sets New Mark," *Morning Telegraph*, 26 July 1908. No page number given. From a clipping file at the New York Public Library for the Performing Arts; Ann Douglas, *The Feminization of American Culture* (New York: Alfred A. Knopf, 1977), 5; See: Richard deCordova, *Picture Personalities: The Emergence of the Star System in America* (Urbana, Illinois, and Chicago: University of Illinois Press, 1990).
107. "Eva Tanguay Dies in Hollywood, 68"; Ed Barry, "Eva Tanguay—'I Don't Care Girl'—Slips Away, Taking an Era with Her," *Variety*, 15 January 1947, 48.
108. "Eva Tanguay Seeks Marriage Annulment," *New York Times*, 9 October 1927, 13; "Eva Tanguay Gets Divorce," *New York Times*, 22 October 1927, 2:5.
109. Tanguay, "I Don't Care," *American Weekly*, 26 January 1947, 7.
110. Tanguay, "I Don't Care," *American Weekly*, 5 January 1947, 17.
111. Tanguay, "I Don't Care," *American Weekly*, 12 January 1947, 6–7.
112. Tanguay, "I Don't Care," *American Weekly*, 12 January 1947, 7.
113. *Variety*, 30 May 1908, 14.
114. "The Absurd Sex," *Bookman*, September 1912, 59.
115. "The New Sex Psychology," *Westminster Review*, November 1909, 501–02.
116. Earl Barnes, "The Celibate Women of Today," *Popular Science Monthly*, June 1915, 551–52.
117. Juliet Wilbor Tompkins, "Why Women Don't Marry," *Cosmopolitan*, February 1907, 470–71.
118. Tompkins, 469.
119. Havelock Ellis, "The Mind of Woman," *Atlantic Monthly*, September 1916, 367.
120. Rafford Pike, "The Woman's Side," *Cosmopolitan*, July 1902, 326.
121. Amelia E. Barr, "Flirting Wives," *North American Review*, January 1893, 69–70.
122. Robert Hunter, "Burdens Borne by Women," *Cosmopolitan*, December 1905, 162.
123. "What Being a Woman Has Meant to Me," *Ladies' Home Journal*, September 1908, 10.
124. Margaret Ladd Franklin, "Woman's Mind," *Nation*, 27 February 1913, 202.
125. Frederick James Smith, "'I Do Care!' Says Eva Tanguay," *New York Dramatic Mirror*, 27 January 1915, 30.
126. *Variety*, 9 May 1908, 7; "Eva Tanguay Wins a Medal," *New York Times*, 13 February 1911, 7:4.
127. *New York Clipper*, 12 June 1909, 437.
128. *New York Dramatic Mirror*, 19 March 1910, 21.
129. "Eva Tanguay on 'Imitators,'" *Variety*, 6 March 1909, 5.
130. *New York Dramatic Mirror*, 16 July 1910, 17; *Variety*, 13 September 1913, 26.
131. "Eva Tanguay on 'Imitators.'"
132. *Variety*, 1 January 1915, 22–23.
133. Tanguay, 12 January 1947, 6; "Tanguay Flashed $1000 Bills at Her Peak; Left $500," *Los Angeles Examiner*, 24 January 1947. No page number available. From a clipping file in the Southern California Regional History Office, University of Southern California.
134. Linton, 601.
135. Ida Tarbell, "The Business of Being a Woman," *American Magazine*, March 1912, 565.
136. James Murray, "Eva Tanguay, 67 Today, Ill, Almost Blind," *Los Angeles Examiner*, 1 August 1946. No page number given. From a clipping file in the Southern California Regional History Office, University of Southern California.
137. "Eva Tanguay Dies in Hollywood, 68"; "Eva Tanguay Sells Home Furnishings," *Los Angeles Examiner*, 26 February 1930. No page numbers given. From a clipping file in the Southern California Regional History Office, University of Southern California; "Eva Tanguay Left $500," *New York Times*, 24 January 1947, 16:2.
138. "Eva Tanguay to Return to Stage," *New York Times*, 2 February 1933, 21:4; "Eva Tanguay, Better, Plans Big Comeback," *Los Angeles Examiner*, 23 October 1932. No page number given. From a clipping file in the Southern California Regional History Office, University of Southern California.
139. Murray. No page number given. From a clipping file in the Southern California Regional History Office, University of Southern California.
140. "Eva Tanguay Has the Grip," *New York Times*, 24 December 1924, 10:1; "Eva Tanguay Convalescing," *New York Times*, 26 December 1924, 15:4; "Eva Tanguay Not Seriously Ill," *New York Times*, 31 May 1925, 24:3.
141. "Eva Tanguay Very Ill," *New York Times*, 30 May 1925, 5:3; "Eva Tanguay Out of Danger," *New York Times*, 2 September 1932, 18:5; "Eva Tanguay Suffers Relapse," *New York Times*, 8 September 1932, 17:5; "Miss Tanguay Out of Danger," *Los Angeles Times*, 1 September 1932. No page number given. From a clipping file in the Southern California Regional History Office, University of Southern California; "Old Comrades Flock to Aid Eva Tanguay," *Los Angeles Examiner*, 28 August 1932; "Stage Idol's Old Friends Rush to Aid," *Los Angeles Examiner*, 18 September 1932. No page numbers given. From a clipping file in the Southern California Regional History Office, University of Southern California.
142. Tanguay, 26 January 1947, 7; "Eva Tanguay Saves Eye," *New York Times*, 20 May 1933, 11:3; "Eva Tanguay Plans to Return to Aid Blind," *Los*

Angeles Examiner, 9 April 1934. No page number given. From a clipping file in the Southern California Regional History Office, University of Southern California; Barry, 48.

143. "Eva Tanguay Recovers," *New York Times*, 12 May 1934, 12:6.

144. "Eva Tanguay Failing," *New York Times*, 11 December 1938, 4:2.

145. Barry, 46; "Eva Tanguay, of 'I Don't Care' Fame, Dies at 68"; "Death Takes Eva Tanguay," *Los Angeles Examiner*, 12 January 1947. No page number given. From a clipping file in the Southern California Regional History Office, University of Southern California; "Eva Tanguay's Funeral Draws Stage Star 'S.R.O.'," *Los Angeles Examiner*. No page number or date given. From a clipping file in the Southern California Regional History Office, University of Southern California.

146. *New York Dramatic Mirror*, 28 November 1908, 17; "Eva Tanguay Taking Cure," *New York Times*, 24 December 1932, 10:3.

147. Unattributed newspaper clipping from the Robinson Locke Collection, series 2, volume 297, page 158, 2 February 1919. New York Public Library for the Performing Arts; Kitchen, 143; Frederick James Smith, "'I Do Care!' Says Eva Tanguay," *New York Dramatic Mirror*, 27 January 1915, 30.

Five— "The Signal of Distress"

1. *New York Dramatic Mirror*, 8 February 1898, 18; *New York Dramatic Mirror*, 23 August 1902, 16; *New York Dramatic Mirror*, 17 January 1904, 17.

2. *Variety*, 10 March 1906, 4; *New York Clipper*, 27 November 1909, 1058.

3. *Variety*, 22 May 1914, 3.

4. *New York Clipper*, 14 February 1914, 22. Robert C. Allen has argued eloquently, if controversially, against motion pictures' status as mere audience-expelling "chasers" on vaudeville bills. For more see: Robert C. Allen, "Contra the Chaser Theory."

5. One such ill-advised revival was staged by Frank Fay, the vaudevillian who gained fame for having originated the role of Elwood P. Dowd in Mary Chase's *Harvey* on Broadway in the 1940s (only to see ownership of the role, on film and stage, pass to Jimmy Stewart). For more see: Andrew L. Erdman, "From Frank Fay to Jimmy Stewart: Broadway, Hollywood, and the Construction of Creativity," *Theatre Studies* 41 (1996): 13–28.

6. See: Robert C. Allen, "The Movies in Vaudeville: Historical Context of the Movies as Popular Entertainment," in Balio, ed.

7. See: Neil Gabler, *An Empire of Their Own: How the Jews Invented Hollywood* (New York: Anchor Books, 1989).

8. "The Case of William Fox," *Fortune*, May 1930, 48.

9. Gabler, 3.

10. See: Gomery, 18–33; William Inglis, "Morals and Moving Pictures," *Harper's Weekly*, 30 July 1910, 12.

11. "The Campaign to Curb the Moving Picture Evil," *New York Times*, 2 July 1911, v, 15:1.

12. See: Russell Merritt, "Nickelodeon Theaters, 1905–1914: Building an Audience for the Movies," in Balio, ed., 85.

13. Merritt, 86.

14. "Europe's Call to Arms," *Literary Digest*, 8 August 1914, 234.

15. Nasaw, 255.

16. See: Nasaw, 241–56.

Selected Bibliography

Albee, E.F. "Keith Vaudeville." *New York Clipper*, 15 February 1913, viii.
———. "Twenty Years of Vaudeville." *Theatre Magazine*, May 1920, 408.
"Albee on Vaudeville in 1912–13." *New York Clipper*, 5 October 1912, 10.
"All About 'Salome'." *Variety*, 1 August 1908, 7.
Allen, Robert. *Horrible Prettiness: Burlesque and American Culture*. Chapel Hill and London: University of North Carolina Press, 1991.
———. "The Movies in Vaudeville: Historical Context of the Movies as Popular Entertainment," in Balio, Tino, ed. *The American Film Industry*. Madison, Wisconsin, and London: University of Wisconsin Press, 1976 and 1985, 57–82.
Anderson, Oscar E., Jr. *The Health of a Nation: Harvey W. Wiley and the Fight for Pure Food*. Chicago: University of Chicago Press, 1958.
"Another Big Keith Deal." *New York Clipper*, 6 September 1913, 1.
"Attorney General Asked to Dissolve UBO" *Variety*, 11 October 1912, 1.
"B.F. Keith Dead." *New York Clipper*, 4 April 1914, 1.
Balio, Tino, ed. *The American Film Industry*. Madison, Wisconsin, and London: University of Wisconsin Press, 1976 and 1985.
Barth, Gunther. *City People: The Rise of Modern City Culture in Nineteenth Century America*. New York and Oxford: Oxford University Press, 1980.
Beisel, Nicola. *Imperiled Innocents: Anthony Comstock and Family Reproduction in Victorian America*. Princeton: Princeton University Press, 1997.
Berger, John. *Ways of Seeing*. London: British Broadcasting Corporation and Penguin Books, 1972.
Bizot, Richard. "The Turn-of-the-Century Salome Era: High- and Pop-Culture Variations on the Dance of the Seven Veils." *Choreography and Dance* 2 (1992) : 71–87.
Black, Gregory. *Hollywood Censored: Morality Codes, Catholics, and the Movies*. Cambridge: Cambridge University Press, 1994.
Cherniavsky, Felix. *The Salome Dancer: The Life and Times of Maud Allan*. London: McClelland & Stewart, 1991.
Cochran, Thomas C. *Two Hundred Years of American Business*. New York: Basic Books, 1977.
Couvares, Francis, ed. *Movie Censorship and American Culture*. Washington and London: Smithsonian Institution Press, 1996.
Cross, Gary. *Time and Money: The Making of Consumer Culture*. London and New York: Routledge, 1993.

Custen, George. *Bio/Pics: How Hollywood Constructed Public History*. New Brunswick, New Jersey: Rutgers University Press, 1992.
_____. *Twentieth Century's Fox: Darryl F. Zanuck and the Culture of Hollywood*. New York: Basic Books, 1997.
Dale, Alan. "Dramatic Censors and Some New Plays." *Cosmopolitan*, June 1909, 517–24.
Davis, Hartley. "In Vaudeville." *Everybody's Magazine*, August 1905, 240.
DeCordova, Richard. *Picture Personalities: The Emergence of the Star System in America*. Urbana and Chicago: University of Illinois Press, 1990.
Dimeglio, John. *Vaudeville U.S.A.* Bowling Green, Ohio: Bowling Green University Popular Press, 1973.
Diner, Steven. *A Very Different Age: Americans of the Progressive Era*. New York: Hill and Wang, 1998.
Douglas, Ann. *The Feminization of American Culture*. New York: Alfred A. Knopf, 1977.
Duffy, John. *The Sanitarians: A History of American Public Health*. Urbana and Chicago: University of Illinois Press, 1990.
"E.F. Albee, Co-Founder of Vaudeville." *New York Times*, 23 March 1930, ix, 4:6.
Emmet, Boris, and John E. Jeuck. *Catalogues and Counters: A History of Sears, Roebuck and Company*. Chicago: University of Chicago Press, 1950.
Erdman, Andrew L. "From Frank Fay to Jimmy Stewart: Broadway, Hollywood, and the Construction of Creativity." *Theatre Studies* 41 (1996): 13–28.
Erenberg, Lewis. *Steppin' Out: New York Nightlife and the Transformation of American Culture, 1890–1930*. Westport, Connecticut, and London: Greenwood Press, 1981.
"Eva Tanguay Dies in Hollywood, 68." *New York Times*, 12 January 1947, 59:1.
"Eva Tanguay—'I Don't Care' Girl—Slips Away, Taking an Era with Her." *Variety*, 15 January 1947, 48.
"Eva Tanguay, of 'I Don't Care' Fame, Dies at 68." *Los Angeles Times*, 12 January, 1947, I, 3.
"Eva Tanguay on 'Imitators.'" *Variety*, 6 March 1909, 5.
"Evolution of Cheap Vaudeville." *Variety*, 14 December 1907, 10.
Ewen, Stuart. *All Consuming Images: The Politics of Style in Contemporary Culture*. New York: Basic Books, 1988.
_____. *Captains of Consciousness: Advertising and Social Roots of the Consumer Culture*. New York: McGraw-Hill Book Co., 1976.
"F. F. Proctor Dead; Dean of Vaudeville." *New York Times*, 5 September 1929, 29.
Fleischer, Rita Mary. "Collaborative Projects of Symbolist Playwrights and Early Modern Dancers." Ph.D. diss., City University of New York, 1998.
"Folks Film Bill Vetoed By Mayor." *New York Times*, 1 January 1913, 6:3.
Fox, Richard Wightman, and T. J. Lears, eds. *The Culture of Consumption: Critical Essays in American History, 1880–1980*. New York: Pantheon Books, 1983.
Fox, Stephen. *The Mirror Makers: A History of American Advertising*. New York: William Morrow & Co., 1984.
Furia, Philip. "Irving Berlin: Troubadour of Tin Pan Alley," in *Inventing Times Square: Commerce and Culture at the Crossroads of the World*, ed. William R. Taylor, 191–211. New York: Russell Sage Foundation, 1991.
_____. "The Syndicate/Shubert War," in *Inventing Times Square: Commerce and Culture at the Crossroads of the World*, ed. William R. Taylor, 147–57. New York: Russell Sage Foundation, 1991.
Gilbert, Douglas. *American Vaudeville: Its Life and Times*. New York: Dover Publications, 1940.
Glickman, Lawrence. *A Living Wage: American Workers and the Making of a Consumer Society*. Ithaca and London: Cornell University Press, 1997.
Goldberg, Isaac. *Tin Pan Alley: A Chronicle of American Popular Music*. New York: Ungar Publishing Co., Inc., 1982.
Gomery, Douglas. *Shared Pleasures: A History of Movie Presentation in the United States*. Madison, Wisconsin: University of Wisconsin Press, 1992.
Goodwin, Neva, Frank Ackerman, and David Kiron, eds. *The Consumer Society*. Washington, D.C., and Covelo, California: Island Press, 1997.

Graves, Harrison. *Chase's Herald: Devoted to Polite Vaudeville*, 26 January 1903, 1.
Haddon, Celia. *The Sensuous Lie*. New York: Stein and Day, 1983.
Hamilton, Marybeth. *When I'm Bad, I'm Better: Mae West, Sex, and American Entertainment*. New York: Harper Collins, 1995.
Hansen, Miriam. *Babel & Babylon: Spectatorship in American Silent Film*. Cambridge, Massachusetts, and London: Harvard University Press, 1991.
Hanson, Patricia King, ed. *American Film Institute Catalog of Motion Pictures Produced in the United States, Feature Films, 1911–1920*. Berkeley, Los Angeles, and London: University of California Press, 1988.
"Harvey W. Wiley: Pioneer Consumer Activist." *Good Housekeeping*, February 1990, 146.
Hays, J. N. *The Burdens of Disease: Epidemics and Human Response in Western History*. New Brunswick, New Jersey, and London: Rutgers University Press, 1998.
Higgins, Harvey Alexander, Jr. "The Origins of Vaudeville." *New York Dramatic Mirror*, 13 May 1919, 720.
"How Martin Beck Became Vaudeville's Chief Mogul." *Variety*, 11 December 1909, 27.
Jasen, David A. *Tin Pan Alley: The Composers, The Songs, The Performers, and Their Times*. New York: Donald I. Fine, 1988.
Jenkins, Henry. *What Made Pistachio Nuts? Early Sound Comedy and the Vaudeville Aesthetic*. New York: Columbia University Press, 1992.
Kanter, Kenneth Aaron. *The Jews on Tin Pan Alley: The Jewish Contribution to American Popular Music, 1830–1940*. New York: Ktav Publishing House, 1982.
Keith, B.F. "What Pleases in Vaudeville." *Criterion*, September 1900, 24.
"Keith's Seventeenth Anniversary." *New York Dramatic Mirror*, 26 January 1901, 16.
Kibler, M. Alison. *Rank Ladies: Gender and Cultural Hierarchy in American Vaudeville*. Chapel Hill & London: University of North Carolina Press, 1999.
Kitchen, Karl H. "Undone by a Song." *Theatre*, May 1913, 143.
Krasner, David. *Resistance, Parody, and Double Consciousness in African American Theatre, 1895–1910*. New York: St. Martin's Press, 1997.
Laufe, Abe. *The Wicked Stage: A History of Theater Censorship and Harassment in the United States*. New York: Frederick Ungar Publishing, 1978.
Laurie, Joe, Jr. *Vaudeville: From the Honky-Tonks to the Palace*. New York: Henry Holt & Co., 1953.
Leach, William. *Land of Desire: Merchants, Power, and the Rise of a New American Culture*. New York: Pantheon Books, 1993.
Lears, Jackson. *Fables of Abundance: A Cultural History of Advertising in America*. New York: Basic Books, 1994.
Lears, T. J. Jackson. "From Salvation to Self-Realization: Advertising and the Therapeutic Roots of Consumer Culture, 1880–1930." In Fox, Richard Wightman, and T. J. Lears, eds. *The Culture of Consumption: Critical Essays in American History, 1880–1980*. New York: Pantheon Books, 1983.
Linton, Lynn. "The Wild Women as Social Insurgents." *Nineteenth Century*, October 1891, 596.
Lott, Eric. *Love and Theft: Blackface Minstrelsy and the American Working Class*. New York: Oxford University Press, 1993.
Mankowitz, Wolf. *Mazeppa: The Lives, Loves, and Legends of Adah Isaacs Menken*. London: Blond & Briggs, 1982.
Marble, Anna. "Women in Variety." *Variety*, 22 December 1906, 14.
Marchand, Roland. *Advertising the American Dream: Making Way for Modernity*. Berkeley and Los Angeles: University of California Press, 1985.
"Martin Beck Dies; Theatre Veteran." *New York Times*, 17 November 1940, 49:1.
May, Lary. *Screening Out the Past*. New York: Oxford University Press, 1980.
McCaw, Thomas K. *The Essential Alfred Chandler: Essays Toward a Historical Theory of Big Business*. Boston: Harvard Business School Press, 1988.
McCullough, Jack. *Living Pictures on the New York Stage*. Ann Arbor, Michigan: UMI Research Press, 1981.
McGovern, Charles. "Consumption and Citizenship in the United States, 1900–1940." In

Strasser, Susan, Charles McGovern, and Matthias Judt, eds. *Getting and Spending: European and American Consumer Societies in the Twentieth Century*. Washington, D.C.: Cambridge University Press, 1998.
McLean, Albert F. *American Vaudeville as Ritual*. Frankfort, Kentucky: University of Kentucky Press, 1965.
McNeill, William H. *Plagues and Peoples*. Garden City, New York: Anchor/Doubleday, 1976.
Mock, James, and Cedric Larson. *Words That Won the War: The Story of the Committee on Public Information, 1917–1919*. Princeton: Princeton University Press, 1939.
Nasaw, David. *Going Out: The Rise and Fall of Public Amusements*. New York: Basic Books, 1993.
Odell, George C. D. *Annals of the New York Stage, VIII, 1865–1870*. New York: AMS Press, 1937.
Pike, Rafford. "What Men Like in Women." *Cosmopolitan*, October 1901, 609–13.
Presbrey, Frank. *The History and Development of Advertising*. Garden City, New York: Doubleday, Doran & Co., 1929.
Rosen, George. *Preventive Medicine in the United States, 1900–1975: Trends and Interpretations*. New York: Prodist, 1977.
Samuels, Charles, and Louise Samuels. *Once Upon a Stage: The Merry World of Vaudeville*. New York: Dodd, Mead & Company, 1974.
Schenk, Joseph. "Inside Vaudeville." *Variety*, 20 December 1912, 33.
Schreiber, Harry N., ed. *United States Economic History: Selected Readings*. New York: Knopf, 1964.
Schudson, Michael. *Advertising, the Uneasy Persuasion*. New York: Harper Collins, 1984.
Senelick, Laurence. *Cabaret Performance, Europe, 1890–1920: Songs, Sketches, Monologues, Memoirs*. New York: Performing Arts Journal Publications, 1989.
Sklar, Kathryn Kish. "The Consumers' White Label Campaign of the National Consumers' League, 1898–1918." In Strasser, Susan, Charles McGovern, and Matthias Judt, eds. *Getting and Spending: European and American Consumer Societies in the Twentieth Century*. Washington, D.C.: Cambridge University Press, 1998.
Slide, Anthony. *The Encyclopedia of Vaudeville*. Westport, Connecticut, and London: Greenwood Press, 1994.
Smith, Frederick James. "'I Do Care!' Says Eva Tanguay." *New York Dramatic Mirror*, 27 January 1915, 30.
Snyder, Frederick. "Theater in a Package—the Origins of Mass Entertainment." Ph.D. diss., Yale University, 1970.
Snyder, Robert. *The Voice of the City: Vaudeville and Popular Culture in New York*. New York and Oxford: Oxford University Press, 1989.
———. "Vaudeville and the Transformation of Popular Culture." In William R. Taylor, ed. *Inventing Times Square: Commerce and Culture at the Crossroads of the World*. New York: Russell Sage Foundation, 1991, 133–46.
Southworth, John. *The English Medieval Minstrel*. Suffolk: Boydell & Brewer, 1989.
Stanton, Donna. *Discourses of Sexuality: From Aristotle to AIDS*. Ann Arbor: University of Michigan Press, 1992.
Stein, Charles, ed. *American Vaudeville as Seen by Its Contemporaries*. New York: Knopf, 1984.
Strasser, Susan. *Satisfaction Guaranteed: The Making of the American Mass Market*. Toronto: Random House of Canada, 1989.
Strasser, Susan, Charles McGovern, and Matthias Judt, eds. *Getting and Spending: European and American Consumer Societies in the Twentieth Century*. Washington, D.C.: Cambridge University Press, 1998.
Stratton, Jon. *The Desirable Body: Cultural Fetishism and the Erotics of Consumption*. Manchester and New York: Manchester University Press, 1996.
Suratt, Valeska. "Personality—That's Me!" *Green Book Magazine*, September 1915, 420.
Tanguay, Eva. "'I Don't Care.'" *American Weekly*, 29 December 1946, 12–13.
———. "'I Don't Care.'" *American Weekly*, 5 January 1947, 17.
———. "'I Don't Care.'" *American Weekly*, 12 January 1947, 6–7.
———. "'I Don't Care.'" *American Weekly*, 19 January 1947, 6–7.
———. "'I Don't Care.'" *American Weekly*, 26 January 1947, 6–7.

Tawa, Nicholas. *The Way to Tin Pan Alley: American Popular Song, 1866–1910*. New York: Schirmer Books, 1990.
Tedlow, Richard. *New and Improved: The Story of Mass Marketing in America*. Boston: Harvard Business School Press, 1996.
Tucker, Sophie. *Some of These Days: The Autobiography of Sophie Tucker*. Sophie Tucker, 1945.
U.S. Bureau of the Census. *Historical Statistics of the United States, Colonial Times to 1970, Bicentennial Edition, Part 1*. Washington, D.C., U.S. Government Printing Office, 1975.
"United Booking Office Cleans Up All 'Big Time.'" *Variety*, 4 May 1912, 5.
"Vaudeville's Clearing House." *New York Clipper*, 29 November 1913, 1.
"'Watch Your Lyric' Slogan Emanates from the UBO" *Variety*, 10 December 1915, 5.
Watkins, Mel. *On The Real Side: Laughing, Lying, and Signifying—The Underground Tradition of African-American Humor That Transformed American Culture, from Slavery to Richard Pryor*. New York: Simon & Schuster, 1994.
Weisberger, Bernard A. "Doctor Wiley and His Poison Squad." *American Heritage*, February/March 1996, 14.
Wells, Herbert George. "Mankind in the Making." *Cosmopolitan*, May 1903, 79.
Westerfield, Jane. "An Investigation of the Life Styles and Performance of Three Singer-Comediennes of American Vaudeville: Eva Tangauy, Nora Bayes, and Sophie Tucker." D.A. diss., Ball State University, 1987.
"White Rats of America." *New York Clipper*, 4 August 1900, 516.
Wiebe, Robert. *The Search for Order: 1877–1920*. New York: Hill and Wang, 1987.
Wiley, Harvey Washington. *History of a Crime against the Food Law*. New York: Arno Press, 1976.
Willensky, Elliot. *When Brooklyn Was the World*. New York: Harmony Books, 1986.
"Williams Sells Theatres." *New York Clipper*, 4 May 1912, 10.
Wightman, Richard and T.J. Jackson Lears, eds. *The Culture of Consumption: Critical Essays in American History, 1880–1980*. New York: Pantheon Books, 1983.
Wilmeth, Don, and Tice Miller, eds. *Cambridge Guide to American Theatre*. Cambridge: Cambridge University Press, 1993.
Wood, James Playstead. *The Story of Advertising*. New York: Ronald Press, 1958.
Woods, Leigh. "Sarah Bernhardt and the Refining of American Vaudeville." *Theatre Research International* 18 (Spring 1993): 16–24.
Wright, Chester W. *Economic History of the United States*. New York: McGraw-Hill, 1949.
Zangwill, Israel. "The Future of Vaudeville in America." *Cosmopolitan*, April 1905, 641.

Index

Abbott, John 78
Acrobatic acts, use of disrobing in *see* Disrobing onstage
Actor's Fund 58
Actresses and dancers, social views of 139–140
Adams, Maud 104
Adgie 9, 89
"Advanced Vaudeville" (of Klaw & Erlanger) 60
Advertising Federation of America 75
Advertising, claims of honesty in 72, 76; claims of purity in 74–75; theories of effectiveness in 73; use of voyeurism in 85
An Affair of Honor (*Une Affaire d'Honneur*) 103
African-Americans: influences of, in the theatre 146; limitations to vaudeville of 7, 169n; vaudeville circuit of 179n
Agoust, Emile 112
Agriculture, United States Department of 78–80
Albee, Edward Franklin 2, 4, 5, 12, 16, 19, 20, 22, 45, 49, 51, 64, 61, 87, 126, 133–134, 141, 143, 165; birth and early life of 46; death of 62
Alcohol: consumption of, by audiences 11, 19, 58; use of, in vaudeville acts 125
Alexander, Louise 98
Alhambra theater, Keith's 109
Allan, Maud 107
Amato, Mlle. 125

American Circuit of burlesque theaters 13
American Weekly 130, 144, 153
Ames, Winthrop 33
Anarchist movement, fear of 33
Ann Arbor, Michigan 152
"Apache" dances 125
Aquatic, bathing, and swimming acts 4, 85, 87, 88, 91–93, 98
Aragon, Virginia 89
Armstrong, Paul 124
Artists' studios, vaudeville acts set in 105
Association of Theatre Managers 34
Association of Vaudeville Managers 53
"Au Bain" or "Suzanne at the Bath" 88
Audiences: behavioral control of 12, 19, 170; blamed for moral indecency onstage 25
Austin, Col. William Austin (partner of B.F. Keith) 44
Ayer, N.W. 73

Baby Alice 44
Bacon, Lloyd 131
Bailey, Frankie 105
Barnet, R. A. 144
Barnum circus organization 44, 46
Barr, Amelia E. 156
Barrasso, F. A. 180n
Bathing acts *see* Aquatic, bathing, and swimming acts
Bayard, Emile Antoine 103
Bayes, Nora 133

Beck, Martin 16, 110; birth and early life of 58
Beecher, the Rev. Henry Ward 74
Belangee, J. 149
Belasco, David 114
Berger, John 132
Berlin, Irving 170n
Bermuda, use of, as motion picture set 96
Bernhardt, Sarah 140
Bertram and Willard theatrical producers 144
Beryl, Simone de 112
Betz, Clara 101
Bijou, Keith's: Boston 47; Philadelphia 47
Bindley, Florence 90
Bingham, Theodore (police commissioner of New York City) 28
Biopics 132
Bird, E. Marion *see* Charmion, Mlle.
Bizot, Richard 108
The Black Crook 23
The Blue Mouse 24
Booke, Alexander 153
Boston 44, 47, 50, 145
Boston theater, Keith's 19
Boyer, Adeline 112
Breen, Harry 158
Brighton Beach Music Hall 153
Britt, Jimmy 122
Brooklyn 28, 109, 159
Brown, George Russell 80
Browning, Bessie 158
Bruin's Bears 62

Bryson, Dr. Louise Fiske 77
Bunnell's Museum 44
Burkhart, Maurice 72
Burlesque 4–5, 10–14, 19–20
Burnham, Charles 24
Burr Robbins circus organization 46
Business management of vaudeville 60–62

Cabaret 19–20, 40
Cahill, Marie 109
Campbell, Rhodes 148
Canada 127
Candler, Asa 69
Cass, J. F. 114
Castle, Cora Sutton 141
Catalogue merchants, rise of 65
Catholic church, Keith vaudeville circuit's relationship to 22, 50, 165
Catholic Men's Society 23
Censorship: calls for, objections to, and attempts at 1, 21, 23, 101, 110, 134, 147; self-, entertainment industry's efforts at 17, 22, 60
Chamberlain, Edward 37
Chandler, Alfred 62, 64
The Chaperones 145–146
Charity and philanthropy, depictions of, in vaudeville acts 125
Charmion, Mlle. 3, 9, 10, 116; comparison of other performers to 93, 115; popularity of 117
Chase, Canon William Sheaf 27
Chase, Mary 185*n*
Chase vaudeville circuit 3, 61
Chicago 56, 114
Chiclets chewing gum 67
Chisolm, B. Ogden 113
Cincinnati, Ohio 99, 163
Circus 20, 44
Cities, vaudeville's connection to 19
Civil War 22, 32, 78
Clarke, Josephe I. C.
Classical antiquity, comparison of vaudeville acts to 39, 102, 104–105
Cleveland Baking Powder 74
Cleveland, Ohio 153
Coca-Cola, rise and marketing practices of 17, 69–70
Coccia, Aurelio 125
Colonial theater, Percy Williams's 72, 88, 157
Colonialism, appeal of, on the vaudeville stage 93, 122
Columbia bicycles 76
Committee of Fourteen 23

Committee on Public Information 33
Commodities, vaudeville performers as 52
Comstock, Anthony 30
Concert saloons 4, 11, 19
"Continuous" format of vaudeville 45
"Coon songs" 146
Coquelin, Constant 140
Corliss, E. W. 144
Corporation Counsel of the City of New York 28
Cosmopolitan magazine 25, 31, 37, 74, 76, 77, 107, 139, 140, 142, 155
Costume changes onstage, use of 87–88
Cracker Jacks candy 67, 68
Crisco 22
Curtis Publishing, "Advertising Code" of 75

Dagmar, Alexandra 85
Dale, Alan 25, 117, 140
Daniels, Frank 145
Dartos dancers 87
Dash of *Variety* 91, 104
A Daughter of the Gods 96–97, 97
Davies, Charlotte 103
Davis, James, United States Secretary of Labor 62
Dazie, Mlle. 108
Deland, Lorin 73
Deland, Margaret 143
De Leon, Millie 23, 107
Denver, Colorado 116
Department store mannequins, sexual qualities of 84, 105
Depersonalization of commerce 65
The Derelict 35, 173*n*
Deslys, Gaby 158
Des Moines, Iowa 117
Detroit 101
D'Eve, Liane 87
"Dime" museums 44
Disease, fear of 24, 70, 76–77, 176*n*
Disrobing onstage 3, 10, 23, 89, 99, 103, 115, 115
Dockstader, Lew 81
Doris & Forepaugh circus organization 44
Dos Passos, John 84
Douglas, W.L. 71
Dowling, Victor 62
Duncan, Isadora 104, 111

The Easiest Way 34
East Liverpool, New York 96
Eastman Kodak 71

Economy of the United States in the Nineteenth Century 63
Eight English Roses 91
Eighty-Sixth Street theater, Proctor's 57
Eis, Alice 13, 14, 60, 120
El Fey Club 160
Ellis, Havelock 41, 156
Eltinge, Julian 111
Encyclopedia of Vaudeville 107, 130, 135, 139
Energetic Eva 136
Engel's theater 59
The Engineer 144
Englander, Ludwig 145
Erlanger, Abraham 36, 55, 60
Estabrook, Howard 136
Europe, vaudeville acts taken from 176*n*
Evansville, Indiana 151
Ewen, Stuart 8
Execution, vaudeville acts depicting 164

Farley, Cardinal/Archbishop 24, 27
Fashion, use of, onstage 90, 117
Fatima Turkish cigarettes 71
Fatma and Smaun 122
Faust brothers 29
Fay, Frank 185*n*
Fechter, Charles 46, 174*n*
Feminism 39, 141
Fifth Avenue theatre: Keith's 13, 38, 85, 87, 98; Keith & Proctor's 153, 158; Proctor's 85
50 Beautiful Ladies 93
Fifty-Eighth Street theater, Proctor's 57
Fitch, Clyde 23, 24
Fleischmann's yeast 70
Follies of 1907 (Florenz Ziegfeld) 108, 147, 150
Fondelier, Fannie 87
Food adulteration and impurities, threat of 78
Food Manufacturers' Association 81
Ford, John 152, 157
Fortune magazine 164, 165
42nd Street 132
Fourteenth Street Theatre 29
Fowler, Nathaniel 73
Fox, William 164
Fox motion picture company 96, 98, 164; *see also* Twentieth Century–Fox
Franklin, Irene 71, 72, 157
Franklin, Margaret Ladd 157
French, Bert 13, 14, 60, 120
Freud, Sigmund 41
Friganza, Trixie 145, 161

Index

Frohman, Charles 36, 175*n*
Fuller, Loie 91

Gaiety and Bijou, Keith's 45
Gaiety Museum, Keith's (Providence) 47
Gane, William J. 158
The Garden of Allah 25
Gaynor, Mitzi 130, 131
Gaynor, William (mayor of New York) 113–114, 118, 172*n*
Gender makeup of vaudeville audiences 4, 11, 14–15
Gerard, Francis 122
Gest, Morris 114
Gibson's Bathing Girls 85
Gideon, Melville 109
Gilbert & Sullivan 47
Gillette razors 67
Gillian, S. W. 81
Gilman, Charlotte Perkins 141, 149
The Girl with the Dreamy Eyes 89
Glazunov, Alexander 111
Gluck, Assemblyman 27
Golden, George Fuller 54
Goodwin, Nat 158
Gordon, Cliff 29
Gordon, Lady Duff 90
Gordone, Robbie 38
Gorham's silverware 74
Grauman, Sid 161
Great Atlantic & Pacific Tea Company (A&P) 63
The Great Depression 151
Green Street Theatre, Proctor's (Albany) 57
Guerrero, Mlle. 85

Hall, Josephine 85
Hall, Pauline 85
Hall & Ruckel corporation 71
Hamm, Arthur 121
Hammerstein, Willie 27, 28, 32, 53, 107, 150
Hammerstein's theater 35, 104, 117, 126, 150
Hardy, Thomas 31
Harman, Moses, charges of indecency against 37
Harris, Charles K. 170*n*
Harris, Henry 33
Harvard University 79, 121
Harvey 185*n*
Hearst publications 128
Heartz, H. L. 144
Henle, James 144
Herlein, Lillian 86, 87
Hess, Clarence 151
Higgins, Harvey Alexander 50
High versus low culture, vaudeville's relationship to 170*n*

Hill, Dr. John Wesley 28–29, 109
Hitchcock, Raymond 47
Hoffman, Gertrude 107, 113
Hollywood 17
Horlick's malted milk 67
Howe, Maud 144
Hub Museum 44
"Hundred-Years-Old Club" 82
Hymer, John 111

"I Don't Care" 146; Eva Tanguay's disdain for 147
The I Don't Care Girl 131, 130–132
Ibsen, Henrik 78
Imperial Music Hall (New York City) 144
Indiana Medical College 78
Industry 62–63; vaudeville's comparison to 17, 61–62
Inglis, William 165
Interstate vaudeville circuit 62
Islam (Mohammadenism), objections to, onstage 25
Ivory Soap 74

J. C. Penney (JCPenney) 63
Jarbeau, Veronica 88
Jean Marcel's Living Pictures 102
Jersey City theater, Keith & Proctor's 28
Jessel, George 130, 132
Jolo of *Variety* 103
The Jungle 81

Kalem motion picture company 120
Keith, Benjamin Franklin 2, 3, 12, 16–20, 52, 54–55, 55, 61, 126, 131, 133, 141, 143, 165; birth and early life of 43–44
Keith, Mrs. 21
Keith, Paul 51
Keith & Proctor vaudeville circuit 125; *see also*: Fifth Avenue theatre; Jersey City theatre; 125th Street theater
Keith theatres: furnishings and cleanliness of 48; public relations efforts of 50
Keith vaudeville circuit 22, 50,105, 116, 164–166; *see also* Alhambra theater; Bijou (Boston); Bijou (Philadelphia); Boston theater; Fifth Avenue theater; Gaiety and Bijou; Gaiety Museum (Providence); Jersey City theater; Keith theaters, furnishings and cleanliness of; Keith theaters, public relations efforts of; New Theatre (Boston);

125th Street theater; Union Square theater
Kellerman, Annette 4, 94, 97, 94–99, 99, 163, 178*n*
Key, Ellen 39
Kid Gabriel and Co. 5, 9
Kipling, Rudyard, use of poems by, as basis for vaudeville acts 120
Kirkland, Winifred 142
Kismet 25
Klaw, Marc 34, 36, 60
Knute Rockne, All American 132
Kohl vaudeville circuit 59
Koster & Bial's theater 3, 12, 85, 87, 88, 89, 103, 116
Krasner, David 180*n*
Kroger's retail chain 63
Ksiaziewicz, Chandas *see* Booke, Alexander

L'Abîme see *No Thoroughfare*
Lackawanna Railroad, "Phoebe Snow" advertising campaign of 75
Ladies' Comedy Quartette 85
La Gai, Louise 85
Lambelle, Edith *see* La Sylphe
La Milo 105–106
Language permitted ontage 2
La Sylphe 107, 112, 113
Lea & Perrins condiments 67
Le Deodima 107
Legitimate stage, vaudeville's differences compared to 23
Legs, exposure of onstage 3
Lennox, Jean 146
L'Épave see *The Derelict*
Leuscher, Mark 27
Levantine Brothers 57
Libraries, public, in New York City and Brooklyn, book censorship and 31–32
Lifebouy soap 67
Lighting, use of, in heightening sexual appeal 91
Linton, Lynn 138, 139, 159
Lion tamers, disrobing women as 9
Littlefield, C. W. 16, 124
"Living pictures" *see* Posing acts, "living pictures," and tableaux 3
Lloyd, Alice 157
Loew vaudeville circuit 17
Lord & Taylor 72
Lorraine, Mlle. 102
Los Angeles 128
Louisville, Kentucky 114, 151
Lowrie, Jeanette 126
Lubin motion picture company 111
Luby, Edna 71

Mackey, Julie 85
Macy's 65
Maher, Captain 29
Male body, undressed onstage 15
Man and Superman 31
Marble, Anna 15
Marbleton, Quebec 127
Mardi Gras, vaudeville performer named 85
Marigold, Millicent 62
Marks, Ted 87
Marriage, vaudeville acts' commentary on 50, 122–124, 154
Marx, Groucho 45
"Mashers" and "mashing" 11, 26, 91
Mass scale and scope of vaudeville 7, 52, 60
Massachusetts 28, 32, 44
Mazeppa, depictions of, in vaudeville 102
McCauley's theater 151
McClellan, George B., mayor of New York 27, 172*n*
McCullough, Jack 22
McGean, Monsignor 24
Medicinal qualities of early mass-market goods, putative 70
Menken, Ada Isaacs 179*n*
Mennen's toiletry items 67, 68
Meredith, Letta 91
Mernereau, Mlle. 104
Merrill, Blanche 72
Methodist church, objections of 28
Metropolitan Opera of New York City 114
Michaelis, Karin 141
Midwest, vaudeville in 62
The Mikado 47
Milwaukee, Wisconsin 15, 114
Mimodramas 120
Mindi and the Musketeers 145
Minneapolis, vaudeville in 60
Minstrelsy, blackface 28, 111
Modern dance, use of, in vaudeville acts 104
Monologist acts (stand-up comics) 124
Montague, Pansy *see* La Milo
Montgomery Ward 65
Morgan, Mervin 103
Morin, Pilar 107
Morris, William 60–61, 98, 151
Morse, Robert 144
Motherhood, views on 40
Motion picture industry: popularity of 166; social attitudes toward 165; vaudeville's differences compared to 17,

21; vaudeville's success compared to 19, 22, 59
Moving Picture World 98
Museum of Modern Art 136
My Lady 144–145
"My Sambo" 146
My Sambo Girl 146

Narcotics, depiction of, in vaudeville acts 124–125
Nation, Carrie 125
National Biscuit Company (Nabisco) 64, 74
National Catholic Theatre Movement 24
Neptune's Daughter 96
Nesbit, Evelyn 32
Netzel & Netzel 160
The New Republic 37
New Theatre, Keith's (Boston) 48, 117
New York City 2, 11, 15, 17, 21, 22, 24, 28, 44, 59, 93, 113, 144, 159, 165; response of theater critics in 85
New York Society for the Suppression of Vice 30
New York, upstate, Proctor theaters in 58
Newark, New Jersey 15
Newman, Louis 150
Niblo's Garden 23
Nickelodeon cinemas 166
1919 84
Nirvana's living pictures 102
No Thoroughfare 46, 174*n*
Nolan and Sweeney 62
Northwestern Christian University 78
Northwestern University 73
Nugent, Maud 16, 87

Odell, Maud 103
Odiva the Living Mermaid 91–92, 92, 135
The Office Boy 145
Olympia theater, Hammerstein's 9, 87
Omaha, Nebraska 62
125th Street theater, Keith & Proctor's 113
125th Street theater, Proctor's 57
The Original Mermaid: The Amazing Story of Annette Kellerman 178*n*
O'Rourke and Marie 89
Orpheum vaudeville circuit 16, 59, 99, 110

Palace theater 13, 59, 125
Pantages vaudeville circuit 62
Parada, Allen *see* Booke, Alexander

Parado, Allen *see* Booke, Alexander
Paramount Pictures 62
Pastor, Tony 5, 11, 12, 15–16, 44, 87, 88, 90, 124
Paterson, New Jersey 33
Patrice 85
Pear's Soap 74
People's Theatre (New York City) 144
Pepsi, early marketing practices of 69
Perkins, Carrie 90
Pertina, Bertha 60
Philadelphia 17, 73, 118
Philip Morris cigarettes 67, 68
Pike, Rafford 139, 142, 156
Pitnof, Rose 98
Pittsburgh, Pennsylvania 114
Plainfield, New Jersey 24
Pleasure Palace, Proctor's 58, 91
Plexo facial powder 67, 69
"Poison Squad" volunteers for food adulteration testing 80
Police actions against vaudeville 29
Poli's vaudeville circuit 53
Pollock, Arthur 139, 140
Ponds lotion 67, 68
Posing acts, "living pictures," and tableaux 3, 5, 22, 38, 50, 101–103, 105
Post offices, proliferation of 63
Posters, theatrical advertising 172*n*
Preston, Jessica 111
Princess Rajah 114
Princess Sita Diva 112
Proctor, Frederick F. 15, 46; birth and early life of 57; regard for performers of 58
Proctor vaudeville circuit *see* Eighty-Sixth Street theater; Fifth Avenue theater; Fifty-Eight Street theater; Green Street Theatre (Albany); Jersey City theater; Keith & Proctor vaudeville circuit; New York, upstate, Proctor theaters in; 125th Street theater; Pleasure Palace; Twenty-Third Street theater
Prohibition 19
Protestant church, objections of 25
Providence, Rhode Island 47, 62, 160
Purdue University 79
Pure Food and Drug legislation 77, 79
Purity, sterility, and safety, promises of mass-market products as to 67–69

Index

Quaker Rice 69
The Queen of the Moulin Rouge 36
Queen of the Sea 98–99, 99

Radha 112
Radio Corporation of America (RCA) 169*n*
Radio-Keith-Orpheum 169*n*
Ranken, Frederic 145
Rawlston, Zelma 88
Redding Stanton Repertoire 144
Regional variability, vaudeville acts 166
Religion, vaudeville and 4
Republican Party of New York State 110
Retail chains, proliferation of 63
Revealing costumes: use of, onstage by men 15, 121, 171*n*; use of, onstage, by women 13, 98, 120
Rialta, Mlle. 105
Ritchie, Adele 88, 89
Roosevelt, Teddy 77
Rough, George 151
Royal Baking Powder 69
Royal Music Hall 59
Royle, Edwin 14
Rubinstein, Ida 111
Rush of *Variety* 5, 13, 91, 93
Russell, Lillian 12
Russia, comparison of United States to 29, 33
Russian Imperial dance troupe 113

Sabbatarian League 27
Safety *see* Purity, sterility, and safety, promises of mass-market products as to
St. Denis, Ruth 104
St. Petersburg Conservatory 111
Salbini, Lula *see* Selbini, Lalla
Salome acts: 103, 107–108, 110–111, 134, 150; artistic bases of 107; cross-dressing and 111; likened to disease 110
San Francisco, vaudeville in 15, 59
Sandow, Eugene 15, 121
Sapho 23
Sapolio, "Spotless Town" advertising campaign of 74
Sarnoff, David 62
Savage, Henry 33
Schallert, Edwin 128
Schallert, Elza 128
Schenk, Joseph M. 17, 52
Schlitz beer 74
Schukai, Arthur 38
Scott, Walter Dill 73

Sears, Richard 18, 65; efforts of, to personalize catalogue retailing 66
Sears, Roebuck and Co. 16, 65
Seaton, Billie 158
Selbini, Lalla 100, 98–101
Sells Brothers circus organization 46
Selznick Pictures motion picture company 136
Sexuality, social views on 36
Shakespeare, William, works of 31
Shaw, George Bernard 31, 166
Shea's vaudeville circuit 53
Sherman Antitrust Act 57
Shredded Wheat 74
Shubert, Lee 33
Shubert theatrical enterprise 175*n*
Silverman, Sime, of *Variety* 13, 90, 98, 99, 103, 104, 108, 118, 121
Sime of *Variety see* Silverman, Sime, of *Variety*
Sinclair, Upton 81
Slide, Anthony 130, 135
Smith, Joe 98
Snyder, Robert 3
Social class, audience makeup according to 12, 15, 163
South, vaudeville in United States 62
Sozodont oral care products 69
Spiegel, May, and Stern 65
Springfield, Illinois 17
Standard Manufacturing Company of Pittsburgh 74
Standard Oil 17
Stanislovsky, Konstantin 111
Starr, Dr. Wendell 161
Sterility *see* Purity, sterility, and safety, promises of mass-market products as to
Stevens, D. K. 144
Stewart, Jimmy 185*n*
Stilwell Bill (limiting Sunday shows) 30
Stone, Fred 11
Strikes and labor actions by performers 55
Strongmen, appearance of, onstage 121–122
Style, personal, use of in vaudeville 118
Suffrage movement, depictions of, in vaudeville acts 126
Sullivan, J. J. (district attorney of Cleveland) 125
Sun vaudeville circuit 62
Sunday shows, objections to 27; *see also* Stilwell Bill
Sunlight Soap 74

Suratt, Valeska 72, 119, 117–20, 158
Sutton, Harry 146
Swann, Paul 104
Swimming acts *see* Aquatic, bathing, and swimming acts
Swirsky, Thamara de 104
Sylvia, Marguerite 9
Syndicate, theatrical 175*n*

Tableaux *see* Posing acts, "living pictures," and tableaux 3
Tammany Hall theater 15
Tanguay, Eva 30, 60, 129, 129–30, 137, 138, 149, 166; attempted comeback of 160; autobiography of 128; birth and early life of 127, 144; costumes of 133, 147–149, 149; dancing of 135; eccentric style of 133, 136; illnesses of 160–161, 182*n*; imitators of 158; income and earnings of 127, 151, 159–160, 163; individuality of 143; lack of information on 182*n*; late life and death of 128, 130, 182*n*; mental condition of 161; obituaries of 130; popularity of 133, 157; reputation for combativeness of 150–151; romantic involvements of 152–54, 157; Salome act of 107–109, 147; sexually suggestive style of, onstage 30, 130, 133, 135, 137, ; writing about 133
Tanguay, Gustave 144
Tarbell, Ida 159
Temperance movement 125
Texas, objections of residents in, to schoolbooks 32
Thaw, Harry 32
Theater Comique in Boston 57
13 Girls in Blue 91
Thit, Toon and Moung 122
Thomas, W. I. 148
The Three Musketeers 144
Times Square 61
Tin Pan Alley 170*n*
Tobacco: depiction of, in vaudeville acts 16, 124; use of, by audiences 19
Tojetti 48
Toledo, Ohio 114
Toluca Lake 160
Tompkins, Juliet Wilbor 155, 156
Topeka, Kansas 17
Treloar 121
Tremont Theatre (Boston) 145
Tucker, Sophie 23, 127, 133, 147, 161
Turkey, comparisons of United States to 33

Twentieth Century–Fox 130, 132
Twenty-Third Street theater, Proctor's 57, 105
Twenty-Third Street theater, Proctor's 105
22 Girls 91
Tylenol, cyanide murders linked to 67

Union Square theater, Keith's 15, 47, 49, 85, 90, 91, 101, 121, 123, 125, 126
United Artists 17
United Booking Office(s) 13, 25, 32, 53, 56, 57, 61, 62, 107, 116, 120, 150, 151; national scope of 54
Universal motion picture company 96
Urquhart, Isabelle 85, 87

Van Amburgh's circus organization 44, 46
Vance, Gladys 124
Van Dyke, Gertie 87
Variety-format theater 11, 19
Vaudeville Collection Agency 54, 56
"Vaudeville," derivation and meaning of the word 12, 31, 170n

Venus on Wheels 89
Victoria Roof Garden 93
Victoria Theatre 145
Vogue magazine 117
Von Tilzer, Harry 170n
Voyeurism, depictions of, on-stage 88
Vulgarity, charges of 2

Wakefield, Willa Holt 150, 151
Walker, Ada Overton 107, 108, 111
Wall Street, relationship to motion picture industry of 180n
Walter, Eugene 165
Wannamaker, John 34
Washburn Sisters 15, 72
Wells, George Herbert 31
Werba, Louis 37
West Virginia 27
Westerfield, Jane R. 98, 133
Western Vaudeville Managers Association 53, 135
Wheeler, the Rev. Francis Rolt 59
White, Stanford 40
White Rats of America 25, 54; strikes of 57
White Rock beverages 55
White slavery 67
Wiehe, Charlotte 32

Wilcox, Susanne 120
The Wild Girl 138, 142
Wiley, Harvey Washington 78–82; birth and early life of 81; late life and death of 82
Williams, Percy 28, 53
Winter Garden theater 60, 113
Witmark, Isidore 114
Women: cultural views of 84; social attitude toward money and 77; social views on unwed 155, 159; social views on the attire of 148, 156; social views on the flirtation of 149; social views on the individuality of 156; social views on the intellect of 142–143; social views on the truthfulness of 141, 157; "spectacularization" of 145
Woodruff, Robert 148
Woolworth's 70
World War I 19, 63
World War II 33

Zangwill, Israel 19
Zanuck, Darryl 1
Ziegfeld, Florenz 132
Zimmerman, C. D. 108
Zittell, C. Florian 77
Zittell, Martha 153
Zukor, Adolph 153

www.ingramcontent.com/pod-product-compliance
Lightning Source LLC
Chambersburg PA
CBHW060300240426
43661CB00060B/2848